Royal Favourites of the Tudor and Stuart Age

Royal Favourites of the Tudor and Stuart Age

April Taylor

First published in Great Britain in 2026 by
Pen & Sword History
An imprint of Pen & Sword Books Limited
Yorkshire – Philadelphia

ISBN 978 1 39907 940 2

A CIP catalogue record for this book is
available from the British Library.

Typeset by Mac Style
Printed in the UK by CPI Group (UK) Ltd, Croydon, CR0 4YY.

The Publisher's authorised representative in the EU for product
safety is Authorised Rep Compliance Ltd., Ground Floor,
71 Lower Baggot Street, Dublin D02 P593, Ireland.
www.arccompliance.com

For a complete list of Pen & Sword titles please contact

PEN & SWORD BOOKS LIMITED
47 Church Street, Barnsley, South Yorkshire, S70 2AS, England
E-mail: enquiries@pen-and-sword.co.uk
Website: www.pen-and-sword.co.uk
or
PEN AND SWORD BOOKS
1950 Lawrence Road, Havertown, PA 19083, USA
E-mail: uspen-and-sword@casematepublishers.com
Website: www.penandswordbooks.com

Contents

Acknowledgements

Nobody writes a book alone. Thank you to Pen and Sword, and especially Sarah-Beth Watkins for taking a chance on an unknown author. The Pen and Sword cover design team who have no peers! To my editors who I know I have driven insane, but who gritted their teeth, summoned their patience and carried on.

Please note that all monetary comparisons have come from:
https://www.bankofengland.co.uk/monetary-policy/inflation/inflation-calculator

Dedication

Team Taylor who have seen me through many years of highs and lows but who are always there – my husband Paul, Nicky Griffiths, Joan Mulqueen and Janet Shell. To all the 'proper' historians who have encouraged me to carry on regardless and never give up.

Finally, to my family, blood and otherwise, Paul, Roy, Alan.

Introduction

Favourites of monarchs have always been necessary. To the monarchs if to nobody else. Everyone must have someone they can trust. Someone with whom they can confide difficulties and discuss solutions. The problems begin when the confider is the most powerful person in the kingdom.

In a letter written in 1887 to Bishop Creighton, Lord Acton said 'Power tends to corrupt; absolute power corrupts absolutely'. How, then, can it be surprising that many royal favourites have found it irresistible to line their pockets at the expense of the monarch in whose sun they shine? Even the miser, Henry VII, had no idea Reginald Bray was creaming money from transactions to build his fortune and power base in Surrey.

At the outset, I must stress I have not tried to make this book a historical textbook, aimed at scholars, but rather an accurate account of what happened between 1485 and 1714, written for anyone interested in this period of time. It is a 'dipping' book, not necessarily one to read from beginning to end. I have also put in some quirky facts about each monarch. These *Fun Facts* appear at the end of each section.

The Tudors and Stuarts are, arguably, two of the most important dynasties in English history. They took us from a medieval England split by the Wars of the Roses, through the tumultuous sixteenth century, into a seventeenth-century dynasty interrupted by the English Civil War and culminating in a queen who is often ridiculed, but who actually did her utmost to ensure she ruled fairly, and handed a peaceful United Kingdom to the Hanoverians.

In 1485, when Henry Tudor defeated Richard III, thus founding the House of Tudor, his first objective was to amass money, but equally he concentrated on putting England on a sounder and more peaceful footing than it had known for half a century. His power was absolute – a monarch who only recalled parliament when he wanted money, and he always got it. By the time Queen Anne died in 1714, the United Kingdom of Scotland, Wales and England was a country where the monarch had lost executive power and was subject to parliament. The monarch does, however, have the power of veto. The last one to use it was good old Queen Anne in March 1708.

One wonders how Henry VIII would have acted had parliament told him to go and twiddle his thumbs, or just how much blood his response would have shed. By the time Elizabeth, his infinitely pragmatic daughter, sat on the throne, parliament decided it could disrespect a mere woman who was, allegedly, illegitimate in any case, and refuse her when they felt like it. Elizabeth wooed them with honeyed words, but honeyed words that held enough bite to remind them whose daughter she was. By the end of the Tudors, the balance of power between monarch and parliament had altered – slightly.

The following century was to completely transform the position of the monarchy. After Elizabeth, England was ruled by two kings who believed to the bitter end in their divine right to rule, the son suffering from the father's stupidity and becoming the only English monarch to be executed – by Cromwell and his less-than-merry band. Cromwell did not want to be king, but he did want his own son to rule after him. Thankfully, the son wasn't up to the job and the joyless eleven years of the Commonwealth ended with Charles II being restored to the throne. With less power, certainly, and no heir, which led to a very able Dutch princeling becoming joint monarch with his wife, who had a better right to the throne. And here we find echo back to Henry VII, whose wife, the eldest daughter of Edward IV, certainly had more right to the throne than Henry did. Mary II declared she would not rule alone, leading to William III doing the donkey work, which was what he wanted all along.

All these monarchs had people in their lives they favoured. Indeed, the last Stuart monarch, Queen Anne, is best known for two favourites, one of whom, when you look at the truth of the matter, was not a favourite in fact, but simply a trusted and devoted *servant*. So, please ignore all the hoo-hah in the 2018 film, *The Favourite*.

So, taking the above-mentioned into account, one would think that, as the power of the monarchy lessened, so would the power of the favourite. But, as you will see from this book, that is not always the case. Monarchy has an aura that still surrounds it, and monarchs still have close friends, of course. However, the monarch has to be seen to be impartial and should not, allegedly, express any political opinions, something that is minutely scrutinised by the media. Charles III has a close and loyal inner circle, but they do not wield the power of, say, John Morton in Henry VII's reign, Robert Dudley in Elizabeth I's reign, the Duke of Buckingham in James I and VI's reign, or Sarah Churchill in the first years of Queen Anne's reign. Although, that said, favour in high places has always and will always open doors.

Henry VII

Francis Bacon completed his biography of Henry VII in 1622, presenting him as a *model* of kingship. Moreover, he presented his book to the future Charles I in the belief that a perfect king distanced himself from all his subjects but chose able, sober ministers. Ministers who, in Bacon's opinion, were very like himself – he'd had something of a raw deal hooking his star to people like the disgraced Earl of Essex, and then the Duke of Buckingham. He ended up as a scapegoat for the latter, being thrown to the mercy of the House of Commons wolf-pack to save his patron. Bacon was dismissive of Henry VII's courtiers, but his opinion remained the most influential one right up until the end of the nineteenth century.[1]

It is true that Henry was wise enough to realise he had to make his court the most sparkling and prominent in Europe, not least to negate the widely held view that his claim to the throne was tenuous to say the least. Indeed, Richard III described him as someone who 'hath no manner of interest, right title, or colour, as every man knoweth, for he is descended of bastard blood, both of father's side and mother's side'.[2] Which was true!

Mindful that his wife's father had cared little for anything in his later years except eating, drinking and sex, Henry knew he had to be different. As his reign went on, he fully realised that gaining the throne many thought was not his was not the end of the battle; he then fought relentlessly to keep sitting on it. Henry became a man who, by necessity, had to maintain control over everything, if only to ensure that nothing in or close to his court could be fomented without him discovering it.

One of his methods was to keep a very – *very* – close scrutiny over every aspect of his government, especially the fiscal side. What we would call his work ethic resulted in him toiling over the minutiae of every entry in his account books. And signing every entry, until in 1504, his failing eyesight meant he signed every page instead.

But Henry was not all work and no play. Gunn tells the story of how, in 1507, despite his failing eyesight, Henry went hunting and hawking every day. One can only imagine how the farmer felt whose farmyard cockerel Henry shot in error.[3]

He also enjoyed gambling, once having to raid the royal coffers in 1492 to pay off a loss of £40 (worth £36,655.48 in 2024).[4]

But how did this outwardly dour young man, hiding a cool, observant, mind under a veneer of polite etiquette, finally manage to fulfil his formidable mother's lifelong ambition and sit upon the throne of England?

Henry Tudor was born in Pembroke Castle on 28 January 1457, coincidentally, the day on which his successor died 90 years later. It was the early days of the Wars of the Roses – sometimes known as the Cousins' War – but the hatred of the previous few years between the houses of Lancaster and York was about to boil over into a sporadic but ever-present conflict that would only end when the child born that January day in a Welsh castle won the Battle of Bosworth twenty-eight years later.

His mother, Lady Margaret Beaufort, a diminutive lady, was only 13 years of age. His father, Edmund Tudor, died of plague before his son came into the world. And what a world it turned out to be.

In 1461, the Yorkist Edward of York, triumphed at the Battle of Towton in Yorkshire. Allegedly the bloodiest battle ever fought on English soil, it made the victor Edward IV and the House of York triumphant. For a while.

The consequences for the young Henry, Earl of Richmond, were profound. The 4-year-old found himself without lands, which were all given to Yorkist followers. He was taken from his mother's care and placed with Sir William Herbert, to be brought up with his children at Raglan Castle.[5]

The problem for the new king was that this latest Lancaster sprig needed careful monitoring. The son born to Margaret of Anjou and Henry VI, Edward of Lancaster – sometimes called Edward of Westminster, but seldom Edward, Prince of Wales – was under the care of his mother, first in Scotland where they fled, but later to France where Margaret set up a court in exile.[6]

Edward IV, a very canny operator, decided to keep the young Henry of Richmond in England, which worked very well. Until, in late 1470, Edward was overthrown and Henry VI was brought out of imprisonment in the Tower of London to be reinstated. The young Henry was briefly reunited with his mother after a gap of some ten years. He was placed with his uncle, Jasper Tudor in Wales. And all looked sunny again.

Except that Edward, having left his pregnant queen – who fled into sanctuary at Westminster – escaped to Europe along with his younger brother, Richard. Edward had absolutely no intention of giving up his throne that easily. He returned to England, landing at Ravenspur on the Yorkshire coast and ingenuously insisting he came only to claim his inheritance as Duke of York.

The following few months were the stuff of which legends are made. Edward, 6′ 4″ tall, handsome, charismatic to the extent he could win over even the most intransigent of men, a joy to behold, especially to women, rode down to London, gaining followers and forming an army as he went. He entered London in triumph. The mistake the then Archbishop of Canterbury made was to parade a confused Henry VI through the streets to gain the loyalty of Londoners. The contrast between the shambling Henry VI in a dirty robe and the magnificent man on a white horse could not have been greater.

Within days, Edward won the second Battle of Barnet and immediately yomped his army to Gloucestershire to prevent Margaret of Anjou and her son crossing the River Severn to her Welsh adherents. The subsequent Battle of Tewkesbury was the dynasty decider and Edward won it.

Jasper Tudor, realising that the 14-year-old Henry Tudor's life was not worth a scabby dog, immediately set sail with his nephew to France and thence to Brittany.

And there Henry stayed. For another fourteen years. Until Edward was dead, a ten-year-old child was on the throne, and the late king's younger brother, Richard, discovered that his brother had once been contracted to marry Eleanor Butler – allegedly. This pre-contract made Edward's marriage to Elizabeth Woodville invalid and *all* their children illegitimate.

Richard went from being a loyal brother and protector of his young nephews, to a usurper who could not abide the prospect of a boy, Edward V, the product of a 'corrupt' marriage, ruling England. The last time either of the young princes were seen was in the Tower of London in July 1483, leading to one of history's most enduring mysteries.

Richard, used to the bluff, plain-speaking of men in the north of England, was noticeably unpopular among the courtiers used to a more *refined*, or if you prefer, *devious*, way of going about things. Disaffected factions began to sound out Henry Tudor across the water, helped by the dowager queen and Henry's mother, of course, who were destabilising Richard from within the court. It helped that the French decided to support Henry as well.

To cut a long story short, Henry and his small army of adherents landed at Milford Haven, marched through Wales gathering more support, and against the odds – helped largely by Lord Stanley doing his usual perfidious about-face when it was convenient – won the Battle of Bosworth, on 22 August 1485.

Henry's first act was to backdate his victory to 21 August, automatically making anyone who had fought on the Yorkist side a traitor and enabling him to do a land and money grab. It was a precursor to the way he reigned.

For the first years of his reign, the new king was very short of money. While exiled, he had accumulated debts that he was determined to repay – and did. But he also had to defend this throne for which he had risked so much. And that cost money, especially when it came to the pretenders, Lambert Simnel and Perkin Warbeck. He had also abandoned Chamber finance, and so, in 1486 and again in 1489, he had to send out tax-gatherers to demand loans from his richer subjects. In the long run, this enhanced his reputation because all those loans were repaid.[7]

That said, a traditional tax called the 'Fifteenth and Tenth' had, against all original purpose, fallen most heavily on the poor. So, when Henry asked parliament to raise a tax in 1489, at which time he was determined to help Brittany from being absorbed by France, and needed money, parliament had to make up the shortfall by reintroducing the 'Fifteenth and Tenth'. An angry mob near Thirsk murdered the Earl of Northumberland, who was responsible for collecting it, and started an uprising.[8]

Henry faced a sea of troubles. England had spent the previous thirty years in a series of sporadic battles. The wars seemed to be over after Tewkesbury in 1471, and Edward IV was a popular king, unlike his brother, Richard. Henry's major concern was to cement his right to be king. His choice of queen was fundamental to this, so it is not surprising, given the alliance of Margaret Beaufort and Elizabeth Woodville, that it was decided marriage to Elizabeth of York, Edward IV's eldest daughter, would not only represent the united houses of York and Lancaster but also be a validation of his claim to the throne. In very short order, Margaret Beaufort had taken the 18-year-old Elizabeth into her keeping and control, where Henry had access to court her.[9]

Henry quickly made those loyal to him a major part of his government. People like John Morton, and Richard Foxe, both of whom we will meet later. But he was also aware that he needed those who were, perhaps, not *quite* loyal in his council, like the aforementioned treacherous Lord Stanley – can you tell he is not exactly a favourite of mine? Included in the not quite loyal camp, was his wife-to-be's maternal family, the Woodvilles.

At his first parliament, he backdated his reign, extended pardons to anyone who acknowledged his right to the throne, and claimed Richard III had been a usurper. He also repealed the *Titulus Regius*, Richard's 1484 Act of Parliament that stated Edward IV's marriage to Elizabeth Woodville to be invalid and their children therefore illegitimate. It was decreed that every copy be found, returned to parliament and destroyed:

> … that the said Bill, Act and Record, be annulled and utterly destroyed, and that it be ordained by the same Authority, that the same Act and Record be taken out of the Roll of Parliament, and be cancelled and brent [burned], and be put in perpetual oblivion.[10]

The proposed marriage to Elizabeth of York was popular, but Henry needed to ensure everybody knew he did not need to marry her to be the lawful king. They were married in January 1486; and in suspiciously short order, the new queen was pregnant. She delivered Prince Arthur, allegedly prematurely, the following September. His name was chosen deliberately to evoke the legendary king and imprint even more that Henry was the rightful monarch.

But the Wars of the Roses were not over. In 1487, funded by Edward IV's sister, Margaret, Duchess of Burgundy, John de la Pole, Earl of Lincoln – Richard III's chosen successor – declared a lad called Lambert Simnel to be Edward, Earl of Warwick, the son of George, Duke of Clarence. Henry met the rebels at the Battle of Stoke Field. The royal forces were superior and the rebels defeated. De la Pole was killed in the battle and, in a gesture of clemency, Simnel was sent to work in the royal kitchens.[11]

There was one last hurrah for the disaffected Yorkists. In 1497, again funded by Margaret of Burgundy, the Cornish uprising provided a perfect opportunity for Perkin Warbeck to be presented as the younger of the princes in the Tower, Richard, Duke of York. Sadly, Perkin did not fare so well as Lambert Simnel.

By this time, Henry was determined to ally himself with the might of Spain through a marriage between Prince Arthur and Katherine of Aragon. Ferdinand of Aragon and Isabella of Castile were concerned at the possible threat posed to the English throne by Edward, Earl of Warwick, (who possibly had learning difficulties), son of George, Duke of Clarence, middle brother in the Edward IV/Richard III sandwich, and Perkin Warbeck, at this time imprisoned in the Tower of London. Warwick had been imprisoned in the Tower since Henry's accession. Warbeck had been temporarily released once he had confessed he was not Richard, Duke of York, but then escaped, was recaptured, and sent back to the Tower.[12]

The Spanish monarchs made it plain that while Warwick and Warbeck were alive, they could not possibly send their beloved daughter to marry the Prince of Wales. Henry arranged for the two prisoners to meet and become friendly. They were then accused of conspiring to rebel against him. In November 1499, Warbeck was beheaded and, five days later, so was Warwick.[13] It was said that the state murder of the unfortunate Warwick was something for which Katherine of Aragon always felt responsible and that her marriage to Arthur originated in blood.[14] The marriage took place, but five months later, Arthur died, possibly of the sweating sickness, a disease that came in with the Tudors, perhaps with Henry's original army that landed at Milford Haven, and it also went out with the Tudors, the last outbreak being in 1561 when Henry's granddaughter, Elizabeth, was queen.

Arthur's death left the 10-year-old Henry as the heir to his father's throne. In 1503, Elizabeth of York died aged 37, shortly after giving birth to a daughter who also died. She was 37. As King Henry grew older, he grew more paranoid and miserly, in some cases not even bothering to find out if the actions of his main ministers, Dudley and Empson, were legal. Thomas Penn in his book *Winter King*, asserts that the case of Thomas Sunnyff was not only blatantly illegal, stripping the man of all his money and imprisoning him, but that Henry knew perfectly well it was illegal. Sunnyff was a respectable, prosperous, London haberdasher, accused alongside his wife of murdering a newborn child. The pair were obviously innocent, as Henry knew perfectly well, but it did not stop him conniving in an illegal act to help fill his coffers.[15]

He also refused to return any of Katherine of Aragon's dowry, at one point apparently even considering marrying her himself. What he left his second son was a stable land, regard for England as a power in Europe, and very, *very* full coffers.

Not a very nice man we might assert. But monarchs are not there to be nice; they are there to reign over their land and leave it to their children. When you consider that for the first twenty-eight years of Henry Tudor's life, he never knew for certain if the next person he encountered had been sent to kill him, one can understand his actions. A more than able administrator, he left the beginnings of a dynasty that, although it only lasted 118 years, has always been a subject of fascination; leading to hundreds of books, plenty of films and television documentaries and series. I have always thought of Henry VII as a 'Marmite' man.

But the one thing nobody can deny about this divisive king, is that he found England in a complete mess, virtually bankrupt, the people ground down by thirty years of conflict, and law and order in disarray. Or that by the time he died in 1509, the country was more prosperous – not least the royal coffers, which were bulging – and he had reigned, with a couple of hiccups, over almost a quarter of a century of peace.

Fun Fact

Elizabeth II was Henry's 14 times great-granddaughter, being descended from Elizabeth of Bohemia, daughter of James VI who was Henry's great-great-grandson.

John Morton (Later Cardinal)

The origin of English public house names has engendered many books. When I was young, there were two names that made me curious. One was called 'The Marquis of Granby'. The proliferation of this name stemmed, I was told, from John Manners, Marquis of Granby, who had a habit of setting up his retiring retainers as pub landlords.

The other name was 'The Morton Fork', the name of a pub in a town a few miles from where I was brought up. For years, I wondered about that name. It was only when I began to study Tudor history that I learned what it meant.

John Morton was born around 1420 in Dorset. He was a cleric, as well as a civil lawyer. Both were useful for the future Henry VII. Morton was educated at Oxford, becoming a Doctor of Civil Law in 1451 and later being elected as chancellor of Oxford University for life. He practised as an advocate in the Canterbury ecclesiastical court, coming to the notice of Thomas Bourchier who subsequently became Archbishop of Canterbury.

In 1456, Morton was assigned as chancellor for the son of Henry VI and Margaret of Anjou. Under the Lancastrian king, he held three clerical benefices, requiring a papal dispensation to hold them all at the same time. When Richard, Duke of York, together with the Earl of Warwick rebelled against Henry VI, lost the Battle of Ludford Bridge and were forced to flee, Morton was involved in drawing up the act of attainder against them. However, the tables were turned at the Battle of Towton, when Morton was captured trying to escape. He was brought before Edward IV in Newcastle and was very lucky not to lose his head, but he did lose all his benefices. He escaped and joined the exiled queen in France, only journeying to England during attempts to reinstate the deposed King Henry VI.

Following the Lancastrian defeat at Tewkesbury in 1471, Edward IV, as was his wont, pardoned Morton who resumed his career in royal service. Edward was nothing if not pragmatic, and he recognised what a very able minister Morton was.[16]

He became Master of the Rolls, second only to the Lord Chancellor and Keeper of the Great Seal if the Lord Chancellor was absent. Once again, he began to gather benefices, around a dozen, all of which filled his coffers. He was also involved in negotiations with the French to extend the truce between the two countries, on the payment of 50,000 crowns to Edward by the French – roughly just over £11 million in 2024.

In 1479, Morton was made Bishop of Ely, at which point he gave up his other posts. The Italian, Dominic Mancini, described him as 'having no small influence' with King Edward. While Bishop of Ely, Morton rebuilt the Bishops' Palace at Hatfield as a red-brick stately home. He also built a 40-mile ditch, Morton's Dyke, between Stanground (near Peterborough) and Wisbech.[17]

All seemed rosy in Morton's world until Edward died very suddenly in 1483. He made preparations to crown the 10-year-old Prince Edward as Edward V, but Richard of Gloucester, the late king's younger brother, had other ideas. Richard arrested Morton, Archbishop Rotherham and Lord Hastings. Hastings was summarily beheaded and the two clerics were imprisoned in the Tower of

London. Rotherham was released, but Morton was sent to Wales and imprisoned there. After failing to unseat Richard during Buckingham's Rebellion, Morton escaped to Flanders. He was subsequently named in an Act of Attainder by Richard and stripped of all his possessions. Richard granted him a pardon, but Morton refused to return to England. And so would I have done!

In 1485, he was in Rome, ostensibly to gain a papal indulgence to repair the dykes in the Isle of Ely and Ely Cathedral, which had been damaged in floods. There are grounds for believing, however, that his primary concern was to gain a papal dispensation for the marriage of Henry Tudor, Duke of Richmond to Elizabeth of York, a requirement deemed necessary, since both parties were descended from John of Gaunt.

After Henry Tudor's victory at Bosworth, the new king called Morton to return to England. He was made chancellor in 1486 and became Henry's trusted advisor, as far as Henry ever trusted anyone. Henry made all the decisions, advised by his council, but his was usually the final decision. Morton *et al.* administered those decisions. When Bourchier died, Morton became the new Archbishop of Canterbury and after significant pressure on the Pope, he was made a cardinal in 1493. He carried out many building works, especially to the manor at Knole, but his favourite residence was Lambeth Palace and he built what is now called Morton's Tower.

He also completed the central crossing tower in Canterbury Cathedral, known as Bell Harry Tower. Morton's falcon, perched on a cask, is displayed on the stonework, showing that it was his project. Morton died at Knole in 1500. It is possible he died from the same plague that may have killed the very young Prince Edmund. For Henry, the loss of his most trusted advisor was beyond description. He had delivered what Henry wanted and what Morton himself believed – described by Penn as 'strong, forceful kingship'.[18] But the truth was Morton was revered and hated in equal measure, especially for his onerous taxation policies.[19]

Which is where we circle back to the name of the pub, 'The Morton Fork'. If we are going to be pedantic, it should really have been called *The Morton Cleft Stick*. Francis Bacon, the first biographer of Henry VII, was scathing of Morton's taxation programme, which probably accounts for why Morton is now considered to be a minor royal aide. Modern Ricardians also believe that Morton disseminated lies about Richard; lies that influenced Thomas More, who later wrote most of the Tudor propaganda regarding Richard that held such sway until the twentieth century.

However, there are those who consider that Morton held Henry back from excesses the king would have like to enact, and it is only after his death that

Henry expanded his royal obsession with gathering as much money as possible, to the point of tyranny.[20]

The *cleft stick* can be summed up in a few sentences. Morton travelled round the country inviting himself to stay with this lord or that lord. If it was discovered the lord in question lived simply, Morton said that in living so frugally, he must have a lot of money saved and was taxed accordingly. If the lord in question lived in conspicuous wealth, Morton averred that by so living, he obviously had a lot of money and could be taxed accordingly. A device worthy of Henry himself. The first Tudor *Heads I win, Tails you lose* situation.

Reginald (Reynold) Bray

Bray is often regarded as firstly, Margaret Beaufort's factotum and general manager of her affairs, and then as one of Henry VII's most astute advisors, described as a sort of 'Tudor Prime Minister and chancellor of the exchequer rolled into one'.[21]

A story told by Penn details the exquisite difficulty Henry VII laboured under, having taken the throne by combat from the 'usurper', Richard, but in some quarters regarded as a usurper himself. Having spent his formative years in the French court, Henry knew that in France, whatever the king said was law, whereas in England, the king had to obey the law.

Penn narrates that in the aftermath of the Cornish Rebellion where the rebels had reached as close to London as Blackheath, Reginald Bray, by then Henry's spymaster, read the report of an exchange between two men who had fought on the royal side to quell the uprising. One man urged his companion to 'pray for Henry VII'. The other replied, 'we need not pray for the King by name, but "pro rege nostro tunc" – just "for our king"'. This was Henry's dilemma and deepest fear. That even those who wanted to maintain the status quo were not sure who should maintain it.[22]

Bray was one of those people who are always at the centre of things, regardless of where that centre happened to be. When Margaret Beaufort was conspiring with Buckingham in 1483, helped by Bishop John Morton, it was Bray who carried messages to the conspirators. Morton described him as 'secret, sober and well-witted'. Bray was, allegedly, the person who found the crown of England in the thorn bush after Bosworth and gave it to Lord Stanley so that he could crown his stepson. It was Bray who is said to have told Henry about the Stafford uprising in 1486.[23]

Reginald Bray was born close to Worcester in 1440. He knew the young Henry Tudor well, having been sent by Margaret Beaufort on missions to him while in exile in France. By the time of the Battle of Bosworth, Bray had been in Margaret's service for over twenty years and was quickly taken on by the new king.

He quickly became adept at raising money for Henry and it is said that some of his methods pre-empted those of Henry's later ministers, Dudley and Empson. Like John Morton, Bray was an inveterate builder, both for himself and giving funding to friends or assisting building projects he believed important. He helped fund the 'Magnificat' window in Great Malvern Priory, contributed to Jesus College, Cambridge, and assisted with the building at Bath Abbey among many others. His major building work, however, was St George's Chapel, Windsor, and it became a major beneficiary during his life and after his death. It is where he is buried, although there is no tomb, but his coffin was, allegedly, found in 1740.

He married around 1475, but remained childless, his widow outliving him by three years. She brought him considerable estates in Sussex, Berkshire and Hampshire, but the greater part of his holdings were gained after Bosworth, partly through royal patronage and partly through exploiting his position.[24]

Henry did not keep many people close to him, but he had known Bray from when he had been at Raglan Castle as a child. Always loyal to Margaret Beaufort, Bray spent the years Henry was in exile making contacts and raising money for the invasion. When he entered Henry's service, Bray's financial astuteness was key because the royal coffers were bare. Penn describes his methods as 'brutally efficient' and his measures gradually extended to the whole country. He was one of the very few people Henry and Margaret trusted. He was known to be blunt and to contradict the king. After the shocking early death of Prince Arthur, when Henry was too grieved to concentrate much on affairs of state, it was Bray who made a list of what needed doing to keep the country running properly. The list included fining jailers who allowed prisoners to escape, the sales of royal wardships, and investigating customs offences. The most important things on the list that Henry had to deal with were auditing the royal accounts and sorting out Henry's will.

But just as Bray ensured the royal coffers were full, he also made equally sure his own were, taking a cut of leases of Crown lands, marriages of rich heiresses and the like. He received pensions for access to the king – otherwise known as bribes – bought up portfolios of estates all over the south of England, mostly through compulsory purchase, and generally embodied the phrase *you're first in the queue after me*. He more than helped Henry to become the tyrant of later years.[25]

And what was it all for? Bray died in 1503 with no issue. His estate was parcelled out to a daughter of his blood brother and the sons of a half-brother.

Giles Daubeney

Daubeney was the eldest son and heir of Sir William Daubeney, MP for Bedfordshire in 1448/49, and Sheriff of Cornwall in 1452/53.[26] He was born in Somerset, in June 1451. Descended from a Norman family that came over with William the Conqueror, his ancestors built Belvoir Castle on the Leicestershire/ Lincolnshire border. Although his forebears in the reigns of Edward I and II were called to parliament, they never held the title until Giles was made a baron by Henry VII.

Under Edward IV, he accompanied the king to France and obtained a licence to make a trust-deed of his lands in Somerset and Dorset before being designated as a squire. Soon after, in the mid-1470s, he was made an esquire of the king's body and granted custody of the king's park at Petherton near Bridgwater. He became the MP for Somerset, after which he was knighted by Edward IV.

However, by conviction, he was a supporter of Henry Tudor, Earl of Richmond and, as such, was consulted by Reginald Bray regarding the Buckingham rebellion and the 1485 invasion. After the failure of the rebellion, he fled to Brittany and was attainted by Richard III, with all his lands being confiscated.

Those fortunes were reversed when Henry VII won Bosworth and became king. He was made a privy councillor, appointed as Master of the Mint, and Master of the king's harthounds. He was also granted the offices of Constable of Winchester Castle, Bristol Castle, and steward of lands held by the Duchy of Lancaster in Hampshire and Dorset, among others.

Henry also sent Daubeney to France to help Anne of Brittany in a treaty against France, but by 1492, Brittany had lost its independence. At this point, Henry sent emissaries, including Daubeney, to negotiate a peace with Charles VIII, but this failed, so Henry invaded France to force the French to the negotiating table. Daubeney was one of the main negotiators.

In 1493, Henry granted Daubeney joint office of chief justice of all the royal forests, along with Reginald Bray, and in 1495, following the execution of Sir William Stanley, who had gone one betrayal too far, Daubeney was made Lord Chamberlain. Being one of Henry's trusted councillors, Henry sent him to Scotland to punish James IV for his support of Perkin Warbeck. However, almost before he had started out, Henry recalled him to put down Cornish rebels, who had massed at Blackheath. He was captured by them but quickly released.

In 1500, he accompanied the king on his journey to Calais to ratify the marriage treaty between Prince Arthur and Katherine of Aragon, and the following year he was made responsible for the Spanish princess' reception in London. In 1503, he witnessed the betrothal of Henry's elder daughter, Margaret, to James IV of Scotland.

By 1504, Daubeney was Constable of Bridgewater Castle and given all the lands in Somerset and Dorset that had belonged to the now dead Elizabeth of York. In the years that followed, he was granted lands in Buckinghamshire and Devon. In February 1508, he attended the gout-ridden Henry on the anniversary of the late queen's death, but later that year, on 18 May, he was suddenly taken ill after riding with the king from Eltham to Greenwich. He was ferried down the Thames to his house in London, where, on 20 May, after receiving the sacrament, he died.[27]

After the execution of Stanley, Daubeney was constantly at Henry's side, and it would appear from his many military forays, that he was Henry's go-to man for anything that required a military presence. Katherine of Aragon allegedly told her father, Ferdinand of Aragon, that Daubeney was the one person who could persuade Henry if that was needed. It is interesting that in 1505, he secured the lease of Hampton Court Palace.[28]

Giles Daubeney was buried where his will had decreed, in Westminster Abbey. He lies in St Paul's Chapel, with effigies of himself and his wife side by side.[29]

Richard Foxe

Richard Foxe – sometimes Fox – was born around 1448 in Ropsley, a village near Grantham in Lincolnshire. Not much is known about his early life, but his parents are believed to have been of the yeoman class, and it is thought he may have studied at Magdalen College, Oxford. That apart, virtually nothing is known about him until the age of around 35.

He may have been studying in Paris in 1484, possibly because he had fallen foul of Richard III. However, he met Henry Tudor there and was quickly taken into the latter's service. What is known is that in early 1485, Richard III prevented Foxe's appointment to the vicarage of Stepney because he was in the company of 'the great rebel, Henry ap Tuddor'.

After the Battle of Bosworth, Henry made Foxe his principal secretary, and soon after the Lord Privy Seal. This would indicate that his previous experience included a good deal of political service. And, of course, Henry preferred to rule through lawyers and churchmen, rather than the lords of the land who were liable to rebel and had been responsible for the Wars of the Roses.

Foxe was then elected Bishop of Exeter, and although he received the salary for that position, he was kept at Henry's side, confined to political and diplomatic roles under the eye of Cardinal John Morton. When that prelate died, Foxe took over his duties, negotiating a treaty with James III of Scotland, and, in 1491, baptising Prince Henry, later King Henry VIII.

In 1494, he was appointed to the see of Durham, possibly because it was richer than Bath and Wells, but also because of its strategic importance, being located close to the Scottish border. He would be at hand to conduct any negotiations which might arise. As they did in 1497, during the Perkin Warbeck uprising, when Scotland invaded the north of England. Foxe occupied and defended Norham Castle.

That said, most of his actions were towards the pursuit of peace, and he was instrumental in negotiating the marriage treaty between James IV of Scotland and Henry's daughter, Margaret Tudor, a marriage that had far-reaching consequences, leading ultimately to proposals for the Union of England and Scotland Act under James I & VI a century later, proposals which were defeated but which James used to style himself King of Great Britain.

Foxe was also involved in the arrangements for the marriage of Prince Arthur to Katherine of Aragon, and, at the end of Henry VII's reign, that of the latter's younger daughter, Mary, to the future emperor, Charles V. That particular marriage did not happen since the new king, Henry VIII, wanted Mary to marry the French king instead.

Lady Margaret Beaufort made Foxe one of the executors of her will. An interesting conundrum about Foxe is his alleged involvement in the creation of Morton's Fork by Erasmus, through Sir Thomas More. It was said of Foxe that he would sacrifice his father to save his king.

When Henry VIII came to the throne, Foxe's powers increased. By this time, he had been appointed Bishop of Winchester. The Spanish ambassador said that the new king trusted Foxe more than any other advisor, but that Henry implied that Foxe's name suited him as he was 'Foxe indeed'. He differed with Archbishop Warham, who was doubtful as to the canonical validity of Henry's marriage to Katherine of Aragon, while Foxe championed it.

However, nothing lasts for ever, and by 1515, another very able advisor outshone Foxe's influence. Thomas Wolsey was firmly in the ascendant, directing an aggressive foreign policy against France and against Foxe's views.

He was edged out of power mainly by Thomas Wolsey's policies with which he disagreed. By the mid-1520s, Foxe had decided to devote himself to his Church duties – and not before time, one might say. He became vocal about monastic 'depravity', but by this time, he had gone blind. However, he hung on to the diocese of Winchester, despite heavy lobbying from Wolsey that he should retire on a pension. Wolsey had to wait until Foxe died before he could add Winchester to his own episcopal holdings in York and St Albans.

Foxe died in 1528 at Wolvesley in Hampshire. One other interesting thing remains to be told. Foxe's greatest achievement was the foundation of Corpus Christi College in Oxford, something greatly praised by Erasmus. Foxe had originally intended it to be for the use of the monks of St Swithins in Winchester, but it is alleged he was persuaded not to do this by Bishop Oldham, who foretold the fall of all things monastic. Foxe also endowed grammar schools in Taunton and Grantham.[30]

His tomb is in Winchester Cathedral, and shows him as a wasted cadaver, something well beyond the bounds of what was considered appropriate at that time.[31]

Henry VIII

Ask virtually anyone to name an English king and Henry VIII will almost certainly come out on top. Maybe with William the Conqueror and Richard III in the mix. Henry has turned into, arguably, the most divisive and fascinating monarch England ever had.

So, what new can be said of him when there are literally thousands of books written about this man, his wives, his ministers, the Reformation, and the rest of it? What turned Katherine of Aragon's *Sir Loyal Heart* into a grotesquely overweight tyrannical monster?

The real question should probably be *is there anything new to say?* The short answer is I don't know, but I am always up for a challenge.

We know the principal order of events in his life.

Henry was born at Greenwich Palace on 28 June 1491. He was a bright boy, and reports suggest that his father paid more attention to his elder brother, Arthur. Understandable since he would be the first heir to the new Tudor dynasty, and Henry was the spare who might well end up in the Church. It is believed that Arthur's early death, when his younger brother was only 10, caused the king and queen to chance another pregnancy to save the dynasty, and, sadly, this led not only to Elizabeth's death, but the death of the baby, who was another girl.

Henry had been favoured by his mother, possibly because she saw characteristics of her father in the boy, who was incredibly close to her. Henry was devastated when she died on her thirty-seventh birthday. This theory is supported by a recently discovered picture of a small, red-headed boy kneeling by a bed, his head in his hands, obviously crying. The bed in question is thought to be that of Elizabeth of York, who died in 1503, only a year after the death of Prince Arthur. Henry was 11.[32]

In his youth and early manhood, he presented as the embodiment of kingship. His skeleton, examined in 1813, was 6′ 2″ (185 cms) tall. The Spanish ambassador said in 1507, 'his limbs are of a gigantic size'. Several sources say he had fair skin and a fresh colour, with auburn hair – evidenced by strands still adhering to his skull. His health was excellent, and his energy and vigour incredible. He was idealistic, generous and genial, but also highly strung, emotional and suggestible. His worst sins were thought to be complacency, self-indulgence, and vanity. It was only as he grew older that he became suspicious and cunning. His later arrogance, ruthlessness, and brutality were masked by his charisma and cordiality.[33]

The young Henry did not know his brother well. Arthur, being the heir, was put in a separate household from a young age, and, since there was a five-year age gap between the two boys, they may well not have had much in common anyway. Cunningham asserts that they probably only met on state occasions and very few other times. Henry VII's entire focus was on creating in Arthur, mindfully named to evoke the mythical king – the perfect king. Arthur's learning ensured he was taught every skill he would need when he succeeded to the throne, 'all of the skills, experiences, servants and advisors needed to reign successfully'.[34]

All that fell apart when Arthur died in the spring of 1502 and deteriorated still further when Queen Elizabeth died the day after her new baby. Henry VII's priority was the survival of his dynasty through his second son. Prince Henry was charming, and blessed with the charisma of his maternal grandfather. In addition, he was handsome and sociable, something his father was not. Because Henry VII's health began to fail after the double blow of losing his heir and wife in short succession, the young Henry found he was immediately expected to take up the slack at the age of almost 13. There is evidence he may have resented this curtailment of his usual pleasures. He was very literate, musical, and had a thirst for learning, but possibly no taste for learning statecraft. Even at this early age, there are signs of the future king who was terrified of disease, understandable when he had lost his brother and mother within the space of 12 months.[35]

Henry succeeded to the throne in the spring of 1509. He quickly proved to be astute in summing people up and using them to do the hard graft, while he had a good time enjoying spending money, something his father had never permitted, but that Thomas Wolsey cultivated and encouraged. Obedient to his father's wishes, Henry married Katherine of Aragon in June 1509, leading to the most controversial wedding night in history and one that would be raked over endlessly some twenty years later when Henry wanted his divorce. While all was not always sweetness and light, the marriage jogged along. Katherine accepted the reality of the birth of a son to Henry's mistress, Bessie Blount, something Henry later trumpeted to prove he *could* sire sons.

And then he set eyes on Anne Boleyn, who resisted all his blandishments and refused to become his mistress. Wolsey, of course, by this time was a cardinal. He made the fatal error of getting on the wrong side of Anne, allegedly because he blocked her marriage to Henry Percy, future Earl of Northumberland.

Thomas Cromwell, Wolsey's protégé, read the runes correctly. He began to move away from his master. Wolsey had taught Henry that the reins of government were best held by one pair of hands, by which, he meant his own. Henry learned that lesson well, so well that when Wolsey could not deliver the annulment of his twenty-year-old marriage, the king decided those hands had better be his own.

The rest is, as they say, history. The Reformation that won Henry his divorce, the doomed marriage to Anne, the disaster of the jousting tournament that had Henry coming off his horse and being unconscious for almost two hours, leaving him with a life of pain and suffering that fed his inherited instincts for paranoia and tyranny. Many historians have posited that his later problems with ulcerated legs that burst open and bled pus, were due to syphilis. But his doctors would have treated that with mercury. Now it is thought that not only did Henry never suffer from syphilis, but the problem with his legs was due to fragments of bone broken off in a riding accident – possibly the one in 1536. The cycle of swelling and intense pain, followed by the wounds being opened and the resultant discharge being allowed to escape support that theory.[36]

Cromwell's bent towards the new religion hastened the Dissolution of the Monasteries. But it channelled huge amount of monies from the dissolved monasteries straight into the royal coffers. This was not just from the wealth of the Church in terms of plate etc., but also the selling off to Henry's – and Cromwell's – favoured lords the lands, for which they paid top dollar. Neither must we forget Henry's desperate quest for a son and heir, only to lose Jane Seymour in childbirth, the disastrous marriage to Anne of Cleves, and the even more disastrous marriage to Katherine Howard, followed by a haven of as much peace as he ever experienced after the early days with Katherine of Aragon, but this time with Katherine Parr.

She did her absolute best to bring his children into his life more fully and be his helpmeet. She, too, only just escaped being trapped and executed because of her reformist leanings, but survive she did because she used her brains and begged Henry's pardon for her actions saying she only sought to take his mind off his constant pain. And during all this, Henry's health deteriorated. His appetite, insatiable as it had always been, never took account of his increasing physical infirmities. His consumption of red wine was prodigious, echoing the last years of his maternal grandfather.

By the time Henry VIII died, on 28 January 1547, he was a mountain of sick flesh, his piggy eyes buried in layers upon layers of fat.

He was taken ill at Oatlands in December 1546, his doctors struggling to keep him alive. Determined not to appear ill, he travelled to Greenwich to celebrate Christmas there, but had to admit he was ill, so he then travelled to Whitehall, ordering that the palace be closed to all but his closest advisors. He fell ill with another fever at the beginning of January 1547. Although Katherine

Parr and Princess Mary travelled to Whitehall, they were denied admittance to his presence. However, on 26 January, his wife was allowed to see him. He said 'It is God's will that we should part' but began to cry and, unable to carry on, sent her away.

The following day he received Holy Communion and was in his last hours, but nobody dared to tell him. At last, Sir Anthony Denny, his groom of the stool, told the king that 'in man's judgement, he was not like to live'. Denny urged him to confess. Cranmer was sent for, but by the time he arrived, Henry was beyond speech and could only squeeze the archbishop's hand to signify he died in the faith of Christ. Henry VIII died at around 2:00 am, on 28 January 1547, the day his father would have been 90.[37]

No matter what opinion you have about Henry VIII, and mine is not rosy, it was a sad end to a reign that started with such promise and the undeniable adoration of his subjects.

Fun Fact

Copper, covered by a thin layer of silver, was used as a substitute for silver in the coinage. Of course, the silver gradually wore away, especially around the nose of the king's forward-facing portrait. This resulted in the red colour of the copper coming through from below. It also resulted in Henry VIII being given the nickname 'Old Coppernose'.

Significant Events in Henry VIII's Reign and Interesting Snippets

Arguably, in many people's minds at least, the schism that pulled England out of the Roman Catholic Church was fuelled by the thrall in which Henry was held by Anne Boleyn. This was at its height between 1529, when it was becoming clear that the Pope would not annul his marriage to Katherine of Aragon, so that he could marry Anne and welcome the male heir she had promised him.

A peek into the Privy Purse expenses for the years 1529–1532 tell us a lot about what Henry was doing. Where he lived (and it becomes clear that he seldom stayed in one palace for more than a month, probably due to the fact that his entourage and hangers-on were so numerous), the palaces soon became stinking midden heaps that needed what my mother called *a thorough bottoming* and what we now officially call *a deep clean*.

The Privy Purse expenses, collated by Sir Nicholas Harris, traces where Henry was on most days of those three years, what he was doing, and on what he spent his money. His accounts were examined by him and signed off each month. It is a book full of interesting snippets.

On 13 March 1530, Bishop Hugh Latimer preached before the king and was given £5 (£3650 in 2024).

On 21 November 1530, Henry moved to Hampton Court Palace. He was definitely there on 14 October, with occasional forays to York Place (Westminster) and possibly Greenwich, which the Tudors considered 'home'. At the end of November, Henry was told Cardinal Wolsey, then being brought back from York, presumably for a date with the executioner's axe, had died at Leicester Abbey. Henry did not leave Hampton Court until 8 December, but was at Greenwich by 19 December, where he and Queen Katherine kept a 'solemn Christmas'. The reports of the festivities are only evidenced by entries of money given to Princess Mary and Lady Margaret Douglas, Henry's niece, for the purpose of celebrating the festive season. The amount given was £2615 9 shillings and sixpence farthing. This, in 2024 terms, equals £1,909,298 and was spent between 21 December 1530 and 6 January 1531.

There are also details that in the early days of 1531, Henry was occupied by his divorce from Katherine of Aragon, receiving many books from different abbots and priors; books that were ferried from palace to palace with Henry. On 28 May 1531, Henry and Katherine moved to Windsor and stayed there until 14 July, at which point Henry moved to Woodstock.

Katherine never saw him again.

By 4 December 1531, Henry was once more at Hampton Court but kept Christmas at Greenwich. However, 'all men sayde that there was no myrthe in that Christemas because the Queene and the ladies were absent'.

In 1532, Henry see-sawed between York Place (Westminster) and Greenwich, despite there being outbreaks of plague in both places. However, parliament was sitting and his presence was necessary, although he was known to flee at the first sniff of plague or the sweating sickness.

He was all over the place in the summer of 1532, Berkshire, Bedfordshire, Buckinghamshire, and Oxfordshire. The records show he was at Windsor by 1 September 1532 because it was on that day that he created Anne Boleyn Marchioness of Pembroke. There is no description of the ceremony in the Privy Purse expenses, and Anne does not appear in them until 19 September, when she is referred to as the Marchioness of Pembroke.

The expenses show that Henry's next move was to get François of France on side, supporting his divorce from the Spanish Katherine and approving Henry's marriage to Anne. And since Anne had spent several years at the French court, François would have known her, and anything to split the English from the Spanish would be music to his ears.

Henry – and presumably, Anne's – journey to France began on 6 October 1532 from Mote Park in Kent to Sheppey by boat. Henry then stayed overnight in

Canterbury and travelled on to Dover the following day, embarking for Calais – still held by the English – on 11 October.

Upon arrival, Anne received gifts of grapes and pears from the Great Master of France. The cost of all the games, gratuities to musicians etc., an unspecified gift of £700 to Cromwell, clothes, and jewels amounted to £3592 (£2,536,284.08 in 2024).

The total cost for the thirty-three-day visit was £4033 (£2,847,670.85 in 2024). Ninety per cent of that sum was for jewellery. Of course, the *huge* fly in the royal ointment was that Queen Claude refused point blank to attend, or be anywhere near Anne Boleyn, so the latter could not appear officially at all. One can only wish to have been a fly on the wall of the English royal apartments at that point.

Throughout these years, the Privy Purse accounts show Henry's favourite occupation to be gambling, at which he was spectacularly bad. His losses over this period were £3243 (£2,289,857.81 in 2024). But he was careful enough of his subjects' morals – or two-faced enough, depending on your point of view – to have issued a proclamation forbidding *them* to play cards or bowls.

That said, the accounts show he supported music and literature, giving gratuities to scholars and universities, and supporting St Pauls' boys' school and other schools in England and Paris. He also loved architecture and building and spent large sums on building new palaces.

As a footnote to the Privy Purse accounts, there is one instance in November 1530, when Henry ordered a pledge of £20 (£14,602 in 2024), when Anne Boleyn had pawned some jewels to help her sister, Mary.

And what about the abandoned Queen Katherine? Her name in the entire period only appears twice. She had been wiped out of Henry's life.[38]

Henry's Health and Medicinal History

By the early 1540s, Henry VIII was suffering from the chronic ulcers he had probably sustained in the 1536 jousting accident. He also suffered headaches, swollen ankles, and constipation, probably as a result of his increasingly sedentary life, plus the fact he did not rein in either his appetite or his consumption of rich food and wine.

In the British Library, a document – Sloane MS 1047 – gives details of two of Henry's own formulations to treat himself. The document itself contains almost 200 recipes. The following is one of Henry's own devising – an ointment to help heal skin sores and ulcers:

Take chamomile flowers, mellilote flowers, rose leaves, honeysuckle leaves – in the same amount equally. Boil these in water of rose and honeysuckle flowers as much as shall suffice, then strain, and take thereof – 1 ounce. Then take hens suett well washed with rose water of province more than luke-warm – 2 ounces. Then take litharge of gold – 2 ounces. Tutie [a crude zinc oxide compound] preperated [rinsed to purify], red coral, – in the same amount – ½ ounce. Pearls – 2 ounces. Unicorn horn – 1 ounce. All these finely powdered, mixed with the decoction [medical preparation made by boiling], and hence, boil them until it be an unguent [an ointment].

'A Pusset Ointment devised by the King Majesty at Hampton Court to heal excoriations' (folio 43v).

Some of the ingredients Henry used were poisonous, others just plain bizarre. 'Unicorn' horn, probably refers to narwhal horn. Narwhals are often called unicorns of the sea and have a horn protruding from their heads. He also used white lead, nightshade and earthworms – I never thought I would feel sorry for a worm, but there you go.

One of the strangest ingredients was Oleum Vulpinium, and from that second word, you will probably have worked out it has something to do with a fox. And you would be right.

Take a whole Foxe, except the bowels, and put hym in a vessel, and powre uppon him Welle water, and salte Water, [and] old oyle. Seeth thys over a softe fyre, with Salte untyll the Water be consumed. Then put it into a vessel and powre to it sweete Water, wherein the herbes were sodden and […] seeth them again, till the Water be consumed.

I hope I am not being optimistic when wondering if they removed the poor creature's fur first. This remedy was supposed to treat backache, arthritis, and gout.[39]

But Henry did not just treat himself. We are also told of, 'a Medycyn for the pestylence' that 'Kyng Henry the Eight' wrote, which apparently 'hath helpyd dyvers persons'. Henry's secretary also wrote in a letter to Cardinal Wolsey that the king had given him 'remedyes as any connyng phisician in England coude do'.

Also included in MS1047 is a medicine containing chamomile and myrhh as 'A plaster for my ladye Anne of Cleve to mollifie, and resolve, conforte and cease payne of colde and wyndie causses'.[40]

Because of his tremendous appetite – and the prevailing belief that vegetables were only fit for animals and peasants – Henry's diet was very rich in protein and sugar. That, together with his prodigious consumption of red wine, meant one of his constant ailments was constipation.

In 1539, Sir Thomas Heneage wrote about one incidence of the king's constipation. Henry was given a 'glister' (enema) which would probably contain dill oil, white wine, chicken and duck grease, butter, egg whites and cassia fistula plant, the common names for which are golden shower, purging cassia, Indian laburnum, kani konna, or pudding-pipe tree. This would have been given during the evening and Henry advised to go to bed.

The next morning Heneage wrote:

I received your letter this morning, although your servant came over night; 'for by th'advice of the physicians the King's Majesty went betimes to bed, whose Highness slept until two of the clock in the morning, and then his Grace rose to go to the stool which, by working of the pills and glister that his Highness had taken before, had a very fair siege, as the said physicians have made report; not doubting but the worst is past by their perseverance, to no danger of any further grief to remain in him, and the hinder part of the night until 10 of the clock this morning his Grace had very good rest, and his Grace findeth himself well, saving his Highness saith he hath a little soreness in his body. And I would have had his said Majesty to have read your letter, but would that I should make to him relation thereof, whereat his Grace smiled, saying that your Lordship had much more fear than required.' I will send your bills as soon as his Grace has signed them. The long tarrying of your servant here was by my command. Hampthill, Friday, between 10 and 11 a.m.[41]

The probable cause of Henry's deterioration, both emotional and physical, has long been attributed to his 1536 jousting incident, but that is not the whole story. That it began his decline is more than likely, given that he was insensible, 'without speech', for more than two hours with a head injury that, today, would necessitate a CT scan. This was also the probable catalyst for Anne Boleyn's miscarriage and her last chance to produce a living male heir, for the child she miscarried was a boy.

Henry's interest in medicine led, not just to acts of parliament and the foundation of professional medical bodies, but also, under the influence of Sir Thomas More, improvements in public health. He oversaw the installation of public water supplies and a basic approach to dealing with outbreaks of pestilence using segregation and disinfection.

His main health issues stemmed from the various accidents he incurred during his sporting activities. We know enough of Henry's character to realise he would have been fixated on being the absolute best and winning at all costs. Coming second was something his pride would not permit, although there are occasions in his early kingship when his great friend, Charles Brandon sometimes managed to win. In the main, those who played against him knew that it was better if they came second, not least for them.

In 1527, he injured his left foot playing tennis and was forced to wear a loosely-fitting black velvet slipper, something his sycophantic followers copied, thus making it a court fashion. Also in 1527, it is thought a possible jousting accident caused him to be stricken with another injury, this time in his thigh. The reference to his 'sorre legge' may well have been an ulcer.

In his twenties, Henry, around 6' 3" (190 cms), weighed about 15 stones (95 kgs) according to his suits of armour. By the time he died in his mid-fifties, he is thought to have weighed around 28 stones (178 kgs). Since his forties, he had needed a hoist to mount his horse – poor creature!

By 1541, he was unable to take any meaningful exercise. He had a wheeled chair, and a stairthrone – a hoist at Whitehall Palace to get him up and down the stairs. However, he was mindful of the threat to his realm and dynasty from France and spent many hours on horseback, personally overseeing coastal defences.

What did not help – and actively hindered – his below the knee ulcered legs was the prevailing fashion of wearing tight garters to show off his shapely calves, a source of immense pride to him. So much so, that those who did not have such magnificent calves were known to stuff their hose with fabric to create the illusion of them.

Henry also refused to reduce his consumption of meat and wine, and his appetite for high cholesterol foods, all of which are documented in the *Ordinances of Eltham*. This aggravated the ulceration of his legs and, at the same time, reduced his capacity for healing. Even in modern times, there is ample evidence that chronic leg ulcers have serious consequences for the sufferer's quality of life.

For Henry, whose physicians frequently lanced the ulcers with red-hot irons, his suffering must have become unbearable.

Is it any wonder that, looking back over his golden youth, and comparing that to his now morbidly obese, pain-racked body, his vicious rages and immense cruelty came to the fore.[42]

The Field of the Cloth of Gold

We talk about conspicuous consumption today, but I wonder if there has ever been anything to rival the Field of the Cloth of Gold in 1520.

First of all, what *is* cloth of gold? It is a silk fabric where the weft is woven with a spirally-spun gold strip – and yes, the gold is real gold.

Henry VIII of England came together with François I of France at this most splendid and gaudy of summits, in the Pale of Calais. The monarchs and their immense entourages were housed in tents and pavilions, all decorated with sumptuous fabrics, most notably, cloth of gold.

The meeting was originally intended to be a celebration of peace between the two realms. However, it turned into a macho battle between two rival kings who sought to prove to each other and the world that each of them was superior in terms of sport, ruling a nation, and being a patron.

As the hordes from both sides massed, two horsemen rode towards each other, as if on the attack. Instead, they doffed their feathered hats, 'saluted each other, dismounted, and embraced like brothers'.[43]

Most commentators view the Field of the Cloth of Gold as a colossal waste of money, especially when, in 1518, most European states had already suffered prolonged periods of war, or unrest. England had come out of the Hundred Years' War in 1453 and almost immediately into the thirty years of the Wars of the Roses.

It made sense to be at peace. Monarchs were expected to uphold the tenets of Christianity, not to mention that war is enormously expensive. Not just in terms of money, but the effects on the monarchs' subjects, their lives and their livelihoods.

Unlike his father, Henry VIII was filled with the chivalric notions of Edward III in the Hundred Years' War. Immediately upon his accession, he made his intention to go to war with France perfectly clear. His council were very much against this, but Henry was still in the honeymoon period with his subjects and kicked against the opinions of the older generation of councillors.

In this, he was supported by Thomas Wolsey, who was already 'training' Henry in how to run a country while encouraging the new king to go and hunt, play tennis and joust all day, leaving the wily Wolsey to rule.

In 1511, the Pope formed a Holy League against France and Henry joined it. However, his first foray into battle with his father-in-law, Ferdinand of Aragon, was a disaster. In 1513, the English cavalry won a skirmish now known as the Battle of Spurs. At the same time, Henry's queen was busy overseeing Norfolk subdue the Scots and win the Battle of Flodden, during which the Scottish king was killed. Katherine sent Henry James' bloodied surcoat.

Then a serious weed floated into Henry's garden. In 1514, the French king, Louis XII, made peace with the newly elected Pope Leo X. Henry demanded that Louis recognise his claim to the French throne, emulating Henry V, and demanding Louis pay an annual tribute of 100,000 crowns. As a sweetener, Henry threw in the hand of his younger sister, Mary, who was not only young, but beautiful. Louis was 52 years of age, his young bride 18. Naturally, Louis was delighted to accept Henry's terms.

This concord set the tone for future relations between the two countries. Mary went, very reluctantly, to her wedding. She was escorted by the then Duke of Brittany, later François I, to her wedding with Louis and François also attended her coronation, despite the fact that, should Mary produce an heir, François' own hopes of the French crown would be dashed.

However, he need not have worried. Louis died within three months of the marriage. Some put his death down to 'excesses in the bedchamber', but in truth, the cause of his death was probably gout. However, all this set the scene for the 1520 spectacle.[44]

The royal journey to France began at Greenwich Palace on 21 May 1520. It was long thought that Henry and Katherine of Aragon stayed at Leeds Castle on their way to embarkation at Dover. Partly this was because the owner of Leeds Castle had been granted a sum of money and, were he to house the entire entourage – numbering almost 6000 people – he would have certainly needed money to host them all. Leeds Castle also had a history of accommodating royalty in this fashion. Cardinal Wolsey had 350 in his retinue, Katherine of Aragon had more than 1250 in hers, just to give an idea of the numbers.

However, more recent investigations have put this overnight stay into question, because there are no surviving accounts that support it. The alternative stopover may well have been the Archbishop's Palace in Maidstone, which was also used as a convenient stop on the way to Dover.[45]

Tournaments like those 'fought' during the Field of the Cloth of Gold had been a part of the entertainment for centuries. For a vivid description, one only has to read the accounts of William Marshal – also known as *the Perfect Knight* – who began jousting at tournaments as a penniless knight but soon became rich through them. In her books about Marshal, Elizabeth Chadwick writes about how the object was to 'capture' enemy knights and hold them for ransom, something at which he excelled.

The displays at the Field of the Cloth of Gold were overblown examples of reconciliation. Indeed, the whole spectacle can be regarded as a very early peace summit. The ostensible reason, apart from sealing the 1518 peace treaty between Henry and François, was to jump-start 'Universal Peace' throughout Christendom. A contemporary poet described one of the knightly jousting tournaments held at the Field of the Cloth of Gold as 'a noise like thunder that resounds to the very stars'.

What its legacy has really become is an obscene display of conspicuous wealth, showmanship, and self-indulgence on the part of the two kings. Both sought to display their wealth and power to the world, so much so that one of the major considerations was that neither king should upstage the other, for it was imperative that both should end up with their pride intact.

The Pale of Calais was in English hands – it would not be taken back by France until 1554 under Henry's daughter, Mary. In return for holding the meeting on English soil, Henry agreed that François was in control of the tournament part of the summit. He organised three competitions: jousting; a tournament between knights on foot over barriers; and a tournament between mounted knights. To do this, a rectangular tilt yard was constructed for the 200–300 competitors, with a special stand for the spectators.

Both kings led teams but never met each other in direct combat. Their performances were judged as 'adequate', but the weather – obviously remembering it was on English soil – spoiled the general standard of jousting.

Apart from the sumptuousness of the tents and pavilions, the conspicuous consumption really came into its own where the feasts and foods were concerned. Henry built a temporary banqueting palace just outside Guines. It was a 10,000-metre square building with a central courtyard, surrounded by brick and timber walls, 9 metres high, and topped by battlements, with four brick-built towers at each corner. Within the edifice itself was a chapel, a suite of rooms for Henry and Katherine of Aragon, Cardinal Wolsey, and Henry's sister, Mary, dowager queen of France. Last, but by no means least, was a banqueting hall. François adapted a building in Ardres and it, too, was highly decorated.

The feast consisted of three or more courses, each course having a choice of around fifty dishes. All were presented and served to fanfares and the accompaniment of music. Table settings of castles and horsemen, all made of marchpane (marzipan) kept the diners amused, and all was ably assisted by the finest wines that could be purchased – French, of course, from the Loire Valley and Bordeaux. Beer and wine were also shipped from England. Post-feast entertainment was a series of complex masques, something both monarchs enjoyed and were skilled at producing.

At one point, Henry, obviously feeling the strain of having to appear to be the equal of his French counterpart, challenged François to a wrestling match. Perhaps both kings were feeling the equality strain, for François agreed and trounced Henry – forgive my inordinate laughter. Then, to rub salt into the wound, François tried to top that by appearing at the temporary castle in Guines and declaring himself to be the English king's prisoner, knowing it would put Henry in an embarrassing position. They compromised by exchanging gifts. Very expensive ones, naturally, and lots of them.

So, what did all this mock competition and subtle intimidation achieve? All it really did was highlight the difference between the two men. A large part of Henry, still labouring under the code of being the perfect gentil knight, wanted to win back from France all those lands that had belonged to Henry II. The lands that made the Angevin empire stretch from the Scottish border to the Mediterranean, and which were lost by King John.

François hoped Henry would support him against Charles VI, who had been made Holy Roman Emperor, and who was Katherine of Aragon's nephew. However, possibly by dint of Katherine's wifely persuasions, Henry sided with the Emperor, and by 1522, England and France were, once more, enemies. One wonders if they always were, despite the over-blown protestations of eternal amity.

There was one way, though, in which Henry did not please his wife. François and Henry were meant to meet after the 1518 treaty, but the election of the new Emperor made that difficult, politically, for Henry. Instead, he sent Sir Thomas Boleyn to express his distress at having to cancel the meeting, and to persuade François and his mother, Louise of Savoy, that he was upset enough to have sworn he would not shave until they met.

Of course, both knew that Katherine of Aragon would be working for the good of Spain against France, but, superficially at least, they accepted the reason. And, for about a year, Henry kept his word. This was at a time when there was a substantial anti-beard trend. Members of the bar were not allowed to grow beards. Katherine of Aragon hated Henry's and frequently begged her husband to shave it off. This he finally did in 1519 and had to send Boleyn back to France on a second diplomatic mission to François and his mother, to tell them he had shaved it off as a domestic decision. They weren't happy but had no option but to accept the reason.[46]

The Lincolnshire Uprising

I am a Lincolnshire lass, born only a few miles from the market town of Louth where the Lincolnshire Uprising began. It was the catalyst for unrest that soon spread to the whole of the north of England and became known as the Pilgrimage of Grace, I hope then, that the reader will forgive me if I concentrate on what happened in Louth in the early days of October 1536, and caused Henry VIII to call my home county 'the most brute and beestlie in the hole realme'.

The year 1536 was an *annus horribilis* for Henry VIII. His jousting accident early in the year not only caused him severe and lasting debility, but almost certainly cost him the boy child Anne Boleyn miscarried. Then there was the whole Anne Boleyn conspiracy, which certainly thinned out the number of courtiers close to the king, as well as leaving Henry for eleven whole days without a queen. One wonders how he managed to cope!

Within 24 hours of Anne's execution, he was betrothed to Jane Seymour and on 30 May, he married her. Then his only acknowledged son, Henry Fitzroy, Duke of Richmond, died, probably of tuberculosis,[47] although rumours were rife that Anne Boleyn, whose execution he attended, had, with her dying breath, put a curse on him. By October, Jane Seymour was still not pregnant and the citizens of Lincolnshire and Yorkshire chose that moment to rebel.

There were rumours flying around that indirect taxes were about to be levied. Taxes had already been altered, and now it was believed that there would be further monies levied on livestock, baptisms, burials and marriages, and food. Had these been enacted, it would have eradicated the protection offered by the high threshold of the current subsidy, allied with its low rate of assessment. This would enable the authorities to tax the poorest element of society with extreme severity.[48]

Part of the problem was that the north of England had always been more entrenched in its thinking than the distant government in London appreciated, plus the north was, almost to a man, still Roman Catholic at heart.[49]

The whole uprising blazed into being in the market town of Louth, where the Church plate, crosses and chalices were fashioned in silver-gilt and decorated with crystals and pearls. All 'to the laude and prayse and honor of Gold and the hole holy company of heffen'.[50]

Many of the people of Louth worked in the service of God, and why wouldn't they? By so doing, they eased their passage through Purgatory.

By the late 1520s, Henry VIII's reputation as a gentil knight was all but gone. By 1533, he declared his first marriage to be invalid by reason that he had married his brother's wife and it was an unclean act. He sent Katherine of Aragon to an unhealthy house at Buckden on the Great North Road – now known as the A1.

By 1534, the Act of Succession and Act of Supremacy became law. Everybody considered 'important' had to take the oaths for each act, enforcing and ratifying his new marriage to Anne Boleyn and any heirs she produced. However, all this was very expensive, so Thomas Cromwell set about trying to replenish the royal coffers, helped by those who still adhered to Roman Catholicism. And England was still a Catholic country, but it was an *Anglo*-Catholic realm and not one that had any truck with the Pope – or The Bishop of Rome, as the Pontiff was now called. Henry was still a Catholic, but he was the head of the Anglo-Catholic Church. He was *never* a Protestant.

First of all, Cromwell tried taxes, but they were, as Bush points out above, wildly unpopular. So, who in the land was very rich? Answer: The Church. And the Church was something Cromwell, a covert supporter of the new religion, considered to be fair game. Soon after the 1535 execution of Sir Thomas More, once a great friend and councillor of Henry VIII, Cromwell went to town on the Church, helped immeasurably it has to be said, by that institution's intransigence and refusal to conform to the 1534 acts.

The early months of 1536 were busy. Katherine of Aragon finally died in January, then Henry fell off his horse, then Anne miscarried, and in March, the Act to suppress the lesser monasteries was passed. England saw commissioners travelling the land, valuing the assets of small religious houses and then dissolving them. Lincolnshire had many such houses.

The Lincoln MP, Vincent Grantham, together with the Recorder, a lawyer called Thomas Moigne, went to London to try and get the lands of St Mary's in Louth in order to restore the city's ailing finances. They failed. The heads of religious houses began to sell off property as best as they could to relatives so they would have it for their own use.

Henry's chosen commissioner for the small priory at the village of Legbourne, five miles outside Louth, was one of the most hated men in the county. He had already had one altercation with the townsfolk of Louth in a case that had gone as high as the Star Chamber.

Thus, Louth was ready for trouble to come knocking. And it did. The ostentatious wealth of St James' church was looked on with acquisitive eyes by Cromwell's men. Rumour ran faster than wildfire. In parts of the county, people were told burials and christenings would be taxed.

In short, Lincolnshire was expecting trouble. When Thomas Foster, one of St James' musicians saw all the silver gilt and decorative accoutrements, he expressed his fears that they would be taken away. He also remembered that in Hull, the church treasures had been sold in the belief the king was about to seize them, and the money was used to pave the streets.[51]

At the same service, shoemaker, Nicholas Melton – soon to be called 'Captain Cobbler' – demanded the key to the 'jewel hous' at St James. On Monday, 2 October, Louth was crowded for the visitation was due. Captain Cobbler and his cohorts were guarding the door to the church.

Mr John Heneage, a local landowner and relative of Henry VIII's groom of the stool, Thomas Heneage, together with a man called John Longland, who was a servant to the Bishop of Lincoln, were forced by the mob to swear allegiance to the Commons.

The Bishop's Registrar, John Frankishe, was also seized. Papers and a copy of the New Testament in English were burned.[52] A group of some 3000 men then marched to Caistor, taking Mr Heneage and Thomas Moigne with them. But Caistor had already risen in protest. The commissioners fled but a servant of Lord Burgh was beaten to death.

Trouble began to spread. Quickly. By Monday night, Horncastle was coming to the boil. A man called William Leach had told townspeople that he had been in Louth that day, that the visiting commissioners had taken away St James' treasures, and that they were coming to Horncastle the next day to do the same.

When the Horncastle church wardens went to their church on the Tuesday morning, they found a weaver about to ring the alarm bell. In short order, a host of men arrived and the rumours spread. The mob then marched to nearby Scrivelsby, the home of the Dymoke family, traditionally the king's champion at coronation feasts.

There is confusion as to whether the Dymokes took the oath to the Commons out of fear or because they were in sympathy with the mob. Leach and Dymoke argued, Leach was determined to cause as much havoc as possible, so he went off raising the countryside while Dymoke tried to calm things down. Moigne, still at Caistor, and having tried in vain to persuade the people to go back and work their fields, tried to escape back to his house in North Willingham, but he was caught and forced to become leader of the rebels. Perhaps he thought that by doing so, he could at least try to persuade the rebels to disperse.[53]

On 5 October, the rebels marched on Lincoln, where they ransacked the Bishop's Palace. They had already sent a list of grievances to the king, mainly saying they were loyal to him, but not to Thomas Cromwell. Having received no reply, they sent another letter. An answer was received on 11 October telling the rebels to disperse or pay the consequences.

On 12 October, the rebels began to disband but the Lincolnshire protests had fired further unrest north of the River Humber. Forces led by Robert Aske marked on York and held it. By 19 October, Hull had surrendered to the king's forces. On 21 October, Lord Thomas Darcy surrendered Pontefract Castle to the rebels. Pontefract then became the rebel headquarters. Men arrived daily from the north, Durham, the Lake District and Cleveland, and were soon joined by forces from Hull and Beverley. The northern uprising became known as the Pilgrimage of Grace.

On 26 October, a truce was agreed, but the rebels omitted to ask for guarantees. Initially, only a few people were executed, including the clergy. Henry VIII had suppressed the uprisings by dint of false promises for mercy. Having made promises that he would spare lives, he broke all of them and embarked on a savage revenge. By July 1537, all the leaders had been executed, along with hundreds of their followers. Aske was hanged in chains outside Clifford Tower in York, to die a slow, agonising death, as was Robert Constable of Hull.[54]

The person for whom I feel sorriest is Thomas Moigne. He was forced, for fear of being killed by the mob, to become their leader. He did his best to persuade them to go back to their fields and work. He did his absolute best to maintain the king's peace. However, the badly frightened king's commissioners needed a scapegoat and Moigne was it. In fact, his fate was sealed when it became known he had spoken to Robert Aske. He was hanged, drawn and quartered in Lincoln. The silver from Louth was melted down and the proceeds used for the relief of the poor.[55]

The Bishop's Palace in Lincoln was obviously refurbished, as Henry VIII and his then queen, Katherine Howard, stayed overnight there on their 1541 progress to York, ostensibly so that Henry could meet the Scottish king – who never arrived – but partly to obtain, in person, their abject, heartfelt, and doubtless shoe-quaking, apologies for the 1536 uprisings.

Isn't karma a wonderful thing? It is alleged that it was in Lincoln when Katherine Howard first committed adultery with Thomas Culpepper, a treason for which the pair paid with their lives. It was said that the news of his wife's adultery was one of the biggest shocks and heartbreaks Henry ever had. I suppose I had better *not* say it couldn't have happened to a nicer man. Oops, I just did.

The Struggle to Produce an Heir and Henry's Health Issues
There have been various theories as to why Henry could not father a male child. Initially, it was considered to be the fault of his wives – well, who else's fault could it be? This long-held belief was stopped in its tracks at the beginning of the twentieth century when research indicated that it is the male chromosomes that dictate the sex of a child. So, actually, it *was* Henry's fault. But then historians and the medical fraternity began to wonder why Henry's wives could produce one child, but all subsequent pregnancies ended abruptly, They linked the likely cause to Henry's increasing paranoid brutality in the last decade of his life.

Early theories suggested that Henry's health was the cause. Syphilis, from which he did not suffer, but was for centuries thought to be a problem, was one suggestion. Others included diabetes and a thyroid problem. But many males suffering diabetes and/or thyroid issues have been able to father male children, so that dog won't jump, either.

In the early twenty-first century, a theory arose suggesting Henry might have suffered from an inherited blood antigen, the Kell antigen, causing impaired fertility. This was posited by Stride *et al.* as something he may have inherited from his maternal great-grandmother, Jacquetta Woodville.[56] The paper studies the history of the issue of Jacquetta's children, which supports the theory that the first pregnancy is fine but the Kell antigen precludes the success of subsequent pregnancies. This pattern is repeated when one looks at the obstetric history of Henry's wives and mistresses.

However, Henry VII and Elizabeth of York, Jacquetta's granddaughter, had four children who all grew to adulthood. The big fly in the ointment here is that Mary, born in 1516 was Katherine of Aragon's fifth pregnancy. Stride *et al.* explain this by suggesting that Prince Arthur, to whom Katherine was briefly married at the age of 15, also inherited the gene, and the pair did, contrary to what Katherine always said, consummate their marriage, resulting in a very fleeting pregnancy and miscarriage. This may well have sensitised Katherine in some way, but only the foetus that became Mary inherited it, too. The authors also mention that Mary might not have been Henry's child at all, that Katherine might have recognised that the fault was not hers, and taken independent action.[57] Robert Hutchinson in his book *Henry VIII: The Decline and Fall of a Tyrant*, is very sceptical of this theory, saying that Katherine's miscarriages and perinatal deaths are not typical of Kell antigen sensitivity.[58] We know Henry had multiple affairs, although he could not be compared with Charles II for example. For Henry, there had to be the element of courtly love, not just sex.

When we look at Henry VIII's history, he is known to have caused at least eleven pregnancies with four women. Three of them were first pregnancies: Bessie Blount, mother of Henry Fitzroy, Duke of Richmond; Anne Boleyn, mother of Elizabeth I; and Jane Seymour, mother of Edward VI. Anne of Cleves was so little to his liking, she escaped, and neither Katherine Howard nor Katherine Parr had any recorded pregnancies. Mary Boleyn is known to have had two children, but Henry never acknowledged them and William Carey, her husband, was recognised as their father at the time.

So, what other causes could there be for Henry's difficulty in producing a living heir? Hutchinson talks about the later Tudors' chronic lack of male heirs, let alone an heir and a spare. He partly puts this down to psychological factors. Henry was never meant to be king, so he had a very cloistered upbringing with carefully chosen companions. His father forbade him from leaving the precincts of Greenwich or Richmond, the palaces in which he spent most of his childhood, except for exercise. His early years were spent mainly in female company, with his adoring mother who spoilt him. He had a difficult relationship with his father, who had put all the dynastic eggs in Arthur's basket and was devastated when his elder son died. Lord Montagu claimed that Henry VII 'had no affection nor fancy' for his younger son. They quarrelled, some claiming that the king had tried to kill the young Henry.

All this possibly led to a mindset that led to his tyranny. When Henry finally succeeded his father in 1509, he would brook no opposition. The French ambassador said: 'I have to deal with the most dangerous and cruel man in the world, for when he is in a fury, he has neither reason nor understanding left'. These problems have led some psychiatrists to believe he had an unconscious craving for an incestuous relationship or an Oedipus complex about his mother. And perhaps that by marrying Katherine of Aragon, he was, indeed, committing incest.[59]

What is certain is that by the time Anne Boleyn was at the end of her reign, Henry was already suffering from impotence. And perhaps that is one of the rumours that reached Henry, accelerating his second wife's execution.

The pictures of Henry from that time and into the 1540s are, according to Hutchinson, all lies. By then, the king suffered from chronic osteomyelitis of his legs, forcing him to walk with the aid of a staff. His weight had ballooned, his temper was more unpredictable than it had ever been, and he had to have a stairthrone to get to his bedchamber at Whitehall.

After the execution of Katherine Howard, he became psychotic and suspicious even of people he held in high regard. Because of his inability to move easily, his weight increased. At the time of his death, it is thought he weighed 28 stones and had a BMI of around 51.9. So, he only travelled to a few palaces close to London. This must have been agony, not only because of his physical infirmities, but because he had a lifelong terror of illness, and that, mixed with memories of the glorious youth he had been, must have been mentally devastating.

Hutchinson explores the theory that Henry had Cushing's Syndrome. This is caused by the adrenal glands secreting excessive amounts of cortisol. Obesity and a 'moon-face' appearance are two symptoms, as are irritability, depression, anxiety, insomnia, detachment from those the sufferer loves, and frequent mood swings. Hutchinson also suggests that Henry's opinion of Anne of Cleves as smelling and not being a virgin, was him transferring his own state of health to her. Some sufferers also become psychotic. Bones and muscles are weakened and even getting up from a sitting position can cause severe pain. Another sign is frequent thirst and diabetes. Henry is known to have sometimes drunk ten pints of beer a day. If what Hutchinson says is true, it may well have stemmed from the 1536 jousting accident, which led to a traumatic head injury. Hutchinson goes on to say that such an injury can cause a loss of testosterone, leading to a low sex drive and low fertility. Today, Henry would have been treated with hormone drugs, chemotherapy, or surgery to remove tumours from the adrenal glands.[60]

Henry VIII and Parliament

I want to briefly look at how Henry changed parliamentary process because it had serious consequences a hundred years later when Charles I fell out with his parliament.

Before the king took England into schism and out of the remit of the Bishop of Rome (the Pope), all the laws that had affected religion especially, had been solely the prerequisite of the Church. Henry changed all that in the 1530s when he founded the Church of England, but it must be reiterated that England was still a Catholic country, not a Protestant one. Indeed, Henry was as vicious as the Spanish Inquisition when it came to any kind of religion that he saw as a threat to his own. The torture and execution of Anne Askew is a case in point, and rather close to home because it is believed that Katherine Parr was a closet-supporter of Anne, something for which she was almost arrested herself.

The Reformation Parliament passed the Acts of Succession and Supremacy – the latter having three incarnations prompted by the execution of Anne Boleyn and the death of Jane Seymour. They ensured that the Church, from being all powerful where the government of England was concerned, as well as the health of people's souls, became side-lined. It was a complete about-face. The Crown, and therefore parliament, gained complete control over the Church. From doctrine to the enormous wealth of the Church, to its property, parliament was omnipotent. Anyone who refused to take the oaths in the acts passed by parliament was executed.[61]

Henry learned that his power was at its greatest when his wishes were ratified by parliament. Thus, in 1531, when the Bishop of Rochester's cook, Richard Roose, decided to play a practical joke on his master's guests and two of them died, Henry forced the 'Acte for Poysoning' through parliament, declaring it to be petty treason. The unfortunate Roose was boiled alive, something many of the spectators, used to a good entertaining execution, found too horrific to watch. When Edward VI came to the throne in 1547, the act was repealed.

Of course, the real architect of these changes was Thomas Cromwell, who, like his previous master, Cardinal Wolsey, was adept at steering the king where he wanted him to go, although Davies, in *A New Life of Henry VIII*, asserts that the driving force of the early 1530s acts was Henry.[62] That said, Cromwell was determined Henry would be recognised as having 'no superior on Earth' and that he was 'the singular protector only and supreme lord and supreme head of the English Church'.

In 1531, the clergy amended that to add 'only as far as the law of Christ allows'. Of course, Cromwell was unhappy with this, and in 1532, the clergy was forced to surrender its legislative independence. This ended up with the 1533 *Act in Restraint of Appeals*, which declared that England was an empire in which spiritual and temporal jurisdiction came from Henry. It was the beginning of national sovereignty.[63]

The Effect of Factions in Henry's Court

> …but this wicked Tower, like a cruel giant in a fairy-tale, must be fed with blood, and that blood must be the best and bravest in England, or it's not good enough for the old Blunderbore.
>
> Gilbert, *Yeoman of the Guard.*

This Gilbert and Sullivan operetta is set in the sixteenth century, although we are not told which reign. Blunderbore refers to a mythical giant who grinds men's bones to make his bread. However, it is an appropriate introduction to the element that factions played in Tudor politics.

It is also very relevant. Henry VIII began his reign in 1509 by executing the hated Empson and Dudley, Henry VII's major money-grabbers. Their crime was high treason. It became a habit throughout the sixteenth century for the victorious court faction to have a rival executed for 'high treason'.

The Earl of Essex, who led a chaotic, fruitless, and arrogant attempt at an uprising in order to unseat Robert Cecil, Elizabeth I's chief minister, also lost his head for high treason, ninety-two years after Empson and Dudley lost their heads.[64]

Faction does not just mean a group of people in pursuit of personal gain. For example, Robert Dudley, a favourite of Elizabeth I and grandson of the Dudley mentioned above, was part of a faction that actively promoted clergy who had puritan leanings.

Faction in Henry VIII's court emerged from the patronage system. Using personal influence became a defining system for moving up the social scale. The aphorism 'It isn't what you know but who you know' as a recipe for social success is still as true in the twenty-first century as it was in the sixteenth.

Patronage was as valuable in a monetary and influential sense to the sponsor as to the protégé; a symbiotic relationship where either or both could fall if they fell foul of a rival in another faction, or didn't change sides quickly enough.

By the end of the Wars of the Roses, the monarch became the major source of advancement and any significant employment.[65] As the sixteenth century progressed, influence moved to those in the privy chamber and a position close to the monarch became key to social power and influence. Councillors did not wield the ultimate power, due partly to the fact the court moved from palace to palace frequently and they could not always be in attendance on the monarch.

The gentlemen of the privy chamber were a constant. They were the monarch's closest confidants. William Brereton was responsible for sending the 1530 petition, signed by peers and clergy, to Rome asking the Pope to annul Henry's marriage to Katherine of Aragon. It was the groom of the stool who was in charge of the king's coffers. Even more vital, it was the gentlemen who had control of the 'dry stamp' at the end of Henry's reign when he was ill so frequently, giving them the power to add his signature to documents.[66]

One of the earliest examples of faction in action, is the downfall of Cardinal Thomas Wolsey, who was a patron of Thomas Cromwell. The cardinal had shone in the light of Henry's sunshine for years, gathering enmity as he went, including that of Anne Boleyn for possibly preventing her marriage to Henry

Percy, Earl of Northumberland. When it became clear Wolsey could not get Henry his divorce from Katherine of Aragon, his enemies undermined the king's confidence in him. It took six months of concerted effort but eventually Wolsey was exiled to his diocese in York.[67] Even then his enemies could not be sure that he would not pull a political rabbit out of his cardinal's hat and return to Henry's favour. I believe that would have been unlikely, if only because Wolsey taught Henry that power was best left to one man, and in his younger days, Henry had been happy for Wolsey to be that man. As he grew older, Henry decided he was the one man. Summoned back to London for what was almost certainly a date with the executioner, Wolsey died en route, at Leicester Abbey.

Possibly the most significant example of the power of faction was the downfall of Anne Boleyn. Her influence over the king was too much for those who thought she threatened their own power. Cromwell, known to have reformist leanings, allied himself with Catholic ministers in a joint enterprise to get rid of Anne, and that began by dangling Jane Seymour, the complete antithesis of Anne – allegedly. It must be remembered that Jane achieved in six weeks what it had taken Anne six years to achieve.

The wording of the attainder against Anne stated that 'she allowed others to "violate" and "carnally know her" and "she tempted her brother with tongue in the said George's mouth". Cromwell's use of such emotive language could not help but foment Henry's rage at his wife. He believed in her guilt mostly because Cromwell said it was true.[68]

However, the Boleyn enemies, who had used the restoration of Princess Mary to her father's loving bosom as a reason to get rid of Anne, overstepped themselves. They believed it had been Anne's malign influence that had separated Henry from his elder daughter, claiming that Mary had been conceived at a time when everyone believed Henry's first marriage to be valid, thus making Mary the heir presumptive.

When her supporters became more vocal, Cromwell, who realised Henry's view of his first marriage had not changed, struck. Two of the king's councillors were dismissed, and Nicholas Carew and Anthony Browne were interrogated. The wife of Mary's chamberlain was sent to the Tower of London. Mary herself was forced to sign documents that confirmed her father as the head of the Church and that she was illegitimate.[69]

> I do freely, frankly and for the discharge of my duty towards God, the king's highness and his laws, without other respect, recognize and acknowledge that the marriage formerly had between his majesty and my mother, the late princess dowager, was by God's law and man's law incestuous and unlawful.[70]

Faction continued to play a large part in subsequent reigns well into the Stuart era. Shephard makes a very valid point: 'You could no more follow Cromwell if you were a convinced Papist than you could attach yourself to Norfolk and Gardiner if you thought that there had been no true religion before Luther'.

He goes on to point out that post-Reformation, court factions had a clear political or religious viewpoint and this became clear in succeeding decades.[71]

Now we have a good flavour of Henry VIII, let us move to his favourites. I have purposely tried to include those lesser known. However, the first, Sir Thomas Wyatt, had an interesting life, so I am including him.

Sir Thomas Wyatt, The Elder

Wyatt was born at Allington Castle near Maidstone in 1503. The events of his childhood are virtually unknown, but he appears as 'Sewer-Extraordinary', something akin to a butler, to Henry VIII in 1516, the year he also entered St John's College, Cambridge. He was married a year later to Elizabeth Brooke, but separated from her in 1525, charging her with adultery. It is believed his interest in Anne Boleyn dates from this time.

Wyatt was knighted in 1535, but quarrelled with Charles Brandon, Duke of Suffolk, Henry's great friend until his death in 1545, and long considered Henry's 'yes-man'. In 1536, Wyatt was suspected of being one of Anne Boleyn's lovers. However, he was returned to the king's favour and sent to the court of the Emperor, Charles V as an ambassador, staying there until May 1540. At some point in 1536, he took Elizabeth Darrell as his mistress for the rest of his life.[72]

An ally of Thomas Cromwell, Wyatt fell foul of Bishop Bonner in 1541, after Cromwell's execution, and was charged with treason. Bonner claimed that Wyatt had been rude about Henry and consorted with Cardinal Pole, the Papal Legate with whom Henry had fallen out when the cardinal refused to support him in the matter of his divorce from Katherine of Aragon. From his cell in the Tower, Wyatt wrote a passionate *Defence*. It is thought he was pardoned due to the exhortations of Katherine Howard, Henry's fifth queen. Once more, he was restored to favour. However, he became ill in 1542 after welcoming the Emperor's envoy and died at Sherborne in October.[73]

Wyatt introduced the Italian sonnet and *terza rima* form, along with the French *rondeau* verse styles into English Literature. *Terza rima* is a poetic format whereby each poem-section consists of three-line stanzas with an interlocking three-line rhyme scheme. He was also a skilled musician, but his main claim to fame, apart from his rumoured love for Anne Boleyn, is his poetry. His style is unusual for that time period because the poems carry a great sense of the

individual. Readers can find more information about his verse here: https://
www.poetryfoundation.org/poets/thomas-wyatt.

From prison in 1536, Wyatt wrote two messages to his friend, Sir Francis
Bryan, using poetry as his medium to hide what he was saying. In the first, he says:

> Sighs are my food, drink are my tears;
> Clinking of fetters such music would crave.
> Stink and close air away my life wears.
> Innocency is all the hope I have.
> Rain, wind, or weather I judge by mine ears.
> Malice assaulted that righteousness should save.

His reference to *fetters* did not mean, as it usually did, the fetters of a life in
the hothouse of the court, but the iron fetters of a prison cell in the Tower of
London. In the second poem he says:

> Sure I am, Brian, this wound shall heal again
> But yet, alas, the scar shall still remain.

The scar refers to the 'proverbial unfading scar', a warning to Bryan that the
latter would well understand since both men preferred 'proverbial wisdom' to
rhetoric. Wyatt used the subjects of friendship with betrayal and loss in his
poetry. With the above words, he is warning Bryan that there are secrets which
must be kept. And, since both men were both courtiers and diplomats, they
shared many secrets.

For Wyatt, his close friendship with Anne Boleyn was far too close for
Henry VIII's liking. In the poem *Forget Not Yet*, Wyatt makes it clear that he
is stepping back from his friendship with her, but he was, and always will be,
associated with Anne. Bryan shared his championship of the 'Great Whore'.
However, by the late spring of 1536, the king's determination to be rid of Anne
came to the boil – I was going to say came to a head, sorry – and both Wyatt
and Bryan found themselves tangled in the mess.

On 8 May 1536, Wyatt learned the full meaning of 'circa regna tonat' – about
the throne, thunder rolls. He found himself in a dingy cell in the Tower, his
time there fluctuating between being told his life was safe and that he would
'suffer with the others'. From his window in the Bell Tower, he watched his
friends meeting the executioner's axe.

Quite how he escaped sharing their fate is unclear, but Brigden puts forward
the theory that Thomas Cromwell secured a ransom from Nicholas Carew for
Wyatt's life. In March 1537, he was sent as an ambassador to the Spanish court.[74]

Sir Francis Bryan

Bryan was close to Sir Thomas Wyatt, but had been in royal service from a young age and was also close to Nicholas Carew. So much so, Cardinal Wolsey did his utmost to get them both exiled from court, because he was suspicious of their influence over the king. Wolsey failed, so he made sure they were sent abroad as ambassadors to European courts to 'haue theym owt off the way'. How ironic that they survived, but Wolsey did not.

Bryan accepted that the minds of princes sometimes change, initially supporting Anne Boleyn, but then becoming one of her most bitter enemies. He navigated court politics so adroitly, he outlived her, too. But that was only after, having been summoned by Cromwell in May 1536 and questioned – one can only imagine how terrifying that was – Bryan did a complete about face, turned against Anne, and joined Nicholas Carew on the winning side. The side that came out of the whole kerfuffle still alive.

In fact, shortly after, Bryan became chief gentleman of the privy chamber and was the man chosen to take Jane Seymour the news of Anne's execution. That said, he was still regarded with suspicion in some quarters, but then most of the people at court were under suspicion at one time or another. Bryan supported Princess Mary and her position as first heir to the throne, even though she had been declared illegitimate. Possibly to test him, he was sent as the spearhead to sort out the rebels in the Pilgrimage of Grace, probably because it was believed his sympathies lay with the rebels rather than the Crown.[75]

Sir William Butts

Sir William Butts was born around 1496 in Norwich, Norfolk. He went to Cambridge and gained his BA in 1506/7, his MA in 1509 and his MD in 1518. In 1516, he married Margaret Bacon. They had one daughter and three sons. He was admitted to the Royal College of Surgeons in 1529.

Butts became a court physician around 1524, attending The Duke of Norfolk and Anne Boleyn's brother, George, Lord Rochford. His salary was around £100 per annum, (around £91,528 in 2024), but he was paid an extra £20 a year (£18,305 in 2024), to look after Henry's illegitimate son, Henry Fitzroy, Duke of Richmond. In 1529, he tried to reconcile Henry with Cardinal Wolsey, telling the former that Wolsey's malady was largely because he had lost the king's favour.[76]

Henry VIII considered himself an expert on illnesses and, as we have already seen, he was not above creating his own remedies. He gave Sir Brian Tuke advice on a remedy to help his kidney complaint. However, Henry was a hypochondriac, who would flee to another palace if illness raised its ugly head.

In 1528, there was an outbreak of the sweating sickness. Anne Boleyn's brother caught it and recovered. But then Anne's maid also caught it, at which point Henry sent her home to Hever to escape the contagion. Notwithstanding, Anne and her father went down with the sickness, so Henry sent Dr Butts to Hever with a letter 'praying God that he may soon restore your health'. God did and Butts returned to London to tell a much-relieved Henry.[77]

Anne was known to sponsor scholars and reformers, some recommended to her by Butts, who was by then 'a considerable man of affairs' in the court and far more radical in his religious views than Anne. He secured chaplaincies for William Latimer and William Betts, who had both been arrested at Oxford for circulating forbidden books.[78]

Butts also seems to have been a genial man. He used his standing to further religious reform, but he also tried to convert the monks at Syon Abbey who had refused to take the Oath of Supremacy. He championed the replacement of Dr Cox as Prince Edward's tutor with Sir John Cheke, and also helped Archbishop Cranmer, especially during the Prebendaries Plot of 1543. This was a plot with Stephen Gardiner, Bishop of Winchester at its heart, to accuse Cranmer of being a heretic and thus stop further reform in Kent and end Protestant influence at court.[79]

Cranmer's enemies were almost ready to pounce, so Butts went to Henry and said that Cranmer was being forced to wait outside the council chamber until his enemies were ready to arrest him. Gardiner survived, as we shall see in the account of the reign of Mary I later on. Henry ordered Richard Cox, his own chaplain to investigate.[80]

Butts was one of the few men Henry trusted. He was given a livery of green and blue damask for himself and two servants and cloth for an apothecary. He was also a supporter of Princess Mary and his wife became one of the Princess' ladies-in-waiting. At one point, Mary had been put in the charge of Lady Anne Shelton, Anne Boleyn's aunt. Having been deprived of her status as princess and told she was illegitimate, Mary, who suffered psychological problems all her life, became ill. Butts went to see her. Lady Shelton had called in an unknown apothecary, whose pills made Mary worse. Butts then proceeded to terrify Shelton by telling her there was a popular rumour in London that she was poisoning Mary and if she died, Shelton would certainly be held responsible.

Ever anxious to aid reformers, Butts became aware of the plight of Richard Turner who had been attacking Papists in Kent and was sentenced to be whipped out of the country. The conservative faction at court used this as a stick with which to beat Cranmer, but the archbishop's secretary, Ralph Morice, wrote to Butts asking for his help. Butts waited until Henry was being barbered and therefore relaxed, and brought up Turner's plight. Henry, who was always a master at balancing his council with conservatives and reformers, asked Butts to read the letter to him twice. He then changed his mind and all charges against Turner were dropped.

It is alleged that Butts was one of the doctors who performed a caesarean operation on Jane Seymour, having been told by Henry VIII to save the child at the expense of the mother. However, Borman, in her book *The Private Lives of the Tudors*, points out that caesarean operations were not performed at this time in England.[81] Indeed, the first operation of this kind where the mother lived was not performed until 1793 by James Barlow.[82]

In 1540, Butts helped Henry enormously by assuring him that he was not impotent but that the problem he suffered in his ability to consummate the marriage with Anne of Cleves was her failure 'to excite and provoke any lust in him'.[83] He then spent the next few months spreading the rumours that Henry was having wet dreams to support the king.

In 1541, the young Prince Edward fell ill, and, in a panic, Henry sent Butts to him. Butts replaced all the rich food the young prince had been eating with broths and soups. Edward wanted meat, so when he demanded that he be fed meat, Butts took it as a sign that the prince had recovered.[84]

At the Royal College of Physicians, Butts was described as 'a man of serious, exceptional knowledge of letters, of individual judgement, of the greatest experience and a doctor of careful planning'.[85]

During Henry's final years, his two main confidants were Will Somers, his fool, and Dr Butts. Butts died of a double quartan fever (malaria) in November 1545. Most sources quote the 22 November as his date of death, but his epitaph in the church at Fulham, where he was buried, quotes 17 November.

Henry VIII sincerely grieved for his friend and physician. Butts' will confirms he had houses in Fulham, on the site of Whitefriars in London, in Norfolk and in Suffolk. He was painted twice by Hans Holbein and his wife was also painted by the famous court painter.[86]

Butts used his medical relationship with Henry to promote a strong influence for radical Protestantism with the court. He was one of the first physicians to make a high-profile lay career rather than a clerical one. He was also only the second physician to be knighted.[87]

Sir Nicholas Carew of Beddington

Sir Nicholas Carew – sometimes spelled Carewe – was born around 1496. He was sent to the future Henry VIII's court at the age of 6, and quickly became a central figure in it. He became skilled at jousting, something that Henry adored, and was considered fearless. Such was his skill, Henry gave him his own tiltyard in 1515.[88] He was summoned, together with Francis Bryan, his brother-in-law, to be a companion in 'a joust of pleasure'.[89]

In the early years of Henry's reign, Carew was at the heart of the court; a principal court favourite and chief among those close to Henry, who were called the 'minions'. His life at court was to be with those who surrounded Henry, played dice with him, hunted with him, played tennis with him, and pursued women with him, too. They were the centre of masked balls, jousts and tourneys and feats of skill.[90]

By 1517, Henry had knighted him. In 1518, in a move instigated by Cardinal Wolsey, Carew was sent away from the court. Wolsey obviously believed, possibly correctly, that Carew had too much influence over Henry. However, his banishment did not last long and he was soon back in favour.

In 1522, he was made Master of the Horse and Master of the Forests, and was chief esquire to the king. In 1526, Wolsey had another go at getting Carew out of the way. In the 1526 Eltham Ordinances, the cardinal finally managed to get Carew dismissed from the privy chamber, but he was back in 1528, when the cardinal was fighting his own battle to stay in favour with the king.[91]

Back at court he might be, but even though Carew was related to Anne Boleyn, he became resentful of her influence over Henry, the more so because he supported Katherine of Aragon and Princess Mary.[92]

By 1531, Carew was actively working against Anne. He sided with Charles Brandon and his third wife, Mary, Duchess of Suffolk, who was the king's younger sister. Neither Brandon nor Mary approved of Henry's association with Anne and Brandon, a close friend and confidant of many years' standing of the king, did his best to discredit Anne. According to Chapuys, the Spanish ambassador, in a letter to his master, he wrote that Anne 'had been accused by the Duke of Suffolk of undue familiarity with a gentleman who on a former occasion had been banished on suspicion'. The gentleman concerned was Sir Thomas Wyatt, whose poetry made many people believe he was in love with Anne. The Duchess of Suffolk agreed with her husband, and when Henry finally separated from Katherine in 1531, she, too, left court. It did not help that Anne was allied with the Duke of Norfolk, with whom Mary had never had an amicable relationship. The difficulties deepened still further in 1532 when the duchess spoke openly of her disapproval of Anne.[93]

In April 1536, Carew had been made a Knight of the Garter, and the major traditionalists at court joined with Cromwell to bring Anne down, even though they stood for everything he despised. Despite many opinions to the contrary, Cromwell and Anne had disagreed about the control of patronage. She was pro-French, while Cromwell was firmly in the Spanish Emperor's camp.[94]

Historian Eric Ives in his biography of Anne Boleyn states that Cromwell, having gained the support of the traditionalists, left Carew and Jane Seymour, with the aid of her brothers, to deal with Henry, presenting Jane as everything Anne was not.[95]

Jane was coached by Carew to ask Henry for the restoration of the Princess Mary. Henry told her she was a fool, and should be concentrating on the future of the children they would have together. But Carew had done his job well. Jane replied that 'in asking for the restoration of the Princess she conceived she was seeking the rest and tranquillity of the King, herself, her future children, and the whole realm; for without that neither your majesty nor his people would ever be content'.

In the end, Cromwell triumphed. He didn't want Mary back at court, but the princess was forced to sign away her legitimacy, and Cromwell was triumphant. Now it was time to get rid of the conservatives. He spent the next two years planting charges of treason on the most important members of the traditionalist faction.[96]

In 1538, Cromwell was presented with, allegedly, treasonous letters implicating Carew in a plot by the Marquis of Exeter. Exeter was considered to be part of the *White Rose* faction, so named because of his connections to Lord Montague, who was the elder brother of Reginald Pole. Their mother, Margaret Pole, Lady Salisbury, was the daughter of George, Duke of Clarence, brother to Edward IV and Richard III. It was stated that Exeter and the others had 'encompassed Henry's death and tried to usurp the throne'.

But, by far the biggest fish caught in Cromwell's trap was Nicholas Carew. That there was some kind of conspiracy is fairly sure, but it was incompetent and had no real chance of getting anywhere. In December 1538, Montague and Exeter were executed. Francis Bryan was dismissed as chief gentleman of the privy chamber.[97]

Tradition says that the final nail in Carew's coffin was during a game of bowls with Henry, at which in response to a question, Carew is alleged to have given an 'indiscreet' answer and 'used opprobrious language' towards him. Of course, that, if true, was something Henry would never allow. It is possible that Henry used the game to let Carew know that he was no longer in favour, but it seems there is sufficient evidence to posit that this was not the cause of Henry's displeasure.[98]

What is clear is that Cromwell wanted Carew out of the way. He was known to be a supporter of the Princess Mary and that was probably enough for Cromwell to manage Henry's growing paranoia.

After a trial, upon which his brother-in-law, Francis Bryan sat in judgement, Carew was executed in March 1539. His estates were given to Walter Gorges, but it is known that Henry took hangings from Beddington Hall to hang at Whitehall.[99] Carew's son, Francis, later had his father's attainder reversed, but he had to buy Beddington Hall back. It continued to be owned by the Carew family into the twentieth century.[100]

Edward VI

When Henry VIII died, he left what he considered to be the best provision he could for the future of his dynasty. After the birth of his second daughter, Elizabeth, Henry passed the Act of Succession that made his elder daughter by Katherine of Aragon, Mary, illegitimate and stating that Elizabeth was now heir to the throne. After the execution of Anne Boleyn, Elizabeth's mother, he passed a second Act of Succession stating that both his daughters were illegitimate. A few days before Anne's execution, his marriage to her was declared invalid because of a pre-contract with Henry Percy, Earl of Northumberland. Which meant, of course, that Henry and Anne had never been married. In which case, how could he execute her for committing adultery one asks?

When Jane Seymour finally gave Henry the son he had craved for the best part of thirty years, and then promptly died, the king passed a third Act of Succession that stated Edward was his heir, followed by Mary and then Elizabeth. He confirmed this in his will in December 1546.[101]

Job done, one might say with some justification. Henry fully expected Edward to stay alive, marry, have sons and carry on the dynasty. Henry's will also made a 'just in case' provision if none of his three offspring produced children. The 'dry stamp' will made in December 1546 excluded the heirs of Margaret Tudor, Henry's elder sister, who had married into the Stuart dynasty of Scotland. He decided the succession should go to the descendants of his sister, Mary, wife of Charles Brandon, Duke of Suffolk. Mary had died in 1533. Best laid plans and all that, because Edward stuck a rather large spoke in Henry's wheel, as we shall see.

So, what did Edward inherit on 28 January 1547? Under his father, the government of the land had changed considerably. Prior to Henry VII, political factions had held sway, but the first Tudor monarch wanted all the strings of government in his hands. The Privy Council assumed more importance, although it was cumbersome, having around forty members, not all of whom attended all meetings. Henry VIII streamlined the Privy Council, so that only people who attended the daily meetings, and thus involved in current administration, were its composition.

Even this changed. By the time Edward was born in 1537, there was a regular number of councillors, around nineteen, and each with a specific responsibility. When Cromwell took charge, a number of departments were set up for different areas of revenue.

This is what Edward inherited on that January day, and he has the dubious honour – not his fault – of having his entire reign ruled by a regent, not by himself as king. The two most influential men at court were Edward Seymour, his elder uncle, and John Dudley, a son of the Dudley who Henry VIII executed in 1509. Seymour made himself not only the Duke of Somerset, but also the Lord Protector – shades of Oliver Cromwell just over a hundred years later. Dudley was initially Earl of Warwick and then Duke of Northumberland.

As the reign went on, these two men effectively prevented the king from wielding any kind of power, even though he showed determination to be involved in decision making. However, this all came to an abrupt halt when he was stricken by tuberculosis in 1552 and from which he died in 1553. But not before upending his father's will and creating chaos.

Edward was 9 years old when Henry VIII died in January 1547. At his coronation in February of that year, Archbishop Cranmer is alleged to have urged the new king to follow the young king of Judah, Josiah, and ensure that only God was worshipped, and to eradicate idolatry.[102]

Most people think of Edward VI as a kind of breathing space between the tyranny of his father and the zealotry of his elder sister. This is far from the case. Edward can be considered as the king who took the English Reformation to new levels and, for the first time, England became a Protestant nation. Henry VIII had eradicated Rome from England but kept everything else about Catholicism. For Edward and other reformers, the Mass was the prime symbol of idolatry.

Later in 1547, the 'Chantries Act' removed Masses being said for the dead. In 1548, with the Order of Communion, followed in 1549 and 1552 by *The Book of Common Prayer*, the Mass disappeared altogether. Church services were said in English and stone altars were replaced by wooden communion tables.

Edward was the only legitimate son of Henry VIII; his mother, Jane Seymour, dying less than two weeks after his birth, following a protracted, painful delivery that lasted for three days. Henry was so grateful to Jane that he now had a son, he directed that he should be buried with her, his favourite wife. Henry, now holding, in his opinion, the only legitimate child he had sired, called Edward 'this whole realm's most precious jewel'.[103]

As a youngster, Edward was a normal healthy child, being both intelligent and athletic. Henry was fanatical about his son's health. Borman tells us that the king ordered a new washhouse to be built at Hampton Court Palace and directed that the prince's quarters should be washed down several times a day – a practice that demonstrates Henry's own attitude to hygiene. Everything that Edward handled had to be washed first. Nobody under the rank of knight was permitted to touch the child, and anyone coming anywhere near him had to be scrupulously clean. Serving boys and dogs were forbidden to come into his quarters.[104]

For his first six years, Edward was raised by women, but then his education began. He proved to have a fearsome intellect, in common with his sister, Elizabeth. He excelled at his studies and as well as studying science, learned Latin, French and Greek.

His final stepmother, Katherine Parr, lit within the boy the light of the Protestant religion. He was on good terms with both his sisters, although his relationship with Mary, twenty-one years his elder, soured because of their differences over religion. Elizabeth, only four years older than Edward, had a much better relationship with her brother, partly due to the fact she was a very pragmatic person in her youth, and more than capable of reading the runes.

Edward was brought up with everything he could wish for, received expensive gifts from visitors and was thoroughly spoiled.[105] When he was 6, Henry VIII signed the Treaty of Greenwich with Scotland, his aim being to unite the two kingdoms. In the treaty, he stipulated that Edward should marry the seven-month-old Mary, Queen of Scots. As part of the agreement, Mary was to be accompanied by an English lord and his wife until she was 10 years old, at which point she was to move to England permanently. The Scottish Parliament repudiated the agreement, fomenting conflict between the two countries for the next eight years. This has become known as 'the rough wooing'.

Following Edward's coronation, his elder uncle, Edward Seymour, Earl of Hertford, made himself – ostensibly with Edward's blessing – Lord Protector and then Duke of Somerset. Other council members were given lands and gifts. Edward was virtually powerless for two years, until John Dudley, Earl of Warwick came on the scene.[106]

In truth, Somerset had good intentions, especially regarding the resolution of social and economic problems, caused in large part by the enclosure laws. Somerset also approached Scotland in an attempt to create a united Protestant realm. Things began to go seriously wrong for him in 1549 when religious and economic changes triggered a series of rebellions.

The worst of these was the Prayer Book Rebellion, which was particularly virulent in Devon and Cornwall, both of which were still largely Catholic. They despised the new *Book of Common Prayer* and the banning of all the Catholic accoutrements. In Cornwall, William Body, sent by Cranmer to destroy Catholic icons, was attacked and murdered. That was just the beginning.

The Act of Uniformity 1549 made Catholic rites illegal. The congregation of Sampford Courtney in Devon persuaded their priest to conduct the traditional service. When Justices showed up to force the use of the new prayer book, another man ended up dead in the subsequent dispute. When Somerset finally sent his troops to restore order, thousands lost their lives.

The best-known disruption is Kett's Rebellion. Robert Kett, a gentleman of Norfolk, was sympathetic to those who had lost grazing land for their animals because of the enclosure laws. After an unlawful feast and performance of a play about Thomas Becket, rebels began to tear down fencing around land that had until recently been common land. When appealed to, Kett agreed to pull down his own fencing and joined the rebels. They sent a list of demands to King Edward and Somerset, who responded by telling them they would be pardoned if they dispersed. They refused.

Kett's army then attacked Norwich and routed the army sent by Edward to disperse them forcibly. Finally, Edward sent the Earl of Warwick and his troops, and the rebels were defeated. Kett was hanged in Norwich.

The other fly in Somerset's ointment was his younger brother, Thomas Seymour, who, although he was made a baron and given a seat on the council, remained jealous of Somerset's power. Thomas was an unthinking hothead who married Henry VIII's widow only a few months after the late king's death, something that scandalised the court. Katherine Parr was by no means averse to the marriage with Thomas; they had been close to each other before Henry's beady eye lighted on her. Poor Katherine had little joy from the marriage, as we shall see later.

Thomas told the young king that his elder uncle, as well as keeping him short of money, was depriving him of his power as king. However, Edward was punctilious about asking the advice of his council on matters before a decision was made.[107]

That said, Edward was overheard saying that the Duke of Somerset 'dealeth very hardly with me, and keepeth me so straight that I cannot have any money at my will'.[108]

At one point, Thomas Seymour broke into Edward's bedroom, allegedly to *rescue* him. Edward's spaniel barked, alerting everyone, and Seymour ran it through with a sword. He was arrested for various 'treasons', but most seriously for a story that had emerged from the deathbed of his wife, who accused him of improper behaviour with The Lady Elizabeth (Princess Elizabeth) when she was staying with the couple at their house in Chelsea. This caused enormous problems for Elizabeth, but more of that later. Thomas Seymour was beheaded in March 1549.

In October 1549, Somerset, knowing his rule was under threat, panicked, kidnapped Edward and took him to Windsor Castle. Edward was furious – 'Methinks I am a prisoner' he wrote. Within a few weeks, Somerset was ousted by John Dudley, Earl of Warwick, later Duke of Northumberland. Edward does not seem to have mourned either uncle. Warwick kept a tight rein on power, but Edward was beginning to grow into his role, and exhibited frequent temper tantrums. Recognising these as Edward becoming more his own man, Dudley massaged the king's ego, but kept an iron control over the privy chamber.

Rumours began to spread that Dudley visited Edward in his bedchamber, discussing and suggesting matters of state to be raised the following day in the council meeting, as if they had originated with Edward.[109]

Yet, Edward had a mind of his own. Whereas the council – ever with a view to the future – was willing to turn a blind eye to the Princess Mary hearing Mass publicly in her houses, Edward was not. He summoned her to court for a confrontation that left both of them in tears. In Edward's eyes, not only was she disobeying and disrespecting her king, but she was also stirring up trouble – which she was. Despite his council's exhortation to let Mary be, Edward refused point-blank, although he backed down enough to allow her to hear Mass in private.

As he entered his teens, Edward grew to understand more about the workings of government. He had a quiet group of unofficial advisors, one of whom was William Cecil. This group was formed to balance the degree of Dudley's power over the council. By now, Dudley was Duke of Northumberland, and keen to stop spending money on foreign wars. To aid this, in 1551, Edward was betrothed to Elizabeth of Valois, daughter of the French king.

England's economy was in a parlous state, so Northumberland debased the coinage. However, with a bit of assistance, by 1552 the economy was on a much sounder footing. 1552 was the year Northumberland finally disposed of his rival. Somerset, who was beheaded on Tower Hill, walked to his execution and was cheered by the populace who liked him and called him 'the good duke'. It was also made plain that they hated Dudley.[110]

Edward proceeded, urged by Cranmer, to continue the English Reformation. Lands of religious houses that had not been sold still brought in a goodly revenue to the Crown. In 1552, the *Book of Common Prayer* was revised and by the end of that year, all was going swimmingly. Which is, of course, when everything started going to the dogs.

At the beginning of 1553, Edward was ill with a bad cough and fever. He seemed to recover but kept relapsing. By May, he was seriously ill. Determined to stop England falling into Mary's Catholic hands, as per Henry VIII's will, Edward drew up his own will. It left both his sisters out in the cold and declared his successor should be Lady Jane Grey, the granddaughter of Henry's sister, Mary.

Initially, the council refused to ratify the will. Edward summoned them 'with sharp words and angry countenance'. Mary, he said 'would provoke great disturbances' (that's an understatement). Edward went on to say he had decided 'to disown and disinherit her together with her sister, Elizabeth, as though she were a bastard and sprung from an illegitimate bed'.

By so doing, Edward is much more responsible for the chaos that followed than most historians will allow.[111]

By July 1553, Edward was bedridden, coughing up blood and mucus. He was clearly in a lot of pain for he told Sir John Cheke, his tutor, he was glad to die.

Edward VI breathed his last on 6 July 1553 at Greenwich. He was buried in the Henry VII Chapel at Westminster Abbey, but his burial place was not marked until 1996.[112]

It is fascinating, if fruitless, to wonder what kind of a king Edward would have made had he grown to adulthood and reigned in his own right. His tutor, Sir John Cheke encouraged him to keep a journal – the only Tudor monarch to do so. It makes dry reading but does give an accurate account of the rest of his time as king. He also had an almost eidetic memory. He could recite the names of all ports, havens, and creeks in England, Scotland, and France. He could also name all his justices, magistrates and any gentlemen who had authority.[113]

As an interesting addition, once the chaos of Northumberland using Lady Jane Grey as his puppet had ended, both had been sent to the Tower of London, and Mary was beginning her divisive reign, rumours began to spread that Edward was still alive. In November 1553, three London tradesman were called before the Privy Council to answer a charge of spreading the rumour. The rumour went underground, but lived on.

In 1554/5, Edward Fetherston, alias William Constable, declared he was Edward VI. Mr Constable ended up in the Marshalsea prison. Even having a *bill* (a poster) in your possession was fraught with danger. One Laurence Trimming of Greenwich was sent to the Tower for it.

The rumour rumbled on throughout Elizabeth's reign; it was said Edward was living in luxury in France … or Spain.

Even as late as 1599, a vagrant called Thomas Vaughan said publicly that Edward still lived, a child having been killed in his stead, and that he had gone to Denmark, married the queen there and was, naturally, king.

Fun Fact:

Edward was crowned with the St Edward's crown and the Imperial crown but they were both too cumbersome and heavy for a 9-year-old to keep wearing, so a smaller, lighter crown was made to fit him. Because of his age, the service was shortened. He was robed with the coronation gown and sandals, but the spurs that completed the ceremony were removed immediately in case they tripped him up.

Barnaby Fitzpatrick

Barnaby Fitzpatrick was the nearest and most dear of Edward's school companions. Born in Ireland in 1535, he was the son of the Lord of Ossory, and was sent to the English court as a hostage for his father's good behaviour. He is first mentioned at the funeral of Henry VIII, one of nine boys all wearing black hooded cloaks and carrying banners.[114]

Barnaby was Edward's companion in both study and sport, developing a friendship with the young prince that only death would sever. In Thomas Fuller's *The Church History of Britain* (1655, ii. 342) is the claim that Barnaby was Edward's 'proxy for correction', in other words, if Edward misbehaved, Barnaby was whipped for that transgression. Markham notes that Fuller gives no source for this claim and states 'the story is not worthy of belief. The idea is very un-English'.[115]

Whilst the young prince was a diligent pupil, he was also a keen sportsman who enjoyed dancing. After Edward's coronation, Barnaby was kept on as a companion in the schoolroom, even though the new king's household was greatly enlarged by officers, henchmen, pages and attendants.

When Somerset fell in 1549, there was a significant change in Edward's position. In the two years he had been on the throne, he had suffered penny-pinching tyranny, was prevented from seeing his sisters and other family, and was constantly spied upon by Somerset's harridan of a duchess, who was instrumental in getting Thomas Seymour, Edward's favourite uncle, condemned and executed.

Edward was now treated like the king should be, with respect and deference. His tutor, John Cheke was knighted, and Barnaby was made a gentleman of the privy chamber. This was probably so that Dudley could gain Edward's favour. That said, Markham notes that Edward became aware of the mismanagement of the past and its effects on the people, even writing a treatise on the subject. During all this, Barnaby was his most constant companion and the two had a long history of writing letters to each other. In one, Edward details the progress of Somerset's trial and execution, but makes no comment about his feelings on the subject.[116]

Of the ten gentlemen of the privy chamber, Barnaby was the closest in age to Edward, being only two years older, whereas the others were more like ten years older, so that must have been a part of the reason the two were so close.

In early 1552, Barnaby, then aged 17, was sent to Paris as part of Lord Clinton's mission. He was to learn French, see the world, and become aware of the operations of war. Edward told him 'to learn French and avoid ladies'. To give him a better social position, Barnaby was made Baron of Upper Ossory.

Edward was anxious for his friend to gain military experience. In consequence, Barnaby accompanied Henry II of France in his first campaign against Charles V, from April to October 1552. Edward's letters show his extreme affection, ensuring Barnaby was supplied with money and other necessities. At the same time, the king secured Barnaby's rights to his lands and inheritances in Ireland. In one letter, Edward complained, while on a progress that summer, that 'there was a little too much banqueting'.

However, by September, it was clear Edward was missing his friend, who had been in France for the best part of a year. He wrote and told Barnaby to come home. In December, Barnaby took leave of Henry II and returned to England. Only death would separate the two friends.

In Edward's final illness, Barnaby was one of a select, small group, who never left the king's side. They held Edward in their arms to relieve his breathing. It is believed that Sir Henry Sidney was holding the king as he died.[117]

In the Lady Jane Grey hiatus that followed Edward's death, his friends managed to remove most of his papers to safety, but it is thought Mary may have destroyed some, including letters between Edward and Cranmer and those from Barnaby to Edward.[118]

After Edward's death, Barnaby was active in suppressing Wyatt's Rebellion in 1554, after which he returned to Ireland. He was in a lifelong feud with the Earl of Ormonde and the Grace family. He was called to court by Mary I in 1555, but did not go because his father was ill.

He is known to have been present at the Siege of Leith in 1558 and by 1559 was sitting in the Irish Parliament. Sir Henry Sidney knighted Barnaby in 1566, although there is an unsubstantiated rumour that the Duke of Norfolk had already done so.

The feud with the Ormonde and Grace families went on into the next century when Richard Grace murdered Barnaby's grandson in 1602. In 1574, his loyalty was questioned, being accused of being a Catholic by the Earl of Ormonde. Barnaby defended himself well and was acquitted.

In 1560, he had married the daughter of Viscount Baltinglass and they had a daughter.[119] In 1580, he was summoned before the Privy Council to face accusations of being involved with rebels and imprisoned in Dublin Castle along with his wife. While there, Barnaby appealed for help to Sir Robert Dudley, but despite intercessions from friends, including Sir Henry Wallop who said of him that he was 'as sound a man to her majesty as any of his nation', he remained imprisoned.

After his death, his friend, Sir Henry Sidney wrote of him that he was 'the most sufficient man in counsel and action for the war that ever I found of that country birth; great pity it was of his death'.[120]

You can read some of the exchange of letters between Edward and Barnaby here: https://archive.org/details/literaryremains00clubgoog/page/72/mode/2up.

Sir Henry Sidney

It cannot be many people who, at the age of 24, have possibly held a dying monarch in their arms. Historians are unsure whether the accolade belongs to Sir Henry Sidney or Sir John Gates, who was 49, and therefore the story is not so romantic. Personally, I am surprised it was not Barnaby Fitzpatrick, since he was Edward VI's closest friend. However, what is certain is that, along with Sir John Cheke, Edward's physician, Sidney was one of those with the king when he breathed his last.

Sidney was born in 1529, the eldest son of Sir William Sidney of Penshurst Place. He was brought up as one of Edward's closest companions. After Edward's death, Sidney served under Mary, but he was an influential courtier at Elizabeth's court too, so was obviously well versed in trimming his political and religious sails to suit the wind. He was knighted in 1550.

He played a prominent part in the Elizabethan Conquest of Ireland, serving three terms as Lord Deputy. But his career was controversial. He expanded the range of English administration to beyond that area surrounding Dublin, known as The Pale. He was in charge during the Shane O'Neill troubles, O'Neill being anxious to be the dominant member of his family.

Around 1559, Sidney resigned and was sent to the Welsh Marches as president of the council there. Although he frequently visited court, he spent most of his time at Ludlow Castle. While there, he established amicable relations with the local gentry, being interested in the Welsh national culture and his determination to preserve records at Ludlow Castle.

Sidney helped develop the iron industry in South Wales aided by skilled labour from Germany, and extracting copper from Mynydd Parys in Anglesey. He mediated between his brother-in-law, Robert Dudley, and Sir Richard Bulkeley in their argument over the forest of Snowdon. He is also remembered as being somewhat lax in prosecuting those of a Papist disposition, something that earned him another censure. It is clear that he was far happier in Wales than in Ireland, declaring 'A better country to govern Europe holdeth not'.[121]

He was obviously Elizabeth's chosen man for anything to do with England's Celtic neighbours, because in 1562, Elizabeth sent him to Scotland to tell Mary, Queen of Scots, the meeting between the two monarchs would have to be deferred for a year. Mary is said to have wept bitterly.

1565 found Sidney back in Ireland, ostensibly to deal with diminishing O'Neill's influence, but he was castigated for targeting ordinary people, not just military targets, joking that he had 'killed so many Irish varlets, he had lost count'. One can understand why he was not popular, and why the kind of actions of English monarchs from Henry II onwards, with their regular, and often unjust, excursions into Scotland, Wales, and Ireland, have made England a target of hatred.

He persuaded Lord Burghley to set up an Irish Parliament and oversaw the opening of it, but his proposal that there should be a military governor provoked several rebellions. Sidney also caused much discontent by an annual tax levy, called The Cess, to pay for a central government militia.

So incensed were the Irish – and with reason – that they sent a deputation to Elizabeth, who backed them and censured Sidney. When he returned to the English court in 1578, Elizabeth is said to have received him coldly.[122]

In 1553, he married Lady Mary Dudley, sister of Lord Robert Dudley, Elizabeth's favourite, and daughter of John Dudley, Duke of Northumberland. Probably reading the runes accurately, he took little part in the Lady Jane Grey chaos. In 1554, he inherited Penshurst Place. On one of his spells of duty in Ireland, his wife was set upon by an Irish mob, but was rescued by William Sarsfield. Sidney knighted him 'for having rescued Lady Sidney from the Irish'.

But he wasn't all bad. In 1562, the nave of Christ Church Cathedral collapsed and Sidney had it rebuilt. He also declined a barony, and made improvements to Penshurst, designing the garden as an Italian Garden.[123]

Despite all the controversy surrounding his actions in Ireland, Roy Foster opines that Sidney was 'by far the ablest of Elizabeth's able band of Irish governors'.[124]

Sidney died in 1586. He is buried at Penshurst, but his love of Wales is confirmed in that he ordered his heart to be interred at Ludlow.[125]

Sir John Gates

Gates is the other candidate for being the person holding Edward VI when the latter died. Gates was given an excellent education and trained as a lawyer at Lincoln's Inn. By 1537, he was a page of the wardrobe, receiving 40 shillings (£1366 in 2024) as a New Year's gift from Henry VIII. Gates inspected the royal wardrobe, kept records, and received clothing, such as that belonging to Thomas Cromwell after his execution, and what is noted in the records as the Duke of Norfolk's 'goods'. By 1542, he was a member of Henry's privy chamber as a groom, and had responsibility for the 'dry stamp', an accepted form of Henry's signature during his increasing bouts of illness, which indicates he was a trusted member of the inner royal coterie.

Gates served Katherine Parr between 1543–45, and was known to share her reformist leanings. In 1546, he was sent to inventory the houses of the Duke of Norfolk and his son, the Earl of Surrey. Both gentlemen ended up in the Tower during the last months of Henry's reign. Norfolk, known as a great escaper, was reprieved from his execution sentence because Henry died the night before the Duke was supposed to be beheaded. Surrey was not so lucky, but we do have a good body – sorry! – of his poetry to remember him by.

In 1551, Gates became Vice-Chamberlain of the Royal Household under Edward VI, and was given a seat on the council by Northumberland. As such, Gates was a useful conduit for Northumberland to access Edward when the king had retired for the night. So good was he at his job, and so loyal to Northumberland, that in 1552 he was made Chancellor of the Duchy of Lancaster.

From 1532 he was a JP for Essex, becoming High Sheriff from 1549–50. He served as a member of parliament for various boroughs; High Wycombe in 1542, New Shoreham in 1545, Southwark in 1547.

Gates was very much involved in the succession crisis of 1553, but sadly, he chose the losing side. As did John Dudley, Duke of Northumberland. As an interesting adjunct, John Dudley's father, Edmund Dudley, was executed by Henry VIII, along with Richard Empson as a popular measure, for being greedy, grasping money-grabbers for Henry VII. The Dudleys rose high in Edward VI's reign, but after the chaos with Lady Jane Grey, to whom John Dudley married his son, Guildford, not only did Lady Jane lose her head, but so did the Dudley father and son. However, the Dudley family fortunes rose highest in Elizabeth's reign with Robert Dudley, who became her closest companion.

Back to the plot – literally. Gates was a great supporter of religious reform, and, as such, not only was he anathema to the devoutly Catholic Mary, but he was also a traitor for trying to deprive her of her rights under Henry VIII's will. He is known to have been a good, loyal, servant to Henry VIII during the Pilgrimage of Grace in 1536. He was very active destroying altars during the Dissolution of the Monasteries, ending up owning some of them as part of his extensive estates in Essex and Suffolk – there's a surprise.[126]

Gates has been described as a 'grasping, greedy thing' – shades of Ebeneezer Scrooge. He was without conscience, sacrilegious, unreliable, ambitious, and unscrupulous. Perfect for an MP! However, he was a very able administrator and had an uncanny ability to align himself ahead of time to the 'right' people. Which worked brilliantly. Until it didn't.

Gates' brother-in-law was Anthony Denny, and he became Denny's right-hand man. He paid suppliers for items such as gloves, hats, satin hose, gold lace, leather and horse-trappings. He was put in charge of Henry VIII's coffer. When Henry went to war with France in 1544, Gates supplied him with 60 soldiers, and commanded over 3000 men in Boulogne.

Unsurprisingly, neither Gates nor Denny thought twice about using their positions for personal gain, especially after 1545 when Gates wielded the 'dry stamp', which gave him enormous power. He rode beside Henry's coffin on its way to Windsor, but even more riches came to him during Edward VI's reign. He was made a Knight of the Bath and Sheriff of Essex. After Somerset's fall, using that ability to read the runes, he had already allied himself with Northumberland. In 1550, he was appointed to the privy chamber.

However, it was in 1550 when the seeds of his destruction were sown. He was sent with a group of cavalry to prevent Mary from escaping England and finding sanctuary with her cousin, the Emperor Charles V. Mary never forgave Gates for thwarting her plan. It would come back to haunt him. By 1551, Gates was Vice-Chamberlain and Captain of the King's Guard, as well as having a seat on the Privy Council.

When everything went to hell in a handcart after Edward's death, both Dudley and Jane Grey tried to use Gates as a scapegoat for the devise in Edward's will taking away the inheritance of both Henry VIII's daughters. By mid-August 1553, Mary was definitely in charge and acknowledged as queen.

Both Northumberland and Gates tried to use recanting to earn a pardon, unlike Jane Grey, who was a brave girl and stood firm in her reformist faith. Gates confessed:

> … we have been out of the way [away from Catholicism] a long time, and therefore we are worthily punished; and, being sorry therefore, I ask God forgiveness therefore most humbly; and this is the true religion.

It didn't do him one iota of good. He was sentenced to be hanged, drawn, and quartered. However, Mary did show a modicum of mercy by commuting that to beheading. He and Northumberland were led out to execution together. They asked each other's forgiveness for any wrongs done, and bowed to each other. Gates had the dubious privilege of living a few minutes longer than his erstwhile patron, but having to watch the latter's execution.

When it came to his turn, Gates asked people to pray for him. He had been given £10 14s 4d (something over £5000 in 2024), to distribute as alms. He refused a kerchief for his eyes, but it took three blows from the axe to sever his head. He was interred in St Peter ad Vincula.

All his lands were confiscated by the Crown.[127]

The Brandon Boys

In 1485, during the Battle of Bosworth, Sir William Brandon, in his role as Henry Tudor's standard bearer, had the dubious honour of dying while protecting his master. His only surviving son, Charles, became Henry VIII's closest friend. Charles married four times, producing a goodly number of daughters, but, in the end, only two sons who survived him.

The first, Henry, had been born in 1516 and died in 1522. His mother was Mary, dowager queen of France, younger sister of Henry VIII and Brandon's third wife. This first Henry died in 1522, so they tried again, and in 1523, another Henry was born. He made it all the way to 1534, outliving his mother by a year, before calling it a day.[128]

Less than three months after Mary's death, in June 1533, Charles married his fourth wife, Katherine Willoughby. Strictly speaking, she had been betrothed to Charles' son, Henry, but dad nipped that in the bud and the following year, his third son called Henry died.

One might think from the foregoing that Charles was very possibly a whizz in the bedchamber but a tad lacking in imagination when it came to naming his sons. However, it was much more likely that he was flattering Henry VIII. Katherine delivered her first son, called … wait for it … Henry, in 1535. King Henry was named as godfather and gave the midwife and nurse a purse containing £4 (nearly £3000 in 2024).

Two years later, another son was born and since the name Henry was already taken, he was named Charles after his father. These two sons would become Edward VI's close friends and companions.

Not much has been chronicled about either child, save that they were close to Edward. Henry was taught by Richard Cox and John Cheke, as was Edward. Their father died in 1545, ironically on the same day, 22 August, as his father had done on Bosworth Field in 1485. There must be some kind of synchronicity there.

When Edward became king, both Brandon boys were knighted. At Edward's coronation, Henry carried the orb. He remained in the royal household, participating in revels and other events.

In 1549, aged 14, Henry was sent to Boulogne as a hostage for the English fulfilment of the terms of the Treaty of Boulogne. These were that the town of Boulogne would revert to the French, upon the payment of 400,000 crowns to England, and French troops leaving Scotland. Whilst there, young Henry impressed everyone with his prowess on horseback while wearing armour, and his proficiency in Latin.

Charles Brandon's will had stipulated that the boys' mother, Katherine, was to be their guardian, and, upon Henry's return to England, she directed that they must begin their education, choosing St John's College Cambridge for the purpose.

Their daily schedule was in sharp – and harsh – contrast to that they had lived at court. They were awoken around 4 or 5 in the morning, attended church, followed by 12 hours of tuition. After that, they ate a simple dinner and went to bed. And suffering that, so would I. There was very little time for leisure or fun.

Sadly, after two years at Cambridge, the city was hit by the sweating sickness. Katherine immediately had her sons removed to Buckden on the Great North Road, now known as the A1, the main artery between London and Edinburgh. It was too late. In July, both boys died of the sickness, Charles outliving his elder brother by about an hour.

Thomas Wilson, one of their tutors said: 'They both were together in one house, lodged in two separate chambers, and almost at one time both sickened, and both departed. They died both dukes, both well learned, both wise, and both right Godly'.[129]

The Suffolk title then went to Sir Henry Grey, husband of Frances Brandon, a daughter of Charles and Mary Tudor. However, after supporting Thomas Wyatt the Younger in a rebellion in 1554 when Mary announced she was going to marry Philip of Spain, Grey was attainted by her, and executed. The title then became extinct.

Lady Jane Grey - A Bit of a Do!

Like as his life was wicked, so was his end. I pray God that I nor friend of mine die so… Should I, who am so young and in my fewer teens, forsake my faith for love of life? Nay, God forbid; and much more he should not, whose fatal course, though he had lived for years, could not long have continued. But life is sweet…God be merciful to us.

Lady Jane Grey speaking about John Dudley,
Duke of Northumberland, from her
prison cell in the Tower of London.

On 9 February 1554, Jane, dressed in black velvet and carrying her prayer book, walked to the block with what was described as a 'heavenly smile on her face, a tender light in her grey eyes'.

In her final speech, she said that she had come to die but was innocent of any crime against the queen, that she had been forced to do what she had done, and was therefore guiltless. She went on to say she died a true Christian woman and asked those present to say prayers with her. Then she opened her psalm book, read Psalm 51, which is all about repentance, gave the book to the Deputy Lord-Lieutenant, and prepared herself for death.

Jane tied a kerchief around her eyes, but then became very confused because she couldn't find the block to kneel down. She was assisted in this, and was heard commending her soul to God before the axe fell.[130]

Jane Grey was born in either 1536 or 1537, so she was about the same age as her cousin, Edward VI. She was the great-granddaughter of Henry VII, the Tudor dynasty's founder, a great niece of Henry VIII, granddaughter of Charles Brandon and Mary, dowager queen of France, and daughter of Frances Brandon and Sir Henry Grey, who was made Duke of Suffolk after the death of Frances' father, Charles.

Educated by John Aylmer, Jane spoke Latin and Greek and wrote nearly all her letters in those languages. She also studied Hebrew. Her father had become a reformist and so Jane became an ardent Protestant. As ardent, in fact, as her cousin Mary was a Catholic.

Jane preferred academia to more active pursuits like hunting. When Henry VIII died, she was sent to live with his last queen, Katherine Parr and her new husband,

Sir Thomas Seymour. When Katherine died after giving birth, Jane was the chief mourner at her funeral, but then she returned to her studies.

In May 1553, she was married to Guildford Dudley, one of the sons of the Duke of Northumberland. As Edward VI lay dying, the Lady Mary – officially the title of Henry VIII's elder daughter – was warned that Northumberland planned to seize her and put Jane and Guildford on the throne. She fled to Kenninghall, her estate in Norfolk, but was prevented from fleeing the country. As soon as Edward died, Northumberland kept his death secret while he put his plans into action to declare Jane queen.

Jane Grey was proclaimed queen on 10 July, and officially reigned until 19 July – the shortest reign in English history. She never wanted to be queen and was quite happy to relinquish her throne to Mary.

When Edward's death was officially announced, Mary wrote to the council proclaiming herself queen. People flocked to her banner and by 19 July, the council proclaimed Mary as queen. Jane and her husband were put in the Tower of London.[131]

The seeds of Jane's destruction were sown by Edward, desperately determined that Protestantism would reign and Mary would not. He wrote his will completely ignoring that of his father, threw both Mary and Elizabeth out of the succession by what was called his *devise* and promptly died, taking himself out of the maelstrom he had prepared.

In truth, the *devise* was partly the construct of Northumberland who saw his power slipping away if Mary succeeded. But if he married Jane to Guildford, it could only cement his power. His miscalculation was fatal. The people were appalled that Great Harry's daughter should be passed over so presumptuously. They rallied to Mary's call. Jane and her husband were imprisoned, but Mary knew full well that Jane had been manipulated, so, although she went along with the formality of a trial, she had no intention of executing her cousin. Jane herself messed that up by pleading guilty and the sentence could only be death, either by fire or the axe, whichever Mary decided upon.

Mary decided to do nothing, probably in the hope that all the furore would die down and, eventually, she could release Jane. And that seemed to be going well until Jane's brainless father decided to rebel along with Wyatt in late 1553/ early 1554. That put Mary back in the cleft stick because it not only sealed Grey's fate, but also Jane's. The execution of the youngest 'traitor' in British history made Jane a martyr. That Mary had 'murdered' her cousin simply in order to marry Philip of Spain started the rot in her popularity.[132]

Jane died only partly because of the actions of Northumberland and her father. She died mainly because throughout the nine days she was queen and all the time she was a prisoner, she continued to condemn Catholicism.

Initially, Mary realised Jane had been a puppet-queen, and that, plus the fact Jane was her cousin, led to her decision not to execute her. It was Stephen Gardiner, Bishop of Winchester, a man I sincerely hope ended up with a much hotter abode after his death than the angelic one he expected, who reminded Mary that Jane would be a Protestant figurehead, and a magnet for those disaffected by the Roman Catholicism that Mary insisted was now the religion of England.

If nothing else, we must remember that the death of Lady Jane Grey became one of the key elements that later become enshrined in the 1701 Act of Settlement; that the monarch cannot be, or marry, a Roman Catholic. This is still in force today and was used when Prince Michael of Kent was forced to give up any claim to the throne when he married Marie-Christine von Reibnitz in 1978.[133]

Fun Fact:

Jane had such a miserable life, short as it was, it is almost impossible to find a fun fact. However, she delighted in books and reading and was proficient in several languages. So, when other young women were out hunting – animals or husbands – Jane would be found ensconced in a book. My kind of girl!

Mary I (Bloody Mary)

I always feel a bit sorry for Mary. She has had a bad press for the most part, and many people do not appreciate how much her upbringing affected her future life and decisions. As the first queen regnant, she was a bit of a trailblazer. The only other woman who had come close was the Empress Matilda, daughter of Henry I, but she was never crowned or called queen, only 'The Lady of the English'.[134]

Mary Tudor, named after her aunt who had married first the king of France and then Henry VIII's great friend, Charles Brandon, was the only child of Henry and Katherine of Aragon to live beyond a few days. She came into the world in February 1516.

Mary spent a happy, pampered childhood for her first ten years, being a precocious child who, at the age of 4, welcomed a French delegation by playing on the virginals, a kind of harpsichord and not, as some might think, Cockney rhyming slang. By the age of 9, Mary could read and write Latin and also studied French and Spanish. Like her Spanish mother, she was also stoical, something that led Henry VIII to boast that she never cried.

In 1525, Henry sent Mary to the Welsh Marches, where she lived in Ludlow Castle. She was treated as the heir to the throne, but, in truth, had no power at all. This also separated her from her mother, which shows Henry had either temporarily realised his heir was Mary or nobody, or demonstrated how threatened he felt by the bond between mother and daughter.[135]

The rot in the Aragon marriage had been a long time in the making, accelerating after Mary's birth, when, following one final miscarriage, Katherine never became pregnant again. In June 1519, Henry's mistress, Bessie Blount, gave birth to a healthy son. Although Henry could not celebrate openly, it proved beyond any doubt, at least to him, that the fault in not producing a male heir did not lie with him but with Katherine.[136]

By 1528, Mary was back in London, but not necessarily at court. And Henry was in the first throes of his unsatiated lust for Anne Boleyn, trying every avenue he could think of to get underneath Anne's linen shift, or have his marriage annulled and make Anne his wife.

From this time, Mary began to suffer bouts of ill health, probably – understandably – caused by stress. Her menstrual cycle was erratic and she suffered from depression. And, with her mother sent away from court, each forbidden to contact the other, her father's new amour heaping humiliation on her at every opportunity, and her father's distaste at her being a mere girl, who wouldn't be depressed?

Henry was quite as cruel to his elder daughter as he was to her mother. By the time Anne had caved in, Cranmer had conjured up a divorce, and Elizabeth was born, Mary had already refused to accept the new queen, or the fact that her mother was now styled 'Dowager Princess of Wales', or that she herself was illegitimate. She had lost the title of princess, and was now 'The Lady Mary'. All this, plus her continued ill-treatment exacerbated her health issues. In what might have been her mother's last letter to her, Katherine wrote: 'Answer with few words, obeying the King, your father, in everything, save only that you will not offend God and lose your own soul; and go no further with learning and disputation in the matter. And wheresoever, and in whatsoever, company you shall come, observe the King's commandments'.

When Katherine of Aragon died in January 1536, Mary was inconsolable. When Anne miscarried in July 1534. Henry, of course, blamed her for the loss of the child. In 1535, on progress, he visited Wolf Hall. Tracy Borman states that this was deliberate because Henry wanted to see Jane Seymour, one of Anne's ladies-in-waiting. He had spotted her at court in 1534 and began paying attention to her. It is clear, at that point, that Henry was becoming fed up with Anne but he could do nothing, because to divorce Anne would mean he had two ex-wives living. This resolved itself when, in January 1536, Anne miscarried again and Katherine of Aragon died, leaving her daughter, Mary, desolate. So, he fabricated evidence against Anne, using Thomas Cromwell, and other people she had upset, to ratify it, at which point Mary's circumstances improved. Somewhat. Elizabeth was also removed from the succession, named as a bastard, and called 'The Lady Elizabeth'. Jane brokered a peace between Henry and Mary, who hadn't spoken in three years. She was still forced, under threat of death, to sign the documents confirming her parents' marriage was invalid and she was illegitimate. What I believe happened after that is that she believed everything in her life had gone bad – her mother was dead, her father's immortal soul was in peril. Cranmer – in Mary's view, the architect of all her troubles – was often at court, and so she turned more to her only solace, her religion. Her sufferings under her brother, plus her genuine worry for *his* soul, her distrust of Elizabeth, not only because her half-sister was young and healthy, but the daughter of the woman who had wrecked her world, Anne Boleyn, set Mary on the road to zealotry.

When Jane died after giving birth to Edward, Mary was made his godmother, and was chief mourner at Jane's funeral. By now, Henry was growing increasingly paranoid, and Mary could never be sure how safe she really was. In 1541, her old governess, Margaret Pole, the only survivor of the old Plantagenet order, was executed at the age of 67 on trumped up charges. In 1542, her father's fifth wife was beheaded.

Mary had a period of respite when Henry married Katherine Parr, who tried to make a family circle for his three children, all from different mothers. However, soon after Henry died, Katherine, not wanting to be married a fourth time to someone she didn't want to marry, gave in to the demands of her long-time true love, Thomas Seymour.

Mary was appalled. However, her own life was no safer under the priggish Protestantism of Edward VI. Constantly under threat for refusing to renounce her Roman Catholic faith, and refusing to only hear Mass in private, Mary decided to escape England and flee to her cousin, Charles V. Her attempt was thwarted by Sir John Gates, an action for which he would not be forgiven.

On his deathbed, Edward wrote his will, repudiating the tenets of his father's will. Edward threw Mary and Elizabeth out of the succession, replacing them with Lady Jane Grey, an ardent Protestant like himself.

Mary came to London on 3 July 1553 to try to see her brother. She was refused and Northumberland was intent on capturing her. However, she fled, taking six days to reach her house in Kenninghall in Norfolk, gathering followers as she went. Five days after that, she was in Framlingham Castle with even more support rallying to her.

At Framlingham, she raised her standard and called on East Anglia and the Home Counties to attend her. It was an unexpected victory and the explanation given by most historians has always been that those areas of England were largely Catholic and conservative. However, not everyone supported her; many took a 'wait and see' approach. In the main, though, the people didn't want Lady Jane crowned instead of Mary, and flocked to support Great Harry's daughter.[137]

Whitestone credits Mary's household, rather than her supporters, for her victory. Not usually one to hold back when it came to her religion, Mary was persuaded to put it on the back burner until she was safely on the throne. Two of her household, Robert Rochester and Edward Waldegrave, who held the most senior positions in her entourage, had both been imprisoned in the Fleet for not upholding the law forbidding Mass to be said in public. During Edward's reign, Mary was the figurehead for Catholicism and many of her household were imprisoned or fined for flouting the law. To be in Mary's service meant hearing three Masses each day as a Catholic. These men constituted a formidable opposition, and one that outmatched anything Northumberland could muster.[138]

In the initial furore after Mary's proclamation as queen, only Northumberland and Gates died.

Mary's first actions as queen were to release the Duke of Norfolk, who had been imprisoned since the late days of Henry VIII, and Stephen Gardiner. She made Gardiner Bishop of Winchester and her Lord Chamberlain. She then imprisoned Thomas Cranmer, Archbishop of Canterbury. It is interesting to note that as Gardiner walked out of his cell, Cranmer walked into it; Gardiner walked out a free man, Cranmer walked out to his execution.

Mary's major dilemma was to juggle her role as a woman – inferior in every way to any man and only put on earth to make sure men's lives were easier – and her position as a monarch. If we add to that the fact that Elizabeth reigned for the best part of half a century, had her father's charisma, and was, in consequence, very popular, Mary often gets left behind as a mid-Tudor aberration.[139]

Mary was determined to marry Philip of Spain, which made her – and him – very unpopular. Most people wanted her to marry Edward Courtenay, whose father had been executed in 1538, accused of plotting with Reginald Pole. Edward had been in the Tower but was released by Mary when she arrived in London in July 1553. He, too, was against the Spanish marriage and was dragged into the Wyatt Rebellion of 1554 and put back in the Tower. However, Wyatt publicly exonerated him in his speech on the scaffold, so Edward was released from prison and sent abroad. He died in 1556.[140]

Even Gardiner wanted Mary to marry an Englishman, but she was obdurate – in fact she was her father's daughter in this regard – and, of course, Simon Renard, Charles V's ambassador, encouraged her. The people believed they would be dragged into Philip's Spanish wars. The Protestants were terrified at the prospect of Roman Catholicism becoming the English state religion again, with the hovering spectre of the Spanish Inquisition. The French weren't desperately chuffed, either. An English/Spanish match threatened France.

However, she had a few obstacles to overcome, not least the men Henry VIII had rewarded with lands and buildings of the dissolved monasteries and religious houses. When Mary asked parliament to rubber-stamp her marriage to Philip of Spain and some members spoke out against it, Mary is said to have retorted 'My marriage is my own affair'. And then proved it by marrying him.

The depth of Mary's religious fervour even unsettled Philip. He knew he would be blamed for her zealotry, but she refused point-blank to temper her unyielding fervour for the cause. Simon Renard warned Philip that 'such cruel enforcement could cause a revolt'. By September 1554, Mary believed she was pregnant. She gained weight and had morning sickness. However, Philip was sceptical, confiding his thoughts to the Venetian ambassador.

By the end of 1554, the heresy acts had been revived, and anyone not a Roman Catholic was in peril. In April 1555, Mary recalled Elizabeth to court so that she could be a witness to the birth of the child who would ensure she could never be queen. Philip began making overtures to Elizabeth, who encouraged them if only to try and safeguard her own life. This awakened Mary's passionate jealousy, further exacerbating the deterioration in her relationship with her half-sister. Philip obviously thought that he would rather have Elizabeth – someone he was sure he could guide and possibly marry if Mary died and he could force the Pope into a dispensation – than Mary, Queen of Scots, who was betrothed to the Dauphin of France.

When it became clear Mary was not pregnant, Philip took his opportunity to get away from her, saying he had to go back to the Continent to look after his own lands for a while. Mary was distraught, more so when Philip insisted Elizabeth be in the retinue to Greenwich to see him off.[141]

The terror began.

In 1555, bishops Latimer, Ridley and Cranmer were burned. Cranmer recanted but Mary was determined on his death, holding him responsible for her parents' divorce, for making her illegitimate, and for 'perverting' her brother, Edward. Cranmer put his hand, the one that had signed the recantation, into the fire first. Immediately after his death, Mary made Cardinal Reginald Pole the Archbishop of Canterbury.

She annulled all clerical marriages which meant wives and children being summarily ejected from their homes, although many priests kept their families hidden. If the priests refused to convert to Catholicism, they were thrown out on the streets.

Richard Spielmann goes into some detail about the circumstances and effects on married clerics. Cranmer had been married since the early 1530s and Matthew Parker, who was to become Elizabeth's Archbishop of Canterbury, married in 1547.[142]

In late 1547, Cranmer had introduced the Act of Convocation, which finally became law in 1549, but it was a reluctant consent that said priests already celibate would do better to concentrate on their job and not on women. That said, the clergy were known down the ages to have had unofficial wives and children. One consequence led to those priests with a bit of cash buying up land and houses to provide accommodation for the wives and children.

Mary knew she had to follow her father's precepts of making Church and State constitutional, in other words, everything had to be ratified by parliament. Her first parliament in 1553 was to gain consent to marry Philip of Spain and recognition of Cardinal Reginald Pole as papal legate. But there was also an act passed 'to repeal Certayne Statutes made in the time of the Raigne of Kinge Edwarde the Syxthe'. Basically, this was to repeal anything Edward had passed that outlawed Catholicism.

She then declared all married priests must be deprived of their benefices, but if the wife had died or the couple swore to abstain – i.e. the priest sent his wife away – the relevant bishop could use his discretion. Many priests went down this route. Some fled to the continent. Some leased their vicarages to the laity, who employed the wife and children and let them live in. Most priests just waited it out.

Because monks who had married were even more of an anathema to Mary than married priests, they were not only deprived of their benefices, but forced to divorce their wives, and be given 'due punishment'. This could be a whipping, public penance, or a fine. Or all three. Mary was nothing if not thorough!

Records are patchy – not uncommon in Tudor England. The nearest accurate figure of clergy deprived of their benefices is 953. The figures for unbeneficed clergy are almost non-existent, but might raise the 953 to around 1500.[143]

In June 1555, a Protestant preacher, Thomas Brice/Bryce began to record the deaths of martyrs, and this later became a prime research poem for John Foxe when writing his *Book of Martyrs*. The poem has a constant final line to each stanza *We wished for our Elizabeth*. To give a flavour of the tone:

> When worthy Watts with constant cry
> Continued in the flaming fire;
> When Simson, Hawkes and John Ardite
> Did taste the tyrant's raging ire;
> When Chamberlain was put to death,
> We wished for our Elizabeth.
> When blessed Butter and Osmande
> With force of fire to death were brent;
> When Shitterdon, Sir Frank and Bland,
> And Hymphrey Middleton of Kent;
> When Minge in Maidstone took his death,
> We wished for our Elizabeth.[144]

Foxe's *Acts and Monuments* is still a prime source that steers our concept of the religious life in Marian England. Sources vary a little as to numbers. Some say 284 were burned, others 288. The total number arrested according to Cavill, is 312, but some were allowed to die in prison. Foxe's *Acts* has shaded every account of the Marian persecutions, but recent reappraisals have questioned his version. Divided into four sections, those who suffered corporal punishment or forfeiture, those who escaped, and a shorter section on those persecutors who died sudden, gruesome deaths. But by far the biggest section covers those who were burned.[145]

Mary's Privy Council has also come in for a lot of criticism. It is certainly true that when Elizabeth took the throne, she reduced the number of councillors from around 50 to around 20, and Elizabeth made sure, as had her father, that all shades of opinion were represented. However, the very fact Mary was a female monarch made all the difference. Before this, the roles of the privy chamber and Privy Council had been intertwined to a certain degree, because the monarch had been male. In Mary's situation, the makeup of the privy chamber was markedly different because some of the women had been with her for a long time, and very few were married to members of the Privy Council, in other words, the privy chamber setup was not political for the most part. David Loades in *Intrigue and Treason: The Tudor Court* also maintains that Mary's court was the only one with no factions in it.

Vroom maintains that Mary had to solidify her position, not only because she was the first queen regnant, but because she had previously been declared a bastard. (Having said that, everyone knew William the Conqueror was a bastard, but then he was a strong, warlike bastard who few argued with, or if they did, they soon regretted it.) The other problem Mary faced was that women had very few legal rights, and the instant they married they had even fewer.[146]

It is estimated that over 800 protestants fled to the continent to escape the burnings. In 1556, Philip's father abdicated. Philip was still in Brussels, negotiating a truce with France, but in February 1556, Henry Dudley, second cousin of the executed Duke of Northumberland, tried to raise an invasion force in France to oust Mary. It failed.

In 1557, Philip finally returned to England for four months, in order to persuade Mary to support Spain in another war against France. Her council refused it outright because it would have meant a lack of supplies and money at a time when England had suffered a series of poor harvests. But some English soldiers did rally to Philip's call. Mary also had another phantom pregnancy, going as far as to decree that her husband would be regent if she died during the child's minority, but nobody believed it this time. In January 1558, the French retook Calais, which had been in English hands since the time of Edward III in 1347. It was the last in a long line of disappointments for the embattled English queen. Religious strife was still rampant, her husband had abandoned her, she couldn't produce a child, there had been disastrous harvests threatening a famine, and now she had lost the last English possession on the Continent.

By May 1558, Mary was forced to recognise Elizabeth as her successor. It is possible she was suffering from ovarian or uterine cancer.

Mary's death is described in Clifford's 1887 biography of Jane Dormer. Jane, who we shall meet a little later, was also ill at around the same time. Mary was at Hampton Court Palace and wanted to go to London (probably Whitehall).

Jane did not want Mary to travel by barge, so sent her own litter in which to transport the sick queen. Upon arrival in London, Mary took to her bed and stayed there. When it became known Mary was ill, it 'made the whole realm to mourn' – yes, I bet it did. Not! Mary kept recounting her dreams seeing little children, like angels, playing before her and singing.

Cardinal Pole was ill at the same time. Two days before they both died, they repeatedly 'confessed themselves', although this writer fails to see what sins they could have committed in between bouts of confession when they were so gravely ill, but there you go. They reach received extreme unction and seemed to rally, being 'much comforted, according to the fruit of that holy medicine'.[147]

Queen Mary died around 7:00 am on 17 November 1558. Reginald Pole followed her into the afterlife about twelve hours later, which almost seems to be a kind of joke on the part of the Almighty; a kind of 'let's get rid of both of them on the same day to save time'.

Mary had decreed she must be buried next to her mother in Peterborough Cathedral, but she was interred in Westminster Abbey, eventually sharing her tomb with the half-sister she despised.[148]

Fun Fact

Mary I was known to be immensely generous and she never forgot a face. Her gifts to her half-sister, Elizabeth, were very expensive, to such an extent that when she became hostile to her, Mary's councillors advised her to keep sending the expensive gifts so that Elizabeth did not suspect the queen had changed towards her.

Lady Jane Dormer: Duchess of Feria

Jane was born in Buckinghamshire in 1538. Her family was split by the events of the Reformation. Her father remained a resolute Catholic; in fact, her great-uncle, Sebastian Newdigate, a Carthusian monk, was executed for refusing to accept the Royal Supremacy.[149] Jane's mother chose Protestantism, but she died when Jane was 4 years old, so the child's upbringing was largely along Catholic lines, even though she was a friend and playmate of the young Edward VI.[150] Her maternal grandfather would send Jane to read, sing, dance and play with the young king.[151]

Although Mary was twenty-two years Jane's senior, she soon became a close friend and confidante. Edward Courtenay was one of those who opined Jane was a beauty and she had a very sweet disposition. Mary was very unimpressed with Courtenay; she did not want Jane to marry, but to remain with her.

However, when Philip of Spain came to England in 1554 to marry Mary, Jane met Don Gomez de Suarez de Figueroa of Cordova, Duke of Feria. He was very close to Philip and was the first Spanish ambassador to Elizabeth's court.

Mary was more than happy to encourage Jane and her Spanish suitor, but their romance was stopped in its tracks when Philip, having stayed to make sure Mary was not pregnant the second time, returned to the Continent, taking Don Gomez with him. Jane stayed with Mary.[152] However, when Mary fell ill, Philip sent Don Gomez back to England, and when the queen died on 17 November 1558, Philip urged the couple to marry immediately, having realised Catholicism in England was not now in the ascendant. Jane and Don Gomez were married in December 1558 without Elizabeth's consent.[153] Jane delivered Mary's jewels to the new queen, Elizabeth, and was, outwardly at least, on good terms with her. Elizabeth also realised the benefits of maintaining a good relationship with Jane if only because her husband was the closest councillor and friend of the newly-widowed Philip.

Under the Act of Succession, as it stood at the time of Elizabeth's accession, her successor was Lady Katherine Grey, sister of the executed Lady Jane Grey. The new Duchess of Feria passed messages from Katherine to her husband, who, knowing how suspicious Elizabeth was of Katherine, plotted to get her out of England. More of Katherine later.

In 1559, Jane, by then heavily pregnant, left England to join her husband in the Low Countries. She was kept waiting in Elizabeth's watching chamber, standing up, for over an hour, before she was admitted to the queen's presence to say her final farewell. The fault for this awful treatment has in the past been put at Elizabeth's door, but most modern historians now put the blame on William Cecil and his hatred of anyone Catholic.[154]

Jane delivered her elder son, Lorenzo, in the Low Countries. Elizabeth sent her 'hearty commendations', which tends to support the theory that the queen still wanted to cultivate Jane. In another letter, Courtauld notes that Elizabeth signs herself as Jane's 'Sovereign and friend'. Jane was also known as 'always a kind lady to the Queen'.

So, it does look as if Cecil's stratagem to foster bad relations between the two women was a failure, but then Elizabeth was nothing if not pragmatic, especially where religion was concerned, whereas Cecil was at heart a Puritan.

Whilst in the Low Countries, Jane and her husband travelled to spend Easter with the Duke of Guise and there met Mary, Queen of Scots. Although the two never met again, they did become good friends, corresponding frequently until Mary's death. Mary signed herself 'your perfect friend, old acquaintance and dear cousin'.

Jane and Don Gomez had two sons, the younger dying when only a few months old. Once in Spain, Jane became a magnet for disaffected Catholics, even though she and Elizabeth maintained their correspondence. Don Gomez died in 1571. He left debts amounting to 300,000 ducats. Jane took over the management of his estates and cleared all debts by the time Lorenzo came of age. She remained a much-respected figure in Spain, and was mooted as governor of Flanders at one point.[155]

In 1609, Jane had an accident, breaking her arm and she never regained her full health. By 1611, she was bedridden. Jane was described by her servant, Henry Clifford, as 'somewhat higher than ordinary; of a comely person, a lively aspect, a gracious countenance, very clear-skinned, quick in senses; for she had her sight and hearing to her last hour'. She died in 1612 and is buried at the monastery of Santa Clara in Zafra.[156]

Susan Clarencius

Susan White was born before 1510, but little is known about this woman who became Queen Mary's closest friend as well as her mistress of the robes. It is believed she was the youngest child of Richard White and Maud Tyrrell, both of Essex, and that she had two sisters and one brother. That apart, we know nothing about her early life.

At some point before 1534, she married Thomas Tonge, who, in early 1534 became Clarenceux King of Arms, an officer of arms at the College of Arms in London. The title allegedly derives from the Clare earls of Gloucester or possibly the dukedom of Clarence. From that time on, Susan was known as Susan Clarencius, that name appearing among the gentlewomen in a 1539 gift roll. Susan's husband, who must have been much older than her, died in 1536 and she never remarried. She was the executor of his estates.[157]

In 1525, Susan accompanied Princess Mary to the Welsh Marches as a maid-in-waiting to the heiress presumptive. However, when Mary refused to recognise Anne Boleyn in 1533, her household was broken up and Susan lost her job. It was only temporary, however, because when Henry VIII bullied his elder daughter into accepting that his marriage to Katherine of Aragon was invalid and that she was illegitimate, Mary was given back her household and requested the return of Susan Clarencius because she had remained a steadfast friend when Mary's life had been very troubled. Susan returned to Mary's service and quickly became a close friend and confidante.

In 1543, Susan was paid an annuity of £13 (almost £9000 in 2024) out of augmentations, a court set up to handle money and lands resulting from the

Dissolution of the Monasteries. Two years later, Susan surrendered this in exchange for the manor of Chepenhall in Suffolk. Her estates in Essex brought in enough income for her to retain her society position among the gentry of Essex, and remain close to her relations, one of whom was William Petrie, principal secretary to both Edward VI and Queen Mary.

Although Susan held no title, the Imperial Ambassador called her 'the chief lady in the princess' household'. She controlled access to Mary and had her own set of keys to the Privy Apartments. When Mary became queen, Susan's influence over her was recognised by ambassadors, including that of Mary of Hungary, who told him that Mary's marriage should only be discussed with Susan.[158]

One of Mary's first acts was to send John Dudley, Duke of Northumberland to the Tower, along with his wife, Jane. Jane was released after a week and travelled to Essex. She wrote a letter to Anne, Lady Paget, wife of Edward's trusted councillor, who had now transferred to Mary's service. The letter begged Anne to ask her husband to intercede to save Dudley's life and that of his son, Guildford, and suggesting that he talk to Susan who was the closest friend of the new queen. There is evidence that Susan and Paget were in contact. It is clear that Susan tried to gain leniency for both men, to no avail. However, her attempt to save William Parr, Earl of Northampton, one of Dudley's close associates, was successful. When Jane Dudley died in 1555, she left Susan her 'tawny velvot jewell coffer'.[159]

Susan championed the cause of Philip of Spain regarding marriage to Mary and she was the only witness present with Mary and Renard, the Imperial Ambassador, when Mary secretly agreed to marry Philip.[160]

Susan stayed close to Mary when the queen believed she was pregnant, reassuring her mistress that she was, indeed, with child. At the same time, she was telling Antoine de Noailles, the French Ambassador that she was doubtful about the pregnancy. She developed a reputation for being devious and greedy. The Venetian Ambassador, Giovanni Michelei, was persuaded by Susan to present his coach and horses to the queen as a gift. He did. Mary gave them to Susan. All the time, she acted behind the scenes as an unofficial councillor.

When Jane Dormer became Mary's friend, Susan joined her household, and when Jane left England for Spain in 1559, Susan went with her. She left her estates in the hands of her nephews, and it is believed Robert Dudley, Earl of Leicester, may have protected them in gratitude for Susan trying to save the lives of his father and brother.[161]

She stayed in Jane Dormer's household in Spain, but there is no mention of her after spring 1564, and it is surmised she died at around that time. There are no records of her having children.

Stephen Gardiner, Bishop of Winchester

We know that Gardiner was born in Bury St Edmunds in 1483, but have no precise date of birth. Neither do we know the name of his father. His mother has been posited as being Helen Tudor, illegitimate daughter of Jasper Tudor, but this is a possible confusion with another cleric called Thomas Gardiner.

In 1511, Gardiner met Erasmus in Paris, at which time he was probably studying at Trinity Hall, Cambridge. He excelled in Greek and the classics – the study of classical antiquity, mostly Greek and Roman literature. Gardiner devoted himself to canon and civil law. By 1520 he was made a Doctor of Civil Law and the following year, a Doctor Of Canon Law. It is clear he was an exceptional student. So much so, he came to the notice of Cardinal Wolsey, who took him on as his secretary. With that post came a sound knowledge of foreign policy, which brought him to the attention of Henry VIII.

In 1527, Gardiner was sent, with Thomas More, to arrange a treaty with the French for war against Charles VI, the Holy Roman Emperor, and later that year, Henry sent him to see the Pope, Clement VII, to negotiate Henry's divorce from Katherine of Aragon to be heard in England. Wolsey also used him as an intermediary with the French to support the divorce. His knowledge of canon law was significant in the final decision that Wolsey would be allowed to pronounce on Henry's marriage without leave of appeal.[162]

Gardiner, being a staunch Catholic, was an opponent of Anne Boleyn, Thomas Cranmer (by then Archbishop of Canterbury) and Thomas Cromwell. The latter, knowing Gardiner's religious views, eased him out of his post as secretary.[163] But Gardiner was very well aware of the influence of the Reformation.[164]

Physically, he was described by George Cavendish as having 'a swarthy complexion, hooked nose, deep-set eyes, a permanent frown, huge hands, and a vengeful wit'. Sounds like a real laugh at parties, doesn't he?

In 1531, he was made Bishop of Winchester and, notwithstanding his religious views, he was still a favourite with Henry. The two were known to argue without any rancour.[165] Despite that, Henry bypassed him for the post of Archbishop of Canterbury, but Gardiner still signed the papers acknowledging Henry as Supreme Head of the Church of England. He wrote 'De Vera Obedientia', a vindication of the Royal Supremacy, basically saying 'Princes ought to be obeyed by the commandment of God; yea, and to be obeyed without question'.

Throughout the following years, he was sent abroad on various embassies to France and Germany. After the fall of Thomas Cromwell in 1540, Gardiner became the chancellor of the University of Cambridge. In truth, Henry needed Gardiner as much as he needed Cranmer, if only to persuade Europe that the king had retained his faith, that he was still a Catholic, but an Anglo-Catholic, not a Roman Catholic. Cranmer was necessary in his role of upholding the Supremacy. This one thing put both prelates on either side of a wide divide, and, essentially, enemies.

In 1546, Gardiner was involved in a plot to bring about the downfall of Katherine Parr, Henry's sixth wife, known to have Protestant leanings. She became aware of the plot, and threw herself on the king's mercy, saying she had not been trying to instruct him, but only take his mind off the constant pain from his leg ulcers. Henry was furious with the plotters, and that might be one reason he did not name Gardiner as a member of the regency council for Edward VI. It may also have been a stratagem on the part of Edward Seymour, who was determined to rule the new young king and wanted no opposition.

During the early years of Edward's reign, Gardiner wrote a series of letters saying that the Protestant reforms were wrong. In 1548, he was sent to the Fleet Prison, and from there to the Tower of London, where he stayed for the rest of the reign. In 1551, he was deprived of the bishopric of Winchester, but one of Mary's first actions when she triumphed over Northumberland and Lady Jane Grey, was to release Gardiner and the Duke of Norfolk from their imprisonment. She immediately restored Gardiner as Bishop of Winchester.

He put the crown on her head at the coronation, and was appointed Lord Chancellor. He is also known to have interceded with the queen, unsuccessfully, to try and save Northumberland. As Lord Chancellor, Mary gave him the responsibility of finding irrefutable proof that she was not illegitimate.

Gardiner approved the new heresy laws, but *not* the extent of Mary's zealotry, and this is where the tale of him being demonised started. What is telling is that nobody in his diocese was persecuted until after his death. In May 1555, he was sent to Calais as a commissioner, and in October of that year, he opened parliament, but fell ill. He died in November 1555 and was eventually buried in Winchester Cathedral.[166]

Gardiner's reputation has undergone something of a change since the early years of Protestant and Puritan hatred. He often appears as a divisive character, vilified from the time of Mary's death. Overall, though, he appears to be a man of deep (Catholic) faith, who often compromised his principles in order to demonstrate his fealty to Henry VIII, certainly one might suppose, in the matter of him negotiating with the Pope to end the king's first marriage.

On the one hand, he is portrayed as 'Wily Winchester', a Machiavellian, malign influence over Mary, interested only in feeding heretics to the bonfires. Part of this is due to Foxe and his *Book of Martyrs*, especially in the case of Robert Barnes.

Barnes was an Augustinian monk who, in the 1520s, became a convinced Protestant. He was used by both Henry VIII and Thomas Cromwell to take commissions to Europe but his great enemy, and the man determined to have him executed as a heretic, was Sir Thomas More. However, the axe fell on More for refusing to acknowledge Henry as the Supreme Head of the Church. So, Barnes, at that time in Antwerp, felt it safe to come home.

Things jogged on nicely for Barnes until Cromwell fell in 1540. Once he had been executed, Barnes had no protector, and he was arrested and attainted as a heretic, which meant he could not answer any charges in court or defend himself. He was burned at the stake with Thomas Garrard and William Jerome. Although they asked the sheriff what the charges against them were, no answer was forthcoming. An observer of the executions said that all three men 'remained in the fire without crying out, but were as quiet and patient as though they felt no pain'.[167]

At the same time, Henry also executed three Catholics, but it was Gardiner who was later vilified for his part in bringing Barnes to the fire, and this fed the fable of him as a monster. Initially, Gardiner was against a foreign marriage for Mary, but once it had happened, he set about returning England to the Catholic fold.

At the centre of his life from the early 1530s onwards, his main antagonist was Thomas Cranmer, and much of that was because despite being on opposite sides of the religious divide, they were, in many ways, similar. Gardiner came from a higher social strata than Cranmer, but the latter's career soon caught up. Gardiner was faithful to tradition; Cranmer believed the old Catholic services were too complicated for the congregation to understand. He wanted simplicity, the people attending services to understand what was happening, which meant services must be in English.[168] It is also known that Gardiner did his best to save Cranmer, Latimer, and Ridley, but Mary was adamant, especially about Cranmer.[169] It is notable that only after Gardiner's death did her zealotry accelerate, with around 270 people being burned between 1555 and 1558.[170] As for Gardiner, his view of religion was essentially a simple one:

The best plaister and medicine that could now be devised, were to leave apart questions and idle talk, and meekly to submit our capacities to the true faith, and not to overwhelm our understandings with search and inquiry, whereof we shall never find an end, entering the bottomless secrecy of God's mysteries. Let us not seek that is above our reach; but that God hath commanded us let us do.[171]

Reginald Pole

In his biography of Pole, Edwards opines that Pole was thought of in Rome as a Lutheran, in Germany as a papist, in the Emperor Charles' court as a supporter of the French, and in the French court as a supporter of the Emperor. In essence, wherever he was, Pole was regarded with suspicion. Edwards also believes Pole was as committed to the Counter Reformation – including the correction and punishments – quite as much as Mary was. This is in direct contradiction to other historians' opinions that he was not as zealous as the queen.[172]

Reginald Pole was born at Stourton Castle in Staffordshire in March 1500. His father was Richard Pole, but it was his mother who provides a frisson for the historian. She was Margaret, Countess of Salisbury. More interestingly, she was the daughter of George, Duke of Clarence, middle brother between Edward IV and Richard III, and Isabel Neville, elder daughter of Richard, Earl of Warwick, styled 'Warwick the Kingmaker'. Margaret's young brother, Edward, Earl of Warwick was executed by Henry VII on a trumped-up charge of fabricating a plot with Perkin Warbeck. Having disposed of the brother, Henry VII married Margaret off to Richard Pole, whose mother was Henry's mother's half-sister. Are you still with me?

The preceding paragraph demonstrates the royal lineage of Reginald Pole, in direct contrast to that of the Tudors, whose lineage came down through two illegitimate lines. In fact, in some ways he had more right to the throne of England than the Tudors who sat on it. This was to have an impact on Reginald, both good and bad.

His early education is subject to debate, but he entered Magdalen College, Oxford in 1512. For the next two years, Henry VIII paid a pension towards his education. He graduated with an Honours degree in 1515 at the age of 16. By 1518, Henry had granted him the deanery at Wimborne Minster. In 1521, Reginald travelled to Padua, with a stipend given to him by the king, and stayed there for the next three years.[173]

By 1527, he was Prebendary of Salisbury and Dean of Exeter. He had several livings including being a canon at York. But he was still not an ordained priest. In 1529, Henry sent him to Paris to represent his arguments at a discussion with theologians at the Sorbonne on the subject of Henry's marriage. Henry expected Pole to persuade the French to give him a favourable verdict, and offered him the archbishopric of York – Wolsey's old archbishopric – or Winchester in the full expectation Pole would support the divorce.[174]

He is known to have warned Henry not to marry Anne Boleyn at around this time. So far, Henry's favour of this Plantagenet scion had paid dividends, but that was to change. Pole wrote a treatise regarding the difficulties Henry faced. Cranmer later wrote to Thomas Boleyn, Earl of Wiltshire, that it was 'much contrary to the King's purpose', but that the arguments were set forth with such wisdom and eloquence that 'were it to be published, he believed it would be impossible to persuade people to the contrary'. Also in Cranmer's letter to Wiltshire, he went on to say that the principal point of the treatise was that 'the King should be content to submit his great cause to the judgement of the Pope'.[175] At this point, Henry almost gave up the fight, but Thomas Cromwell, regarded by Pole as the spawn of Satan, persuaded his master to carry on.

Pole was very anxious as the 1530s progressed to do nothing that might invoke a civil war. Thomas Starkey, urged by Henry, asked Pole for his opinion on two points; first whether the divine law of marrying a deceased brother's wife was permissible, and second, whether papal supremacy was a divine institution. Henry added that he wanted Pole to state his honest opinion. Pole prevaricated. In 1534, Henry asked Cromwell to write to Pole reminding him that he was still waiting for answers. They soon arrived, and were the cause of the final break with Henry.

In 1536, four months after the death of Katherine of Aragon, Pole answered the questions with a treatise, 'Pro ecclesiasticae unitatis defensione'. Pole disputed Henry's position on his marriage to Prince Arthur's widow, one of the king's primary theological arguments asserting his marriage to Katherine was unlawful. He also denied the Royal Supremacy and, to make matters worse, urged Europe's royals to depose Henry.[176]

Naturally, Henry was a tad miffed by this ingratitude. He wrote to Pole's mother, Margaret, who, with other members of the family, wrote to her son castigating him for his folly. She knew better than anyone the risks involved. Except they weren't risks for Pole because he had fled to the Continent. The Pope made him responsible for helping those rebels involved in the Pilgrimage of Grace, although neither the Emperor, Charles V nor Francis I supported that move.[177]

Henry was determined to get Pole, whom he now regarded as a traitor, back to England. Hiding his anger, he again urged the family to write letters urging Pole to return. His friends in Italy begged him not to. Henry was further enraged when the Pope made Pole a cardinal. He tried again to persuade Pole to return to his homeland and Pole did indeed start to return. He reached France, but Henry had demanded that Francis I hand him over as a traitor. Pole fled to Cambray, at that time neutral territory. The English ambassador demanded he be captured. English agents did their best to kidnap or assassinate him, but eventually he managed to scrabble back to Italy.[178]

Henry, unable to get hold of Pole, took revenge on his family. In 1538, the important people in the family were arrested and charged with treason, including Pole's mother. Their lands were seized. Even though Cromwell opined that they had not really offended, the only one who had committed an offence being Reginald, Henry didn't care. Eventually, they were all executed. Margaret, aged 67, made the blundering executioner follow her as she ran around the block, refusing to accept she was a traitor, while he hacked at her. This last lady of the Plantagenets was beatified by Pope Leo XIII in 1886.

By that time, Cromwell, too, had fallen. Pole stayed in Europe. In 1542, he was one of three papal legates presiding over the Council of Trent, responsible for attempting to build a counter-reformation against the Protestants. At one point in 1549, he had 26 out of the 28 votes he needed to become the next Pope. He was still not an ordained priest.

When Edward VI died, Pole tried to return to England as Papal Legate, but Charles V was worried he would speak out against the Spanish marriage, and it was only when Mary was safely married to Philip that Pole returned. He presented his credentials to Mary and Philip. Gardiner, Bishop of Winchester was present as Lord Chancellor and Pole was made responsible for driving the necessary legislation to return England to the Catholic fold through parliament.[179]

He began his restoration of the Catholic Orthodoxy at Oxford and Cambridge. However, the political manoeuvrings of Pope Paul IV, siding with the French, while Mary sided with her father-in-law, the Emperor, put Pole in a cleft stick.[180]

When Cranmer was deprived of the archbishopric of Canterbury, Pole was made an administrator of the See of Canterbury, but he was *still* not an ordained priest. Until 1556, when he finally took holy orders, was immediately made Archbishop of Canterbury and became Mary's chief minister.

In 1555, Mary began burning heretics; in all about 280 died in the three years between 1555 and her death in 1558. During these years, Pole's health was failing, so his involvement in the burnings is open to question. There is evidence he preferred a more lenient solution to the one Mary insisted on pursuing. Three heretics from Bishop Bonner's diocese who were due to burn appealed to Pole, who pardoned them on the promise of a penance and then gave them absolution.

Mary's zealotry ruined Pole's desire for a Catholic Reformation in England. Her actions turned the people against her, and against Catholicism for centuries to come. The Pope agreed with Mary, reproving Pole for not being severe enough. He tried to recall him to Rome to face a charge of heresy and suspended his role as papal legate. Mary refused to let Pole go, although she accepted his suspension. In November, his health plummeted, and he caught influenza. He died twelve hours after his queen, on the evening of 17 November 1558.[181]

Rex Pogson sums up Pole's character as being mostly incompetent. He was criticised for not calling on Jesuits to re-convert English heretics, when at that time in 1554, Jesuits were being very successful at doing just that. Ignatius Loyola, a Catholic priest and theologian, suggested to Pole that he should call on Jesuits to persuade English heretics to return to the Roman Catholic fold. Pole ignored him, whether through apathy, jealousy or incompetence is impossible to know.[182]

The Emperor, Charles V believed Pole to be incompetent, but the general opinion was that Pole's spiritual piety impeded practical decisions. The Duke de Feria called him lukewarm and lethargic. Even Philip acknowledged that Pole preferred contemplation over action.

One counter to this argument is a lack of time to do what needed to be done. Pole was already ill by the time Cranmer died and he was made Archbishop of Canterbury. From that time his health slowly deteriorated. In truth, Pole only had two and a half years to overturn twenty years of religious confusion, and he was probably only beginning to realise the size of his task by the time he died.[183]

What is interesting and a good point to end this section on Mary I and her favoured courtiers, is Edwards' opinion that, at the time of their deaths, on 17 November 1558, both Pole and Mary were defying the Pope quite as much as Henry VIII had ever done.[184]

Elizabeth I

In the 2007 BBC poll on the subject of who was England's greatest monarch, Elizabeth polled 48% of the vote. The next nearest was Victoria with almost 20% and Henry VIII with a measly 13%.[186]

While that is a subjective conclusion, there is no doubt at all that from a distance of over 400 years, people are still fascinated by this younger daughter of Henry VIII. That she inherited many of her traits from her father is not up for argument. Narcissistic, vain, proud, wily, she certainly was. She used her gender to her own advantage when it suited her; keeping her council, including the devious William Cecil, Lord Burghley, on its toes, by pretending to be indecisive because it meant she kept her options open. Even the love of her life, Robert Dudley, Earl of Leicester, was not immune from the very sharp edge of her tongue.

She was arrogant, insecure, subject to appalling rages – in 1575, she broke Mary Scudamore (née Shelton)'s finger – for daring to marry without the queen's permission, something they quickly put down to an 'accident'. What made her the person she was? Because until we make some attempt to understand Elizabeth, it is difficult to be anything other than speculative about the how and why of what she did.

The beginning of Larissa Taylor-Smither's psychological profile quotes a poem by the unfortunately named Reverend Thomas Bastard:

> Mother of England, and sweete nurse of all,
> Thy countries good which all depends on thee,
> Looke not that countries father I thee call,
> A name of great and kingly dignitie;
> Thou dost not onely match olde kings, but rather,
> In thy sweet love to us, excell a father.[187]

Taylor-Smither's first comment is that Elizabeth was an enigma to her people and we can include her courtiers, Privy Council, and advisors in that.

The life of Elizabeth I has been documented so many times, there is little need to reiterate here what others have written in greater detail. Suffice it to say that throughout the summer of 1533, England was the centre of European interest. Foreign ambassadors to the court of Henry VIII sent frequent despatches to their masters, the subject being one thing.

The English king had divorced his wife of over twenty years, brought his realm into religious schism by declaring that he, and he alone, was the Head of the Church in England. Furthermore, the Pope could only be referred to as the Bishop of Rome.

And for what? Well, that was the question. Would Henry's much-hated second queen, Anne Boleyn, deliver the son she had promised? The answer came on the afternoon of 7 September. The baby was a girl. Let's say Henry was not too chuffed.

They named the child Elizabeth after her paternal grandmother. From her father, she inherited red Tudor hair, his charisma, his intelligence, and his energy. From her mother, she inherited charm and flair. She would need all those traits to carry her through the next almost seventy years.

Unlike her father, Elizabeth did not make decisions quickly. Indeed, she was prone to change her mind. Frequently. And while some would say that was a flaw, it kept everyone guessing, not knowing what she would do next.

During the first ten years of her life, the child had three stepmothers, but it was not until 1543, when Henry married his sixth and last wife, Katherine Parr, that Elizabeth experienced the environment of being part of a family. The new queen sought, and largely succeeded, in making this disparate group of three children from three different mothers, plus an increasingly ill, aging, and vicious father, into something approaching a cohesive unit. One wonders if the 1545 plot against Katherine Parr failed not just because she was forewarned and threw herself on Henry's mercy, but because his final years had elements of the one thing he had craved all his life. A loving family environment.

Like her elder half-sister, Elizabeth was declared illegitimate after her mother's execution on what most people now believe were trumped-up charges. Henry dictated in his will that should Edward not produce children, the throne should pass to Mary and if there were still no children, to Elizabeth. Edward changed all that, but Mary triumphed. Elizabeth had been in trouble when the Thomas Seymour treason became public in 1549, but under intense interrogation, she refused to admit any guilt, nearly driving Robert Tyrwhitt demented.

During Mary's reign, Elizabeth had to conform to the Catholic Mass, outwardly at least. But she was a natural Protestant, although not a Puritan.

She ended up in the Tower for two months in 1554 after Wyatt's Rebellion, but when no proof could be found against her, despite Gardiner wanting to put her on trial, she was put under house arrest at Woodstock in Oxfordshire under the supervision of Sir Henry Bedingfeld.

Mary called her back to court so that she could flaunt her swollen stomach and make Elizabeth the new heir's attendant. It didn't quite work out that way, and Philip of Spain, with one eye on the future, championed the embattled princess.[188]

On 17 November 1588, her time of waiting was over. And for about 300 years afterwards, *Queene's Day* was celebrated with bonfires by the English as a symbol of their release from Catholic oppression.[189] Elizabeth spent the next forty-odd years still keeping everyone guessing, but bringing a degree of peace to her realm that made the people love her and call her *Good Queen Bess*. If nothing else, she, like her father, know how to work the crowd.

It almost came undone in 1562 when she nearly died of smallpox. Her reputation also took a hit in 1560 when Amy Dudley (Robsart) was discovered dead in suspicious circumstances, an event that if it *were* murder, has often been laid at William Cecil's door.

Elizabeth had many suitors from all over Europe, including her ex-brother-in-law, Philip, his cousin Charles, Archduke of Austria, a couple from Scandinavia, and then Henry, Duke of Anjou, and his younger brother, François, Duke of Alençon and then Anjou. This last real chance of her marrying occurred when Elizabeth was in her mid-late forties, and was, possibly, the nearest she came to actually tying the knot. She is known to have told the Imperial Ambassador 'If I follow the inclination of my nature, it is this; beggar woman and single, far rather than queen and married'.[190]

In her fifties, she had to finally deal with the Mary, Queen of Scots situation, and then five armadas – all failures – sent by the Spanish to defeat this heretic queen who had murdered an anointed sovereign. Her final crisis was when the foolhardy Robert Devereux, Earl of Essex, tried to raise an army against her. That failed, too.

The succession question hung over Elizabeth's Privy Council for her entire reign, until in the latter years, Robert Cecil, William's son, was in regular touch with James VI of Scotland. When Elizabeth fell ill in March 1603, she refused to go to bed, but sat on cushions. Eventually, she was pressured into going to bed against her will. This is described by Robert Hugh Benson's essay on the deaths of Mary and Elizabeth:

'About six at night', writes Sir Robert Carey, 'she made signs for the Archbishop and her chaplains to come to her…. Her Majesty lay upon her back, with one hand in the bed, and the other without. The Bishop kneeled by her and examined her first of her faith, and she so punctually observed all his several questions, by lifting up her eyes and holding up her hand, as it was a comfort to all beholders. Then the good man told her plainly what she was, and what she was to come to; and though she had been long a great Queen here upon earth, yet shortly she was to yield an account of her stewardship to the King of kings. After this he began to pray, and all that were by did answer him…. The Queen made a sign with her hand. My sister Scrope, knowing the meaning, told the Bishop the Queen desired he would pray still. He did so for a long half-hour after, and then thought to leave her. The second time she made sign to have him continue in prayer. He did so for half an hour more, with earnest cries to God for her soul's health, which he uttered with that fervency of spirit as the Queen to all our sight much rejoiced thereat, and gave testimony to us all of her Christian and comfortable end'.[191]

The younger Cecil had already smoothed James' path to the English throne. He became James I and VI. It would be another 104 years until the Act of Union united the two nations.

Having covered the basics of Elizabeth's life, rather like I have done with Henry VIII, I intend to examine several events during her reign and how they affected the queen, and England, before I look at some of her lesser-known favourites.

Fun Fact

When she died at age 69, Elizabeth I was the oldest monarch in English history, beating Edward I by a year. This remained the case until George II died in 1760 at the age of 76

Elizabeth and the Succession

The instant Elizabeth's royal behind hit the throne, the only thing that concerned her advisors and MPs was her marriage. Elizabeth was very honest and frank with them. When parliament met soon after the coronation, the House of Commons asked her to marry so as to provide an heir to the throne; she stated she had no intention of ever marrying, 'and in the end, having reigned such a time, lived and died a virgin'.[192]

Elizabeth's refusal to name her successor is something that has echoed down the years. Parliament was sitting at the time Mary died. The Lord Chancellor, Nicholas Heath, announced her death and that the crown now went to Elizabeth, adding 'of whose most lawful right and title to the crown, thanks be to God, we need not doubt'. It was, as historian David Starkey says, an extraordinarily smooth accession when we consider how perilous Elizabeth's journey to the throne had been.[193]

Within four days, Elizabeth and Cecil had chosen her council and the business of government ran on smooth wheels. However, after that first plea by parliament for the queen to marry and produce an heir, and her response, which of course, none of them believed, it was not until the early 1560s when she had made no move to even look at a prospective husband, preferring to keep them all dangling, that parliament decided she needed a reminder.

J. E. Neale discusses a paper written in Elizabeth's hand, and found in the British Museum, and the events surrounding it. It proves how much Elizabeth squirmed under parliament's obsession with the succession, but how pragmatic she could be.[194]

The first parliament that began to pressure her regarding the succession question was in 1562, and it continued until she imprisoned Peter Wentworth in 1593 for saying it was parliament's right to discuss the succession. He died in the Tower in 1596.

To be fair, parliament had a point, especially when she fell ill with smallpox and almost died in 1562. The members knew that all that lay between them and chaos was a sick woman. The Commons decided to join with the Lords and petition her. But they did it in separate petitions. Neale asserts that the Commons petition and the Lords petition were not made at the same time, but the first in 1562 and the second in 1566.[195]

Her response to the Lords was that the marks on her face were from smallpox, not age, and God could still send her children. She further told them 'they had better consider well what they were asking, as, if she declared a successor, it would cost much blood to England'. She merely fobbed the Commons off by saying she needed time to consider their petition. So, off they went, confident she would come back to them shortly, and voted her the money she had asked for, instead of making the money dependent on her answer to their petition.

What Elizabeth knew from bitter experience was the danger to the monarch if people in power knew who would succeed to the throne after the current incumbent. She had lived through Mary's reign, only avoiding execution because the Lieutenant of the Tower questioned the warrant sent by Gardiner, and consulted Mary who knew nothing about it. Add to that the heavy fumes of conspiracy over Mary, Queen of Scots, and you can quite see Elizabeth's point.

Parliament wanted, at the very least, for Elizabeth to make a will and name her successor. She died forty years later never having made a will. So, she sent the Commons away 'answerless' every time, and if they got above themselves, she turned on the charm, lulled them into a false sense of security until they voted her the money or supplies she needed, and then dissolved parliament.

The problem was, the longer this went on, the older Elizabeth became and the more urgent the succession issue became.

By 1566, parliament had learned to not give the carrot away first. They linked the tenets of the Subsidy Bill with an answer to the issue of the succession. They debated a motion to re-present the petition to her asking her to name her successor. She vetoed that *and* any further discussion on the matter. The House then debated for over a day about whether the queen could inhibit their discussions, and petitioned her to allow a free discussion in parliament. She said no and sent for the Speaker, emphasising her decision before the House could reconvene the debate.

What did not help either side was an MP called Dalton, who had discovered a poem doing the rounds saying that James of Scotland was a prince of England. He spoke about it in parliament and Robert Melville, one of Mary, Queen of Scots' agents, lodged a complaint with the Privy Council. Dalton was seized and examined before the Star Chamber. Elizabeth believed that this was all part of the succession plot by parliament and it meant to defy her wishes. The Commons thought she was treating them like naughty boys and the issue became one of privilege, not the succession. It all became very messy.

In the end, parliament thanked the queen for her promise to marry – and give the country an heir – adding pointedly that they hoped God would hasten her fulfilment of her promise. The Commons then requested 'leave to discuss what liberties it did have'.

By doing this, parliament was telling Elizabeth she either gave way or dissolved it, in which case she would lose the supplies under the Subsidy Bill she had asked for. She lifted the veto but asked the Speaker to silence any member who raised the subject of the succession. Thus, she had partially given way and that pacified the moderates in the Commons, at the same time appealing to their chivalric side to accept that she would, at some point, fulfil her promises. However, this was the second time she had forestalled her parliament and some members were not happy, so they decided to incorporate her promise as a preamble to the Subsidy Bill, in which the queen was reminded that the safety of her people, not herself, should determine the time when she nominated her successor. To say Elizabeth was not thrilled at all is an understatement, but she was always pragmatic when it came to the pinch. She agreed, the bill was passed, and she dissolved parliament. However, before she dissolved it, she addressed both Houses. She reproved them, whilst being conciliatory, and identified herself as being responsible for the welfare of the country. She lost money on the bill, and didn't punish Dalton. By so doing, she avoided a parliamentary crisis, but at the same time, she stopped all discussions of the succession in its tracks.[196]

Elizabeth and Religion

Jasper Ridley's biography of Elizabeth, published in 1987, states that her actions regarding religion in the early months of her reign, plus the Treaty of Edinburgh in 1560, resulted in what he calls 'a complete victory for Elizabeth and the Protestant cause'.[197] These two things set the tone for the rest of her reign. In other words, Elizabeth started how she meant to go on.

Her first parliamentary assembly was preceded, as was customary, by a Mass to inspire parliamentary deliberations. Elizabeth was approached by swinging censers, held by monks, and burning tapers. Her reaction was to the point; 'away with these torches, for we see very well'. The preacher, Richard Cox, had been Edward VI's tutor. His sermon preached against monks and accused them of being responsible for the Marian persecutions. Elizabeth's reaction to his sermon is not recorded.

Her prime task, she was told by the Speaker, was the 'well making of laws for the according and uniting of the people of this realm into a uniform order of religion'. He stated that debates should not contain insults such as *heretic* or *schismatic* or *Papist*.

Elizabeth wanted to avoid extremes. Her middle-of-the-road approach was attacked by both sides, which ended in a more radically Protestant settlement than she wanted.[198] She is famously quoted as saying she had no wish to 'make windows into men's souls …there is only one Jesus Christ and all the rest is a dispute over trifles'. However, at that time, England was, by law, a Catholic realm, and confronting that head-on was dangerous. So, she didn't. She prevaricated and delayed.

Elizabeth was crowned with Catholic ceremonial. That said, she forbade the elevation of the host, something that six weeks previously would have sent her to the fires. She liked her priests to wear vestments, but she appears to have had no intention of keeping faith with the Pope. The reformers petitioned her to get money back from the clergy who had increased their wealth on the back of the Catholic religion during Mary's reign.

What she tried to do was steer a middle course on the basis that both sides worshipped the same God. She wanted to restore the situation as it had been in the time of her brother, Edward, but keep some of the Romanist practices so as not to alienate the Catholics.

She ordered the *Book of Prayer* to be revised, ordering all clergy not to teach or preach anything other than the gospel and epistle of the day, spicing up the order with the threat of punishment if they disobeyed her.[199]

Sadly, as in the world today where religion is concerned, the middle ground is anathema to either view. However, Elizabeth knew she had to appease the Catholics while the committee revising the prayer book wanted only to please

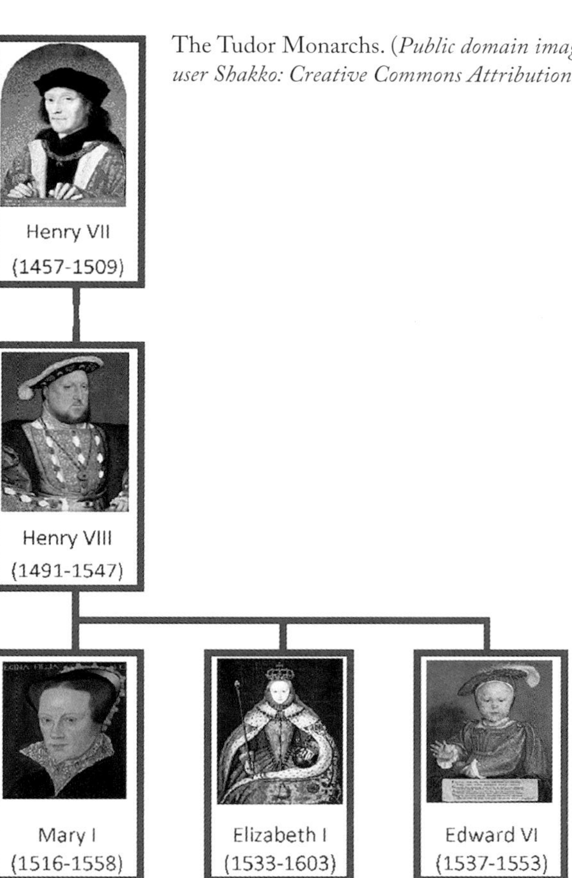

The Tudor Monarchs. (*Public domain image, via Wikimedia Commons; user Shakko: Creative Commons Attribution–Share Alike 4.0*)

Church of St Peter and St Paul, South Petherton — tomb chest of Sir Giles Daubeney. (*Public domain image, via Wikimedia Commons; Mike Searle*)

Field of the Cloth of Gold. (*Public domain image*)

Sir William Butts,
Henry VIII's physician.
(*Public domain image*)

Sir Thomas Wyatt the Elder.
(*Public domain image*)

Charles Brandon the Younger, 1537–1551, a friend of Edward VI. (*Public domain image*)

Stephen Gardiner Bishop of Winchester. (*Public domain image*)

Lady Jane Dormer, a favourite of Mary I. (*Public domain image*)

Blanche Parry, nurse and then favourite of Elizabeth I. (*Public domain image*)

Portrait usually identified as Helena Snakenborg, later Marchioness of Northampton. (*Public domain image*)

James I and VI. (*Public domain image*)

Esme Stewart, First Duke of Lennox, a favourite of James I and VI. (*Public domain image*)

Charles I. (*Public domain image*)

Henry Jermyn, a favourite of Charles I.
(*Public domain image*)

James Stanley, 7th Earl of Derby, a favourite of Charles I.

Charles II. (*Public domain image*)

Louise de Kerouaille by Peter Lely.
(*Public domain image*)

James II. (*Public domain image*)

John Drummond, Earl of Melfort, a favourite of James II. (*Public domain image*)

Lords and Commons presenting William and Mary with the crown. (*Public domain image*)

Hans Willem Bentinck. (*National Portrait Gallery (London) artwork ID mw05101; william-bentinck-1st-earl-of-portland-158599*)

the Lady Apsly Grandmother to the Earl of Strafford and to the Lord and Lady Bathurst

Frances Apsley, a favourite of Queen Mary II. (*Public domain image*)

Queen Anne. (*Public domain image*)

Robert Harley, Earl of Oxford, a favourite of Queen Anne. (*Public domain image*)

Abigail Masham, a friend of Queen Anne. (*Public domain image*)

the Protestants. She sent William Cecil with a paper asking the committee to retain the image of the cross in churches, to allow processions, vestments, and kneeling to receive communion. She met with a blank refusal, their response being that images were odious, and processions superfluous.

The result was a prayer book more suited to the Puritan element than anything else, but the Commons made it law in the Act of Uniformity, while it barely squeaked through the Upper House, by three votes. There was no leeway for conscience; that would be left to the decision of a court. The act also changed Elizabeth's title from Supreme Head of the Church to Supreme Governor. That suited her; it was merely a play on words.

Basically, Elizabeth didn't give two hoots who believed what, so long as they acknowledged her as Supreme Something. However, she partially won the vestments argument, but only those worn in the reign of Edward VI were permitted.[200]

Elizabeth was more anxious that Henry VIII, still revered, should be remembered as a Protestant champion, which he was not. She glossed over the fact that he persecuted Protestants, and portrayed him as an opposer of Popery, and that she was the same.

All the bishops refused to take the Oath of Supremacy and they also refused to officiate at services. When the queen appointed Matthew Parker as Archbishop of Canterbury, no bishop would consecrate him. They had to find three elderly bishops from Henry VIII and Edward VI's time to do it. Bishop Bonner insisted on celebrating the old Catholic Mass, and the Bishop of Llandaff was allowed to sign a declaration, but not take the oath. He kept his see. All the others were deprived of theirs.

This was meat and drink to the Spanish Ambassador. Nobody would ever have dared defy Henry VIII like this, so it was clear a 25-year-old girl held no fears for any of them. All this forced Elizabeth to depend on the Protestants more than she wanted to. Ridley makes the point that had Mary still been alive, Protestants would have been burning the bishops in the summer of 1559, but those who opposed Elizabeth were ousted from their sees or imprisoned because 'Elizabeth was the daughter of Anne Boleyn, the stepdaughter of Katherine Parr, the pupil of Ascham and Grindal, and the friend of Cecil, Robert Dudley, Parry, and Francis and Katherine Knollys'.[201]

Matthew Parker became her ally when he was made Archbishop of Canterbury. He stopped the more stringent Protestants banning the use of organs in church, the sign of the cross, or kneeling to receive communion. The bill made its way through the Commons, but the Lords threw it out.

In Elizabeth's final years, many Protestants believed her reforms did not go far enough and there were still too many Popish elements in the Church. Since, at that time, the climate was cooling down and a few volcanic eruptions added to the mix, making the 1590s a time of bitter winters and failing harvests, they latched on to the view that God was punishing them and had turned against England.[202] It is a shame they didn't look back to the reign of Edward VI, where there were more failed harvests than successful ones.

If we juxtapose how fast Elizabeth had the Protestant religion largely up and running, albeit with hiccups, to the Protestant revolution in Scotland under the leadership of John Knox, it was little short of amazing that England and Scotland became Protestant nations.

It was Knox who pointed out that no woman could hold office unless it was as Head of State. He had believed Elizabeth to be a Catholic since she conformed during Mary's reign, but when Cecil assured him she was a Protestant, Knox replied that she was a Deborah chosen by God to lead her people to salvation. Knox helped form the Congregation, which opposed the Catholic Mary of Guise, mother of Mary, Queen of Scots, at that point queen of France and Scotland.

Elizabeth made a compact with Mary of Guise that neither would support the other's rebels. Cecil wrote to Sir James Croft, Governor of Berwick, that the rebels must be supported, firstly with promises, and then with money, and, if necessary, arms. In that order.

Normally, Elizabeth would not have touched this with a barge pole. As far as she was concerned, rebellion against an anointed sovereign was anathema. However, events in France, including Mary of Guise's brother putting down an uprising with wholesale executions after promising he wouldn't, made Elizabeth opine that the Guise family were planning to take over Scotland. It took some time, but the queen gave money and troops to help the Congregation to expel the French, ending in the Treaty of Edinburgh, whereby the French agreed to leave Scotland to decide its own religious future, and England agreed to withdraw the demand for the return of Calais, lost under Mary in 1558.

Jasper Ridley goes on to say that although these events made England and Scotland Protestant states, and were a complete victory for Protestantism, it was much less a victory for Elizabeth. It set a precedent that a parliament could force its anointed monarch to accept a religion against his/her will. And that is exactly what happened eighty years later when parliament executed Charles I.[203]

Elizabeth: Marriage and Men

If there were two subjects upon which Elizabeth exasperated her council, one was the issue of the succession. The other was marriage. From the instant the crown was placed upon her head, her Privy Council began their fruitless campaign to saddle her with a husband – and I use the term advisedly.

For the next twenty odd years, all these clever men thought about was getting this difficult, self-willed, contradictory, but fearsomely intelligent woman to marry and have a (Protestant) heir. She outwitted them at every turn. Elizabeth was not prepared to obey any man, unlike her half-sister, and look how that turned out! But as we have seen above, she did tell them at the outset she would never get married and the 400 plus years since then have been full of theories, sensible and otherwise, as to why she refused to marry. My own view agrees with some historians who believe her upbringing taught her how treacherous men could be, especially when it came to their climb up the greasy pole of power.

We know much about the men in her life: Thomas Seymour, whom she later labelled as a fool; Robert Dudley, probably her one, true, lifelong love; and Robert Devereux, with whom she became completely infatuated, but not infatuated enough to allow him the privilege of storming into her bedchamber before she was dressed, made-up and bejewelled. Or infatuated enough to stop his execution for what was an ill-conceived, chaotic and fatuous attempt at a revolt.

We also know much about her life during Mary's reign; the sojourn in the Tower, her house-arrest at Woodstock etc. We know Mary hated – or perhaps more accurately, feared – her half-sister, claiming that she would grow to be like her mother. Which in some ways, she did, but always to her own advantage. When Mary insisted parliament pass an act that voided the annulment of her parents' marriage, and confirmed her legitimacy, it also upheld Elizabeth's bastardy.

So much so that Mary was determined, quite as much as Edward had been, to change the tenets of Henry VIII's will. She declared that she would repeal the statute passed in 1544, remove Elizabeth completely from the succession, and instead, make Lady Margaret Douglas, her cousin as the daughter of Henry's elder sister, Margaret Tudor, her heir. In preparation for this happening, Margaret Douglas was accorded precedence at court over Elizabeth, and was brainless and arrogant enough to create a noisy, smelly, kitchen in her own rooms since they were directly over Elizabeth's bedchamber. It was something she later regretted.[204]

The fallout from this was that Mary's advisors, with an eye to the future, told Mary this would cause more problems than it solved and she had to back down. But Elizabeth was twice-tarnished with the bastardy issue. Renard, the Spanish Ambassador obviously considered her of no further importance because Elizabeth had 'too doubtful lineage on her mother's side'. The Venetian

Ambassador described her as 'the illegitimate child of a criminal who was punished as a public strumpet'.[205]

Elizabeth, unlike her mother, who had a reasonably happy childhood, a pleasant time at the French court and then, until almost the end, a charmed life in England, had at times a wretched childhood, at one point causing Margaret Bryan to beg Cromwell for money to buy the growing child clothes. The Thomas Seymour affair taught her that men could be charming, and I do not believe there is any doubt her head was, temporarily, bewitched by him. But his fate was a lesson she never forgot. She was determined no man would be her superior, at the same time demanding all men should adore her, flying into jealous rages if her ladies dared to marry. And if they became pregnant, they were supposed to leave the child at home and come back to court.

At one point, when it became clear Robert Dudley was flirting, if not worse, with Lettice Knollys, she rounded on him:

> God's death, my Lord, I have wished you well, but my favour is not so locked up for you that others shall not participate thereof. And if you think to rule here, I will take a course to see you forthcoming. I will have but one mistress and no master.[206]

Then, of course, there are the conspiracy theories about the myth of the virgin queen. Kaara Peterson examines these in depth. Was Elizabeth capable of childbirth because of various anatomical deformities? In 1579, when the Anjou marriage raised its head, Elizabeth was examined by her doctors who averred she would have no difficulty in producing children. Therefore, we can at least put the fable that she was really a man to bed, so to speak.

Peterson also makes the point that Elizabeth gave strict orders her body was not to be opened up or embalmed when she died, and this, of course, led to more rumours. Was this order given because she was internally deformed, or maybe simply deflowered, and not a virgin? She also had issues with leg ulcers, something Mary Stuart wrote about in 1585, opining that these were caused because Elizabeth had impeded menstruation and it was well known that this caused bodily dysfunctions. Mary was certain Elizabeth would die soon because of this and then she, Mary, would be able to sit on the English throne.[207] How wrong can you be?

Mary, Queen of Scots claimed Elizabeth was incapable of having sex, while at the same time informing her guardian, Bess of Hardwick, that Elizabeth had such an insatiable sexual appetite, she had seduced many men, most frequently, Robert Dudley, and that the English queen was a sexual predator.[208]

Those beliefs, plus how dangerous life was for post-menopausal women because of the physical and mental imbalance it may cause, do not hold water, since the queen outlived most of her (male) courtiers, including Cecil, Walsingham, Dudley and Hatton. Her half-sister was embalmed, despite a similar gynaecological history, although since she was married, nobody would be surprised to find she was not a virgin. Did Elizabeth expect there would be a different conclusion if her body were to be embalmed? This question has continued, and will continue to fascinate Tudor historians.[209]

The nearest Elizabeth came to actually getting married was to François, Duke of Anjou. She had been mooted as a wife for his elder brother, Henry, when *he* was Duke of Anjou, and François, when he was Duke of Alençon. When, in a weak, jealous moment – possibly after discovering that Robert Dudley had married Lettice – she agreed to marry Anjou, she soon wriggled out of it.

Dudley, of course, was very much against the French marriage. One of his servants, Henry Goldingham, wrote a poem called 'The Garden Plot' against the marriage, especially as Elizabeth was over twenty years older than Anjou.

The people didn't like it either. Another foreign, Catholic prince brought back shades of the Smithfield fires and religious persecution. Elizabeth's council, for the most part, was not keen on it. When Anjou visited in 1579, the opposition grew ever more vociferous. John Stubbes published a booklet describing the French prince as 'an ill companion to live withall'. He famously lost his right hand for the publication, shouting *God save the Queen* before fainting when his hand was severed.[210]

Goldingham's poem is important because research indicates it was written during the time of the marriage negotiations, and is, thus, a contemporary source of information. In the Elizabethan realm, people believed drama and poetry answered all the problems of the world, so when, in 1579, the Earl of Sussex entertained Elizabeth with masques and pageants promoting the marriage, it was a clear signal he supported it. So much so, his opponents on the council, including Dudley, put quills to paper to convince Elizabeth not to marry Anjou.

In 1581, a pageant where virtue defeated desire (echoes of Thomas Seymour, one wonders?) was seen as promoting the queen's celibacy over the French marriage. From the get-go, Robert Dudley, by then Earl of Leicester, was the principal opponent. He wanted his cake as well as eating it, and could not bear to have his place in Elizabeth's affections supplanted. Not to mention the numerous 'presents' the queen bestowed on him. That said, his last throw to persuade her to marry him, with his 1575 display of entertainment when she stayed at Kenilworth, just about bankrupted him. By the time of the Anjou negotiations, Leicester's dog-in-the-manger attitude wanted marriage to Lettice but a virgin queen who depended on him. That said, one can understand that

Leicester wanted – needed – an heir, but he knew full well what Elizabeth's attitude would be, should he talk to her about it. What made it worse was that Lettice, also red-haired, was younger and more attractive than the aging queen, and had a good bloodline.

Burghley knew the marriage would be wildly unpopular with the people. Apart from Stubbes and his pamphlet, ballad singers bawled their opposition. And, to Elizabeth's fury, some courageous preachers railed against it from their pulpits. Others who were more cautious, wrote private letters to her.

The biggest issue was that by 1579 when Anjou actually travelled to England, Elizabeth was 46 years old and well past childbearing. So, what was the point? The point, as several historians, including Conyers Read in 1925 argue, was that a French marriage would cement relations with France and have an effect on Anjou's actions in the war with Spain over The Netherlands.

However, logical as that seems, and there is no question that Elizabeth took foreign policy very seriously, many other historians argue that she kept chopping and changing her mind to keep her advisors constantly on the back foot, in what has been likened to an elaborate game of chess, in which she outwitted them all.[211]

As a last word on the subject of Elizabeth and marriage, it is interesting to note that when John Knox published *The First Blast of the Trumpet Against The Monstrous Regiment of Women*, he maintained the biggest threat was that female rule meant, on marriage, the realm would be run by strangers. In other words, the husband. At that time, Elizabeth was newly enthroned and Mary, Queen of Scots was queen of France, but her husband died in 1560.

John Aylmer wrote back to Knox saying that if England could provide a king for your queen and you a king for our queen, England and Scotland would be strong.[212]

It is interesting to wonder what the future of the two countries would have been if that had, indeed, happened.

Elizabeth and Mary Stuart, and How the Spy Network Doomed Her
Shakespeare begins *Romeo and Juliet* with the words:

> Two households, both alike in dignity,
> In fair Verona, where we lay our scene,
> From ancient grudge break to new mutiny,
> Where civil blood makes civil hands unclean.

One might well apply those words to the relationship between these two queens, Elizabeth and Mary Stuart, who is mostly known as Mary, Queen of Scots. I shall call her Mary Stuart not only because it is shorter, but because it separates her from Mary Tudor, Elizabeth's elder half-sister.

The two sovereigns were so very different in character. Mary the pampered darling, sent to France by her mother to save her from Henry VIII's 'rough wooing', having a happy, if very short, marriage to François before he died, but then being sent back to Scotland, at the age of 18. At which point, it all started to go horribly wrong.

And Elizabeth, with her mother executed before she was 3 years old, spending the next twenty-two years more or less learning to live on her wits before coming into smoother waters when she ascended the throne.

If our lives are moulded by our experiences, then, really, Mary didn't have a hope in hell. If Elizabeth learned through experience not to let her heart rule her head, Mary appears to have been the opposite once she got back to Scotland. In fairness, she had a lot of opposition to her religion, and especially to her practising it in her new realm. From the instant Mary returned to Scotland, Cecil was aware that the recent religious question would soon clash with the new, young queen's faith. He began to form the spy network that, with the aid of Francis Walsingham, became the main obstacle between the Catholic cohort who wanted Elizabeth dead and keeping the English – Protestant – queen alive.

Walsingham looked and was uncompromising. His keen brain made him ideal to help England's foreign policy, involving forgery, heading what was effectively a secret police force that had bagloads of dirty tricks. He was not only responsible for gathering information and analysing it, but trapping and destroying anything and anyone who threatened the queen's safety. He used techniques known to modern security services, such as dead letter boxes, complex ciphers, and secret writing. He was not averse to extortion, forgery or blackmail and excelled in turning agents into double or even triple agents. And torture was not a problem for him if his targets refused to talk.[213]

Sir William Cecil, Lord Burghley, arguably qualifies for a top five place in the 'Wiliest of British Politicians' hit parade, and I use the word *hit* on purpose. A reformer by inclination, he conformed or dissembled, whichever verb you prefer, during Mary Tudor's reign. The instant Elizabeth was queen, he took over the reins of her government and spent the next forty years keeping his monarch safe, often against her will.

Cecil realised the extent of Catholic hatred not just in England, but throughout the Catholic world, for this bastard, heretic daughter of the whore, Anne Boleyn. He took Francis Walsingham under his wing in the late 1560s. Between them they built arguably the finest, most devious and effective security service before or since.

The scene that haunted Cecil for all of those forty years was what would happen to Protestant England if Elizabeth was assassinated. The likelihood was that Philip would invade, the Protestants would go into the fire, and England would become a satellite of Spain. The most effective way to prevent this was espionage, surveillance, a robust treason law, the use of torture, and anti-Catholic propaganda.[214]

The Pope blundered in some ways when he excommunicated Elizabeth in 1571, and his bull was nailed to the gates to the Bishop's palace. Elizabeth's parliament responded with the Treasons Act, which basically gave the Privy Council carte-blanche to define what the word *treason* encompassed in any given situation.

Two years earlier, in 1569, the Ridolfi Plot to put Mary Stuart on the throne alongside the Duke of Norfolk, was the first of the three major plots to oust Elizabeth. Parliament demanded, and was granted, the execution of Norfolk. It also demanded Mary be executed, but Elizabeth refused to kill an anointed sovereign. For almost twenty years after her arrival in England asking for protection in 1568, Mary was an unwanted, uninvited, guest, but a guest nonetheless of the English queen. She was believed to be complicit in the murder of her second husband, Lord Darnley, she was hostile to Elizabeth, and she never stopped plotting with Catholic Europe to usurp her English cousin and execute her as a heretic.[215]

Things calmed down a little for twelve years after Norfolk's execution, but Cecil and Walsingham never ceased their surveillance of Mary, her servants, and her agents, but beefed up their spy networks in France, Spain and Italy.

In 1583, the Throckmorton Plot came to light. In many ways it was inept and clumsy. Francis Throckmorton, cousin to Bess – wife of Sir Walter Raleigh and like him an ardent Protestant – became involved in a plot that Spain and France would join together to invade England under the generalship of the Duc de Guise. When Guise's forces had subdued the heretic English, Elizabeth would be executed, and Guise's niece, Mary Stuart, would be put on the English throne. What actually happened was that one of Walsingham's spies alerted his master to a suspicious exchange of letters by the Spanish Ambassador, Mendoza.[216]

Walsingham set his spies to find out all the facts, before arresting Throckmorton. He was tortured on the rack in the Tower of London on 16 November 1583, but refused to talk. Walsingham gave him a couple of days to think about his position, then on 18 November, he sent a warrant to the Lieutenant of the Tower suggesting Throckmorton should be threatened with another dose of the rack if he wouldn't come clean.

'I suppose the grief [pain] of the last torture will suffice without any extremity of racking to make him more conformable than he had hitherto showed himself',

Walsingham wrote. And he was right. The threat made Throckmorton talk, although he initially tried to blame the letters on a household servant. The Earl of Northumberland was also implicated and he, too, ended up in the Tower.

Further enquiries revealed the extent of the invasion plans. They also revealed the daughter of the Lieutenant of the Tower helped smuggle a letter to Throckmorton's wife revealing the existence of a small casket. Further information came to light, enough to give Elizabeth an excuse to dismiss the Spanish Ambassador.

It didn't stop Guise, though. He still wanted to go ahead with the invasion and if you think about it, his niece had, until the death of her first husband, been queen of France. How much greater would his own influence be should she sit on England's throne? What stopped him in his tracks was the death of Elizabeth's onetime suitor, the Duke of Anjou, which precipitated a succession crisis for the French throne.[217] Throckmorton was executed in July 1584. Northumberland was found dead in suspicious circumstances soon after.[218]

The strongest and final nail in Mary Stuart's coffin was the Babington Plot. It became a perfect storm for Mary and a perfect planet alignment for Cecil and Walsingham. R. Kent Tiernan's examination of Walsingham's entrapment of Mary Stuart begins in the best James Bond style. And in many ways, the final downfall of this irritating Catholic magnet in England proceeds very much in the style of an old-fashioned ripping yarn, depending, of course, which side you favour.

What is revealed is a sophistication in the art of spying. The deceptions, the elegance of the ciphers, the double-agents, allied with the naivety of the Scottish queen, all made her destruction inevitable. Tiernan goes on to comment that the same things are still happening today, instancing the Russian attempts to influence the US Presidential election in 2016.[219]

One example suffices to demonstrate the latter and compare Mary to Elizabeth. Sitting in the National Archives is the *Tide Letter* Elizabeth wrote to Mary Tudor, then queen, in 1554. It is, probably *the* most vital letter Princess Elizabeth ever wrote. She had been accused of being involved in the Wyatt Rebellion and was about to be taken to the Tower of London, the place her mother had been executed. She wrote slowly so that the tide under the arches of London Bridge would be too low for her to be taken that day, and thereby gaining an extra day. But where she displayed her intelligence and cunning was scoring diagonal lines across the empty page at the end of her letter between the last words and her signature at the bottom of the page, so that nobody could insert any text.[220]

Mary showed no such sense, especially in the *Gallows Letter*, written by her to Anthony Babington in July 1586. Walsingham opened it and amended it before sending it on to Babington.[221]

There is little doubt that the threat to Elizabeth increased massively from 1560 onwards, something that led Cecil and Walsingham to overhaul their intelligence system. They began monitoring and infiltrating the Catholic community in the early 1580s. After the Throckmorton and Parry plots in 1583 and 1584, they tightened Mary's security by moving her to Tutbury Castle, a place she hated. They then proceeded, with Elizabeth's help and some sweeteners, to alienate Mary from her son, James VI. By the time, in January 1586, when Mary was moved to Chartley Hall, their spy network was in place and the plan to ensnare the Scottish queen fully worked out.

Thomas Phelippes, Walsingham's cipher-clerk extraordinaire, had complete access to every communication between the Babington plotters and Mary Stuart. And once Phelippes had deciphered each letter, Walsingham read it and could, if he so desired, manipulate every item going in either direction. To quote Moist von Lipwig in *Going Postal*, by Terry Pratchett, 'It was masterly. The bastard'.

Cecil and Walsingham did all this without telling Elizabeth anything, so she could not stop them, but could also truthfully say she didn't know. They knew better than anyone that the queen was friendless in Europe and needed to be rid of Mary Stuart and what she represented. In other words, by the time it came to Mary writing the *Gallows Letter*, so called because Phelippes drew a gallows on it to denote she was doomed, every stage in the conspiracy could be proved under any scrutiny, passing any inquiry.[222]

So, really, the big question is why did Mary Stuart choose Protestant England to fly to in 1568 and not Catholic Europe where she would have been safer? The general consensus seems to be she expected her cousin, a fellow female monarch, to help her regain her Scottish throne. Elizabeth was, I believe, torn between the loyalty due to an anointed monarch, and the Scottish government that wanted rid of their Catholic queen.

Mary never believed she would end up essentially a prisoner of state under permanent house arrest. To support her in this belief, Spain was suppressing Protestants in the Netherlands and the St Bartholomew Massacre in Paris in 1572 signalled that Catholicism was more than alive and well and intent on eradicating the 'enemy'. The assassination of William of Orange in 1564 had escalated the religious conflict on both sides. Catholics saw it as a sign they would triumph. But for Cecil and Walsingham, it was the signal they needed to upgrade their security systems. For Mary, the Catholic *successes* only served to convince her that her communication systems were perfectly safe since the English government had more than enough problems on its hands.

Apart from Anthony Babington, who comes over as naive as the queen he served, the most dangerous plotters were John Ballard, a Jesuit priest and Thomas Morgan, one of Mary's confidants and spies. But they were up against Cecil and Walsingham, who, apart from years of experience keeping Elizabeth safe, had almost limitless resources at their disposal; and a certain Gilbert Gifford, a Catholic subversive who was promised his life if he turned his coat.

After Mary wrote the *Gallows Letter* in July 1586, she was a dead woman walking. The letter gave her approval for the Babington plot to go ahead. She told Babington to 'sett the six gentlemen to woork'. In other words, to assassinate Elizabeth, free Mary, overthrow James, her son and do 'some sturring in Ireland'.

Walsingham amended several passages of the letter, asking Babington to name the six assassins before sending it on, but that amendment probably alerted Babington, who fled. He was finally arrested, as were Mary's secretaries, who confessed to writing the letter at her instruction. Babington was hanged, drawn and quartered in September 1586.[223] Mary was put on trial at Fotheringhay Castle, the birthplace of Richard III, in October 1586. She was found guilty of treason. But Elizabeth dallied and prevaricated about signing a death warrant. This woman had Tudor blood running through her veins. She was an anointed queen. What was simple for Cecil and Walsingham was an appalling dilemma for Elizabeth and it almost broke her.[224]

Elizabeth was badgered by her advisors, her own preference being that someone should simply and quietly murder this wretched woman at Fotheringhay so she could claim she knew nothing about it. She asked Amyas Paulet to do it for her but he vigorously refused. It was not until February 1587 that Elizabeth caved in and signed the warrant. Her junior secretary, William Davis, rushed along the corridors to give it to Cecil. Cecil immediately sent it to Fotheringhay, almost before the ink had dried on Elizabeth's signature. The execution was carried out before Elizabeth even knew the warrant had been sent. Cecil told her the Scottish queen was dead.

Elizabeth was both furious and terrified. She insisted Davis be hanged, but he escaped that, only to be put in the Tower. She banned Cecil from her presence and went into mourning.[225]

But the die was cast, the precedent set for the scene outside Whitehall in January 1649 when the English Puritan government executed its anointed sovereign, Charles I.

When we think of Elizabeth I, and her court, many people appear to focus on the favourites we have all heard of – Robert Dudley, Earl of Leicester, William Cecil, Lord Burghley, Sir Walter Raleigh, Robert Devereux, Earl of Essex, and Kat Astley, her chief attendant, who caused so much trouble for Elizabeth during the Thomas Seymour scandal. You will, I hope, be pleased I am not going to write about any of them.

The three people I have chosen are still famous, but, perhaps, lesser known. The first is the lady who was with Elizabeth from the time of the Princess' birth and was chosen by Anne Boleyn to be in her household.

Blanche Parry

Blanche was born a year or so before Henry VIII ascended the throne. Born in the Welsh Marches, her surname was Ap Harry, later changed to Parry. Blanche's father was Sheriff of Herefordshire and a relative of the Earls of Pembroke. She was bilingual, and there is a possibility that, on her mother's side, one of her ancestors was the Lollard, Sir John Oldcastle.

Blanche came to court with her aunt, Blanche, Lady Troy. Appointed by Anne Boleyn, the latter became lady mistress to the baby Elizabeth and then to the infant Edward. Our Blanche was, therefore, with Elizabeth from her earliest days.[226]

Blanche was put in charge of the four maids who rocked the child's cradle and it was said that she sang Welsh lullabies to the child. It is also probable that when Mary Tudor sent Elizabeth to the Tower in 1554, Blanche was one of the two ladies allowed to attend on her. Apparently, in later life, when she and Elizabeth, then queen, wanted to hide the subject of their discussions, they would use Welsh vocabulary.[227] In 1552, Blanche was paid 100 shillings (about £2290 in 2024) with an allowance to feed horses.

When Elizabeth came to the throne, Blanche was made second gentlewoman of the privy chamber.[228] She controlled much of the access to Elizabeth, and was responsible for the queen's jewels, her personal papers, furs and the many books Elizabeth received as gifts. She also passed on information, such as the time her nephew warned of unrest in the north of England, that led to the Northern Rebellion of 1569/70, and which intended to depose Elizabeth, replacing her with the Catholic Mary Stuart. This early intelligence helped quash the rebellion.

Blanche wrote Elizabeth's letters and also received petitions from parliament on her mistress' behalf. She gave the queen many gifts of jewellery, and wrote the inventory, now in the British Library, of Elizabeth's jewels.[229]

George Ballard, in his 1752 book, calls Blanche a 'worthy gentlewoman who appears to have been a lover of antiquities, and to encourage learning in others'. Ballard also avers that when John Dee was at a low point 'distressed by the lubricity of fortune' Blanche mentioned him to Elizabeth who agreed to help him. Lubricity means smoothness or oiliness, what a fabulous word.[230]

At Elizabeth's coronation, Blanche was given seven yards of scarlet, fifteen yards of crimson velvet, and one and a quarter yard of cloth of gold. Her salary from the time of the queen's accession was £33 6s 8d (about £16,000 in 2024). That sum never altered during the reign.[231]

In temperament, Blanche was quietly assiduous and ideally suited to a position of trust. She had impeccable morals, was utterly devoted to Elizabeth and never married. A stabilising presence, Blanche became the benchmark by which Elizabeth measured all her other ladies.[232]

Elizabeth Norton in *The Lives of Tudor Women* states that when Elizabeth came to the throne, Blanche would have been ideally suited to the post of chief gentlewoman of the privy chamber, but Katherine Champernowne (later Astley), was a much more vivacious and forceful character and the post went to her. When Lady Troy retired, Henry VIII replaced her with Katherine because of her 'learning and the distinguished teaching' she could provide. What is certain is that Elizabeth was devoted to both women.[233]

By the 1580s, Blanche was one of the very few people who could remember Anne Boleyn, and who had shared Elizabeth's childhood. There is no doubt that Elizabeth trusted her as she did very few, and loved her. There appears to be a disagreement over the year of Blanche's death. Having become blind during the 1580s, she remained at court with her mistress. Her cousin, William Cecil, also of Welsh ancestry, supervised the drawing up of the two wills Blanche made. In either February 1589 or February 1590, this most devoted of servants died. Elizabeth was in 'great sorrow', naturally. Since Blanche had held no titles, Elizabeth, notable for her stinginess, paid for a funeral fit for a baroness. Blanche's body was buried at St Margaret's, Westminster. Her bowels were buried at the church in Bacton, Herefordshire, where she was born.[234]

In her will, she left £500 for the building of an almshouse in Bacton, and enough money 'as Lord Burghley should think sufficient' to repair Bacton church and its steeple.[235]

As an interesting final note, in Bacton church, there is a monument to Blanche. She had intended moving back to her home village when she retired. In 2016, the altar cloth in the church was recognised as a piece of Tudor embroidery. It was eventually confirmed as the sole survivor of Elizabeth's wardrobe and made part of an exhibition in 2019. The stained-glass window, originally in Bacton church, was moved to St Eata's, Atcham, near Shrewsbury by a descendant of Blanche's. It depicts Queen Elizabeth with Blanche at her side. It states her date of death as 1589.[236]

Helena Snakenborg

A fascinating lady, Elin Ulfsdotter Snakenborg, Marchioness of Northampton, was known as Helena and Helena the Red because of the colour of her hair.

She was born in Sweden around 1548/49, the younger daughter of Ulf Henriksson of Fyllingarum, a supporter of King Gustav I. Helena is said to have been beautiful, with large brown eyes and a pink and white complexion.[237] She always signed herself as *Elin* and was independent and strong-willed.[238] Hardly, one would suppose, a good mix for a lady-in-waiting to Queen Elizabeth I!

It has been claimed that her Viking ancestors were the Earls of Orkney, but there is not enough evidence to prove this. What we do know is Helena was among six Swedish maids of honour to accompany Princess Cecilia of Sweden during her 1564 visit to England, her objective being to persuade Elizabeth to marry her half-brother, Eric.

The journey was perilous, because at that time Sweden was in conflict with Norway and Denmark, so their long detour to avoid those countries took a year, and ended in a very rough channel crossing from Calais. Helena had become – and still was – ill on the journey. By the time she landed at Dover, and the bedraggled party was met by William Parr, Marquis of Northampton, Helena was still suffering.[239]

William Parr, brother to Elizabeth's stepmother, Katherine Parr, was 53 years old, Helena was 16. He was immediately struck by her and insisted on paying for her medical treatment. Helena was later to write to her parents in a letter that spoke of affection rather than love. 'The marquess has been both father and mother to me, and most kind in every detail.'[240]

When the visitors arrived in London, Elizabeth agreed to meet them. Helena was soon being seriously courted by the lovestruck Parr, and, when Cecilia left England to escape her creditors, Helena stayed behind, becoming one of Elizabeth's maids of honour. She never returned home, but became a gentlewoman of the privy chamber. Elizabeth gave Helena lodgings at Hampton Court Palace and a horse.

Parr, still lovesick, hoped to marry Helena, but there was an impediment. Well, two impediments, both emanating from Elizabeth. The marriage had to be put on hold because Elizabeth hated any of her ladies to marry. Parr's second wife had died, but his first wife, whom he had divorced, was still living. Elizabeth used as her excuse, her disagreement with Cranmer's conclusion that Parr's first wife, Anne, had committed adultery and was therefore at fault. She told the couple they must wait until Anne died. During the wait, Parr was pushing Elizabeth to marry and produce an heir. She told him he would be better employed thinking of arguments to let him marry Helena 'instead of mincing words with her'.[241] I don't suppose he had the courage – or perhaps, more accurately, the stupidity – to reply that he would stop urging Elizabeth to marry if she allowed him to marry.

Anne died in 1571 and Elizabeth grudgingly gave her consent to the marriage. Sadly, for by then Parr was 60 years old, five months after their marriage, he died. Worse still, he had had no time to make provision for Helena and she was virtually penniless. Elizabeth paid for Parr's funeral and then employed Helena again and gave her lands worth £400 a year (approximately £173,000 in 2024).[242] In 1574, Elizabeth also gave Helena the manor of Hemingford Grey in Huntingdonshire. This was later the house where the children's author, Lucy Boston, lived, the manor house becoming her inspiration for the Green Knowe fantasy books.

Thomas Gorges was Anne Boleyn's second cousin. He and Helena fell in love, but Elizabeth refused her consent – no change there, then! So sometime around 1576, they married in secret. When the queen found out, she was incandescent. Thomas was sent to the Tower and Helena was exiled from court. Thankfully, and possibly due to the influence and intervention of the Earl of Sussex, Thomas was released and Helena reinstated.

Gorges was far beneath Helena in rank, and while Elizabeth was not happy about that, she became godmother to their first child. They were to have eight children between 1578 and 1589, and in 1582, it is believed that Helena accompanied her husband as an envoy to the Swedish court, where they met her family.

In 1586, Gorges was knighted. Helena was with Gorges in 1586 when he escorted Mary Stuart from Chartley to Tixall. For some reason, Elizabeth believed the pair were plotting against her, but in the queen's defence, she was under a lot of strain since the discovery of the Babington Plot. She is said to have 'raged and stormed and showered invectives on Gorges and his mistress'.[243]

However, Elizabeth continued to hold Helena in high regard, and, as Elizabeth's health deteriorated in her declining years, Helena often deputised for her at important baptisms. Because Elizabeth was notorious for not wanting the impediment of children to affect the smooth running of her court, but she wanted to keep Helena on side, she gave the couple an ex-monastery at Sheen, so they could live with their children, but still be close to the court.

When Elizabeth died, Helena was chief mourner at her funeral, because Arbella Stuart refused and James (VI & I) was still dilly-dallying on his way to London, handing out honours left, right and centre. Thomas and Helena attended James' coronation and then moved to their property at Longford, but

Helena was made Keeper of Richmond Palace and acted as a go-between for James with Sweden.

Thomas died in 1610 at the age of 74. Helena retreated from public life, although she was an ardent member of the Church of England. Eventually, she went to live with her son, Sir Robert, in Somerset. She died in 1635, aged 86, and is buried in Salisbury Cathedral.[244]

Sir Christopher Hatton

In his biography of Sir Christopher, Neil Younger makes a sound case for disagreeing with the long-held view that Hatton was a lightweight. From 1571 until his death in 1591, Hatton was a major figure at court, moving from being a favourite to a privy councillor in six years. He was, Younger avers, one of the last heavyweights at Elizabeth's court in her final years. His contemporaries dismissed him as a lightweight, but he maintained the royal favour for over twenty years and became influential in matters regarding the Church during that time.[245]

John Guy, who wrote *Elizabeth: The Forgotten Years*, agrees with Younger. He says Hatton shifted his focus from seduction towards building his reputation as a statesman, working with Leicester at the time of the Anjou marriage negotiations. He also became a friend of Francis Walsingham, who often turned to Hatton for help with the conflict in the Netherlands.[246]

Where Hatton really shone was as Elizabeth's spokesman in parliament, at the time of the Babington Plot. So just who was this man, who has always been regarded as worthy of little more than an afterthought?

Christopher Hatton was born in Holdenby in Northamptonshire in 1540 and educated first at St Mary Hall, and then Oxford University, after which he joined the Inner Temple.[247]

He came to court 'by the galliard for he came thither as a private gentleman of the Inns of Court, in a masque, and for his activity and person, which was tall and proportionable, taken into the Queen's favour'. He first came to Elizabeth's notice in 1564 in a play at the Royal Court. He was accomplished, talented and charming, soon winning Elizabeth's favour, after he became one of her bodyguards. He was known to be a good dancer, earning the soubriquet 'The Dancing Chancellor'. He was also very practised in the art of courtly love, but, despite the usual rumours, including those put about by Mary Stuart, there is absolutely no evidence that his and Elizabeth's mutual affection went any further than that.[248] And we must always keep in mind Elizabeth's statement, 'I do not live in a corner. A thousand eyes see all I do'. Plus, after the vagaries, accusations and scandals surrounding her younger days, there is no way the queen would have put herself in such an invidious position. She was, as she knew, the lantern of Protestantism in a Catholic world.

Elizabeth showered Hatton with valuable grants of land. When he voiced a wish to own land and the house belonging to the Bishop of Ely, the bishop initially refused. Elizabeth wrote to him: 'You know what you were before I made you what you are now. If you do not immediately comply with my request, I will unfrock you, by God. Elizabeth'. Not quite what I would term a polite request, but it had the desired effect.[249]

Elizabeth's nickname for Hatton was *Liddes*, no doubt to accompany Leicester's nickname of *Eyes*. He called himself her sheep.

By 1572, Hatton was Captain of the Queen's Bodyguards and the parliamentary representative for Northamptonshire. He was active in the prosecutions of John Stubbes over the publication of his pamphlet regarding the Anjou marriage and William Parry's half-baked plot in 1584.

In 1577, he had been made a privy counsellor and Vice Chamberlain of the queen's household. He also became Sir Christopher Hatton. A natural Puritan by nature, he accepted Elizabeth's version of Protestantism, although he sided more with Leicester's hard-line anti-Spanish attitude, rather than Cecil's more conciliatory approach.[250]

He was one of those appointed to arrange the Anjou marriage, although he tried to persuade Elizabeth against it, and was a vigorous critic in parliament of Mary Stuart. In common with other favourites, Hatton sent the queen presents. One was a ring to be worn at the breast, 'the virtue to expel infectious airs, and is … to be worn between the sweet duggs [breasts] the chaste nest of pure constancy'. Constant he was. He never married and his loyalty to his queen never wavered.

In his post as Lord Chancellor, he was not overly brilliant, but was sensible and demonstrated sound judgement. Some labelled him a Catholic in all but name, but in reality, he was a religious moderate, one of the reasons he was so anti-Spanish, but not necessarily anti-Catholic.

He gained wealth due to his career progression and Elizabeth's gifts. He built Holdenby House, the largest private house in England at that time, which, to show his wealth, had 123 windows at a time when glass was very expensive. It was as big as Hampton Court Palace, and contained a state room for Elizabeth to use should she grace him with her presence. Sadly, she never did.

The house was ruinously expensive, so Hatton began to invest in Drake's voyages, including the piratical ones! During the circumnavigation of the world, Drake named his ship *The Golden Hind* in honour of Hatton's coat of arms. That voyage made Hatton £2300 (approximately £882,000 in 2024).[251]

Hatton's role was, essentially, that of the perpetual suitor who forever worships an earthly goddess with unwavering devotion – a devotion that cannot be fulfilled but never wanes.[252]

He became Elizabeth's spokesman in parliament and opposed Peter Wentworth on the latter's view that parliament could discuss whatever it wanted. Hatton replied that the Church was a matter for the royal prerogative alone.[253]

Where Hatton really shone was during the Babington Plot. As mentioned above, he was a friend of Walsingham, and was given an active role in the examination of the Catholic conspirators. He sat on the commission that tried Mary Stuart for treason in 1586, and was one of the courtiers who urged Elizabeth to sign the death warrant. It took almost five months, but when the queen did sign it, Hatton was one of those who urged William Davison to despatch it immediately.

He sided with the Puritan Archbishop of Canterbury, John Whitgift, working with him to formulate policies. In 1587, Elizabeth made Hatton her Lord Chancellor, and in 1577, he was made a Knight of the Garter and chancellor of Oxford University.[254]

Despite the huge amount of money he had made from Drake's voyages, Hatton was deeply in debt when he died. His health declined in 1591, so much so, that Elizabeth visited him on 11 November. This favoured courtier died nine days later at Ely Place. Elizabeth gave him a state funeral.

He is remembered today, partly for the London jewellery quarter, Hatton Garden, which stands on the site of his London home. Although he never married, his line continues from his nephews and cousins as the Finch-Hattons.[255]

James I and VI

'James I slobbered at the mouth and had favourites;
he was thus a Bad King.'[256]

I shall call this monarch James I for clarity. Apologies to anyone who is a native of Scotland.

A lot of what befell the Stuarts in the seventeenth century was directly the fault of James I. Jonathan Keates puts it baldly, but accurately: 'Pig-headed obstinacy and refusal to face facts, an overweening sense of regal entitlement and a failure to grasp the importance of mutuality in the relationship between sovereign and subject'.[257]

James Charles Stuart was a strange man, but, given his upbringing, that is not surprising. Called 'the wisest fool in Christendom', he was also the first monarch and one of the first people to travel in a submarine.[258]

In contrast with some other monarchs, such as Richard II, Richard III, and even Charles I, there has never been a concerted effort to rehabilitate James. Marc Schwarz believes this is partly due to a general repugnance of his lifestyle, and it is the case that many modern historians seem to enjoy wallowing in his less than acceptable traits and ignoring the good things he achieved.

James has never been seen as a heroic monarch. Childhood rickets left him with what Schwarz describes as a 'Chaplinesque gait'. His tongue was too big for his mouth, so instead of drinking normally, he gobbled his drinks. He was also very frightened of violence – unsurprising when you consider the many plots that surrounded him, even when he was in the womb. Scared of weapons, he wore a sword-proof vest, and was known to pile beds in front of the door if he thought he was in danger. This is not exactly the portrait of a Richard the Lionheart or a Henry V.

His much-vaunted learning was narrow and conceited; one biographer called his writings 'tantrums in print'. That said, he was politically astute. From his time as king of Scotland, he knew how to steer clear of trouble before it caused confrontation. Trevor-Roper considered this policy came to a head when James' successor, Charles I, did what his father had lectured him to do, leading directly to his meeting with the executioner. Generally considered a mediocre monarch, James' actions led to the Civil War.[259]

No historians defend James' thriftless spending, which never improved and was in direct contrast to Elizabeth I, known as penny-pinching in the extreme. Maurice Lee describes this as 'his worst failing as a king'. However, he also opines that James brought a high degree of peace to the country after the religious to-ing and fro-ing since Henry VIII divorced Katherine of Aragon. Lee also points out that after years of uncertainty, the succession under James was assured, even after the death of Prince Henry in 1612, which made Charles, the next son down, the heir. James was also open-handed, which helped to solidify the dynasty.[260]

His parents were equally complicated. Mary Stuart, normally called Mary, Queen of Scots, possibly to differentiate her from her cousin, Mary Tudor (Bloody Mary), had been whisked away to France by her French mother to escape Henry VIII's 'rough wooing', when he wanted Mary to be betrothed to his son, Edward, later Edward VI. Just as well in hindsight, since Edward became a priggish Protestant, and Mary was a wholehearted Roman Catholic. Of course, Henry didn't mind that at the time, since he was not to know that Edward would espouse Protestantism, and since he was an Anglo-Catholic, I do not suppose he foresaw any problems with the proposed match.

James' father, Henry Stuart, Lord Darnley, was, through his mother's side, a claimant to the English throne, his maternal grandmother being Margaret, elder sister of Henry VIII. His marriage to Mary Stuart took place without Elizabeth I's permission. Since the groom was an English subject, she was furious. Not an uncommon occurrence.

In character, Darnley was vain, arrogant, unreliable and a drunkard with violent tendencies when under the influence. He was incensed when his wife would not grant him the crown matrimonial, which would have meant he succeeded to the Scottish throne, should she die. He was also insanely jealous of Mary's private secretary, David Rizzio, and, when Mary was heavily pregnant, Darnley and his adherents stabbed Rizzio 56 times, unsurprisingly killing him. Mary kept her husband sweet until the birth of her child, James, and contrived to keep him onside until he was murdered, when James was eight months old, at Kirk o' Field, his body being discovered in the orchard, with no discernible wounds. The house was blown up, and a post-mortem showed internal injuries that could have caused his death. Quite how he found his way to the orchard – or was, more likely, dumped there has led to a centuries old mystery.[261]

However, back to baby James. He was born in Edinburgh Castle in June 1566, immediately becoming the heir and Duke of Rothesay. He was described as 'well proportioned and like to prove a goodly prince'. Soon after Darnley's death, Mary married James Hepburn, Earl of Bothwell. Whether Bothwell kidnapped her, raped her and then forced the marriage, or whether Mary was a willing wife is yet another mystery.

The marriage, however it came about, was desperately unpopular, partly because Scotland was Protestant, and Mary insisted on celebrating the Catholic Mass, and partly because of the cloud of suspicion over her following Darnley's murder. In June 1567, Protestant rebels imprisoned her in Lochleven Castle. James was taken away and she never saw him again. She was forced to abdicate the following month in favour of her baby son.

James was anointed king of Scotland at the age of thirteen months, the third consecutive Scottish monarch to succeed to the throne as an infant, the second being Mary herself on the death of her father, James V.

When Mary was deposed – or abdicated, depending on your point of view – her half-brother, James Stewart, Earl of Moray, was appointed regent. Baby James was brought up, as a Protestant, in Stirling Castle by the Earl and Countess of Mar. The Privy Council appointed, among others, George Buchanan to be the young prince's tutor. Buchanan beat the child frequently, but he instilled in him a lifelong love of literature and learning, so I suppose that makes the beatings OK. Or perhaps James was just a bratty child – we do not know and beatings were considered normal.

What is true is that his childhood and early adulthood experiences were, as in most people, responsible for the way he turned out. Buchanan wanted James to become a God-fearing Protestant, who was aware of the limitations of the monarchy.

In 1568, Mary escaped from Lochleven in an attempt to regain her throne, but the whole thing turned into a fiasco, so she fled to England, landing Elizabeth with the greatest state headache she ever had. Mary, of course, hoped Elizabeth, a fellow queen, would send troops to aid her regain the Scottish throne. Sadly for Mary, Elizabeth just kept her under house-arrest for almost twenty years. Bothwell fled to Denmark, dying insane, in a Danish prison.

In 1570, Moray was assassinated – the first leader of a nation to be shot by a gun. James' paternal grandfather then became regent. He lasted a year, before being mortally wounded by Mary's supporters. He was replaced by the Earl of Mar. He also lasted a year, dying after attending a banquet given by the Earl of Morton.

Unsurprisingly, Morton then became regent. We could say it's déjà-vu all over again or perhaps James was just singularly unlucky in his regents. Quite! In 1579, James was declared an adult ruler and took over his royal inheritance. Morton, who was obviously not desperately popular, was executed in 1582, accused of being complicit in the murder of James' father, Henry, Lord Darnley. More of him later.

James then made the current Earl of Lennox the only duke in Scotland. He was a major influence on the young 15-year-old king, but was very unpopular with Calvinists who accused him of leading the King into 'carnal lust'. Also in 1582, James was taken prisoner by the Ruthven clan and Lennox was exiled. James soon escaped, however, and began to take control of his kingdom, although he proved hopeless with money, one trait that never improved.

All went well until 1600 when another of the Ruthvens allegedly assaulted James and was run through by the king's page. Since James owed the Ruthvens a huge amount of money, there is some doubt as to the veracity of his account of the incident.

James has been portrayed as something approaching an idiot, but he was very intelligent even if he did not always show it. His Roman Catholic mother was as much an embarrassment to him as she was to Elizabeth. The main thrust of his foreign policy was that, as a Protestant, he should succeed the Protestant virgin queen of England. So much so, that in 1586, when Mary was conspiring with Babington, her son signed the Treaty of Berwick, which was described as a 'league of amity'. In other words, a peace agreement between England and Scotland. After Mary's execution, at which James sent a fairly minor rebuke to Elizabeth when you consider it was his own mother who had been executed, and during the 1588 Armada crisis, Elizabeth kept James sweet with an annual subsidy that gave her influence in Scottish affairs.

James showed little interest in women, being praised for his chastity, although he is thought to have had one mistress. However, Anne of Denmark came onto the marriage market, so to speak, and, after a proxy marriage service, she set sail for Scotland. Storms blew her fleet onto the Norwegian coast. In what historian David Harris Wilson calls 'the one romantic episode in his life', James immediately set sail and went to fetch her.[262]

In March 1603, James became one of the few monarchs to reign over two kingdoms simultaneously. England and Scotland did not, however become one realm, officially, until the 1707 Act of Union. He had something of a baptism of fire, with two plots – the Bye and the Main, and then the biggie, the Gunpowder Plot – within two years of taking the throne.[263]

Reams have been written about the Gunpowder Plot, but it was caused in part by James' attitude towards parliament. During the later years of Elizabeth I, parliament and the queen had clashed over free speech, her marriage, the succession and Mary, Queen of Scots. In 1601, a member of the Commons spoke openly about the difficulty of making parliamentary decisions when Elizabeth used her royal prerogative to overthrow them.

James' later years in Scotland had hardened his belief in absolute monarchy, so clashes with parliament were inevitable, especially when he raised Robert

Cecil to the peerage so he was no longer able to argue the king's point in the Commons. Indeed, Cecil spent much of his time trying to undo James' meddling, not helped by the king telling the Commons they were 'rash, over-inquisitive and apparently distrustful'. By 1605, the country's Catholics were ripe for conspiracy. Fawkes' desire was to rid the country of the ruling classes. When asked by James why he had conspired against him, Fawkes replied 'a dangerous disease requires a desperate remedy'. He wanted to get rid of king, queen, heir, lords, bishops and the Commons. It has recently been established that Fawkes had twice the amount of gunpowder needed, even taking into account deterioration of it, to ensure that nobody in Westminster would have survived.[264]

Robert Cecil, son of the great Elizabethan, William, Lord Burghley, took over the reins of the day-to-day running of the country, and was made Earl of Salisbury. This left James time to concentrate on his plan to unite England and Scotland, and on foreign policy. Not to mention his leisure pursuits, of which, hunting was his favourite.

His plan to join England and Scotland foundered when both countries opposed it. The Commons refused him the title 'the King of Great Britain', so James adopted it anyway, and used it on official documents in both realms.

James' relationship with parliament was fraught mostly because he was so financially inept, but the rate of inflation did not help him. In 1610, Salisbury proposed the 'Great Contract', whereby James would be granted money to pay off his debts of £600,000 (£142,421,678.97 in 2024), and given an annual grant of £200,000 (£47,473,892.99 in 2024). This did not go down at all well with parliament, so James dismissed it. He told Salisbury 'ye ever expected to draw honey out of gall'.

The same thing happened in 1614 – the *Addled Parliament*. He dismissed that too, and reigned without parliament until 1621, employing astute money men and selling honours to gain money. Gosh! Where have I heard that before?

At one time, he considered marrying his heir, Prince Charles, to the Spanish Infanta, as a way of staving off issues with Spain, who continually pushed James to lessen the stringent anti-Catholic laws. James strung the negotiations out for almost ten years, so Charles decided to take matters into his own hands and go and woo the Infanta in person. Very bad move. She detested him and insisted part of any marriage settlement must repeal the laws against Catholics. For once, Charles, parliament and the country were united. So much so, Charles believed parliament had tacitly agreed to a war with Spain. Silly boy!

Since James' accession, he had had trouble with the extremes of the Puritans on one side and the Catholics on the other. The Puritans wanted to abolish Church confirmations, wedding rings and the term 'priest' among other things. James was fairly conciliatory towards Catholics, so long as they took the Oath of Allegiance. This was possibly because, like Elizabeth, he tried to balance the two sides. His attitude may also have had its origins in the political shenanigans during his childhood, and he possibly thought he might need Catholic support. And if so, who can blame him?

In 1611, James issued The King James Bible. Early on in his reign, in 1604, James had ordered further changes to be made to the *Book of Common Prayer*, a revision of the 1559 one under Elizabeth. Later the Civil War would abolish the prayer book, after which, in 1662, a revised version would be issued, and remains the official prayer book of the Church of England today.

Regarding his personal life, James, in direct contrast to Elizabeth's flirtatious behaviour, was of a more scholarly bent. Where historians have always looked askance at him, is the continual rumours that he took male lovers, most notably Esmé Stewart, Earl of Lennox, Robert Carr, Earl of Somerset and George Villiers, all of whom we will meet in due course. Some historians have maintained these male friendships were not sexual, pointing out that Anne of Denmark gave birth to eight children, or some sources say nine, but only three lived to maturity.[265]

When Salisbury died in 1612, he was not greatly mourned, being considered a hangover from the Elizabethan era. However, from 1612 onwards, James took the reins of government into his own hands, and his administration fell into notoriety and decay. James became his own minister of state, but he had neither the focus nor the concentration to be efficient or effective.

In 1613, the Carr/Overbury scandal – which we will read about later – became public and further tarnished the reputation of the court. In his later years, James drank heavily, suffered from gout and kidney stones, and lost all his teeth. The Duke of Buckingham then allied himself with Prince Charles in order to keep his status close to the seat of power. There is a theory that James suffered from porphyria, but some of the symptoms are synonymous with kidney stones, so this is not substantiated.[266]

In religious matters, James tried to navigate the middle of the road between the Catholics and the Puritans. He once said 'my care for the Lord's spiritual kingdom is so well known, both home and abroad, as well as by my daily actions as by my printed books'. At the end of his reign, he refused to sign a proclamation against the proliferation of Popish books until a balancing clause against Puritan tracts was added. He stated that Puritan pleas for specialist treatment were 'an excellent argument for the papist'.[267]

He is massively criticised for his absolute adherence to the divine right of kings. 'The state of Monarchie is the supremist thing upon the earth. For kings are not onely God's lieutenants upon earth, and sit upon God's throne, but even by God himselfe they are called Gods.'[268]

In early 1625, James succumbed to recurrent bouts of gout, arthritis and fainting fits. He died in March of that year and was buried in Westminster Abbey.

Generally speaking, his people loved him or at least had a good opinion of him. He reigned over a peaceful England at a time when taxes were quite low, although Elizabeth was still remembered with much love. The one disfavour James did his son was to bequeath to Charles an absolute belief in the divine right of kings, plus contempt for parliament.

Both things would literally end in a fight to the death.

Fun Fact

James I believed utterly in the existence of witches. He took a somewhat unhealthy interest in their torture and trials. He also wrote a treatise called Daemonologie.

Esmé Stewart – 1st Duke of Lennox; 1st Earl of Lennox; 6th Seigneur D'aubigny

Born *c*.1542, Esmé Stewart was described as 'of comely proportion, civil behaviour, red-bearded and honest in conversation'.[269]

He met James in 1579, when the latter was 13 years-old and Esmé was 37, married and with children. He was the first cousin of Henry, Lord Darnley, which made him James' first cousin, once removed. Son of a French nobleman but with Scottish forebears, he appeared an exotic figure in the grim Scottish court, and James was utterly fascinated by him.[270] Newly arrived from the French court, he must have seemed like a breath of fresh air for the adolescent king who was surrounded by dour, controlling noblemen. Men who were more concerned with not just their own path to power but by maintaining control of the king. Esmé soon had James openly showing his affection to this French import.

John Matusiak maintains he was a secret agent of the Guise family, sent to Scotland to promote the cause of Catholicism and Mary, Queen of Scots. The latter had given Esmé 40,000 gold crowns for use at the Scottish court to save the Catholic faith and get her back on the throne occupied by her Protestant son.[271] Mary wrote to Henri III of France asking him to support Esmé and help her regain her throne.

By March 1580, James had not only appointed Esmé to the Privy Council of Scotland, but had created him Lord Darnley and Earl of Lennox. Esmé took great pains to maintain his popularity with officers of Scottish burghs, gaining in one instance, fishing rights in Aberdeen, which proved lucrative.[272]

Whether or not he had been dispatched as a secret agent, there is some evidence to believe he played double agent to the Guises, Mary, Queen of Scots, the Scottish Kirk, and Elizabeth I, all in the pursuit of personal ambition. He soon discovered his influence over James was such that it was much easier to maintain that to gain what he wanted, and leave the Guises etc. behind.[273]

Esmé arrived at the Scottish court as the influence of James' last regent, the Earl of Morton was waning. Needless to say, he was not popular with Morton or his adherents, or most of the old nobility.[274]

Within months of his arriving in Scotland, James was not just endowing Esmé with titles, but with a fair bit of Mary, Queen of Scots' jewel collection. The Great H(arry) of Scotland was a chain of rubies and diamonds. That and a cancan (a jewelled collar) of diamonds were just two of the items that had belonged to James' mother.

The open affection James showed to Esmé was shocking to those who witnessed it. The English ambassador reported that 'few or none will openly withstand anything that he would have forward'. This was, of course, considered very dangerous, not just because of the moral aspect, but because Esmé was a Catholic in a very Protestant court and realm, with a Protestant king, born of a Catholic mother. The religious entente was a fragile thing that could collapse like a delicate flower, and as quickly. Esmé converted to Protestantism, but most people at court did not believe he was sincere and trusted him even less.[275]

What anybody with two brain cells to rub together would have realised was that James had been abandoned as an infant, crowned at the age of thirteen months, controlled by grim men intent only on their own advancement, and schooled by a bully, who obviously believed beating the child was the best kind of education. And then along comes this charismatic, magnetic man, who showed him how fabulous life could be because – hey! – he was the king. Add to that the fact that Esmé was physically virile, handsome and everything James was not.

At first, Esmé maintained an unassuming mien, fooling his enemies, who were won over by his 'courteous and modest behaviour'. If he could fool them, how much easier would it be to fool James? That said, we must remember, he was the king's cousin. He would see how James' childhood had not exactly been happy and being the character he was, Esmé probably wanted to bring some joy into the king's life and thumb his nose at those who had made James' life so bleak.

Morton certainly misunderstood this Frenchman. It is possible he believed him to be a dilettante, the friendship merely a passing whim, and of no threat to him. Wrong! James had, by this time, formally taken power over his kingdom, but Morton still pulled the strings. It was probably this that made Esmé take instruction about the Protestant religion from James, and officially convert, which he did, signing the 'Articles of Religion' in the Chapel Royal at Stirling Castle. After which, James and Esmé went on a progress around Scotland.

It was Elizabeth I who read between the lines of her ambassador's reports and those of other spies at the Scottish court. She did not trust Esmé one inch. So much so, she wrote to Morton advising him to 'lay violent hands' on the Frenchman. At the same time, she wrote to James advising him that it was dangerous to prefer 'any Earl of Lennox before a Queen of England', demanding Esmé's removal from the Scottish Privy Council, and hinting for the first time that she was considering naming James as her successor.

What actually happened was that James and Esmé plotted to get rid of Morton for good. It shows what a devious, manipulative mind the favourite had, for he suggested raising the spectre of James' murdered father as the weapon. He inveigled Sir James Balfour, brother of the man who had owned Kirk o'Field, and who was himself a suspect in Darnley's murder. Balfour played ball – there's a surprise. He publicly claimed to possess a bond signed by the Darnley conspirators, one of those signatures being that of the Earl of Morton.

This was absolutely masterly, because apart from shoving Morton into the middle of a morass of treason, the claim 'proved' that Mary, Queen of Scots was completely innocent, and thus exonerated from any blame in the matter of Darnley's death. Add to that it gave James a stick to beat the English with about how they were treating his royal mother, and one can see just how agile Esmé's brain was. Esmé had also covered his back by marrying his sister to the 60-year-old John Knox, proving, were any proof needed, that he was not just capable and confident but politically astute as well.

However, not everyone was taken in. Sir James Melville hated Esmé, labelling him 'a scorner of all religion, presumptuous, ambitious, covetous, careless of the Commonwealth, a despiser of nobility and of all honest men'.

Morton's downfall was not dissimilar to that of Thomas Cromwell. During a meeting of the Privy Council of Scotland, Esmé burst into the room and channelling his best melodramatic abilities, flung himself on his knees before James, pointed at Morton and accused the earl of murdering James' royal father. In the ensuing shouting match, Esmé pretended that, only being able to speak French, he had no idea what was being said – yelled.

Morton was manhandled to a kangaroo court, convicted of treason and beheaded. Elizabeth sent 2000 men to save him but she was too late, and James basically told her to push off. To say Elizabeth was angry is an understatement. She called James a 'false Scottish urchin'. What she, too, failed to take into account was that, as Matusiak points out, while James' upbringing had taught him to be cunning, it was Esmé Stewart who taught him to be duplicitous.

Under Esmé's tuition, James came to regard the Scottish clergy in the same light as his French counterparts regarded the Huguenots. Disturbers of the peace.[276]

Four months after Morton's execution, James made Esmé the Duke of Lennox, the only duke in Scotland, and certainly one not of royal blood! Naturally, as far as the Scottish nobility was concerned, this state of affairs could not continue. In 1582, in what came to be called the *Ruthven Raid*, James was kidnapped while he was out hunting. The king was effectively given a deal he could not refuse, which probably majored on *if you want to stay king, Lennox must go*.[277]

And go Lennox did. To Paris. However, he carried on a secret correspondence with James and, much to the disapproval of the French, he remained a Presbyterian, so perhaps all the doubters were wrong and James' teaching had converted him. Esmé died in Paris in 1583. After his death, William Schaw, James' architect, took Esmé's heart back to James, who had always believed his friend's conversion was sincere. James wrote a poem, 'Ane Tragedie of the Phoenix', likening Esmé to a phoenix; an exotic, beautiful bird, killed by envy.[278]

Robert Carr, Earl of Somerset

Robert Carr was born in Somerset around the year 1587, although some historians date his birth year as 1590.[279] Described by some as 'handsome and full of life', to others at James' court he appeared coarse, shallow and less than cultured.

In 1601, Carr became page to Sir George Home, the first Earl of Dunbar, who was a member of the royal household, and James' Chief Scottish Advisor. Whilst in this post, Carr met Sir Thomas Overbury, an English poet and essayist, and the two became close friends. When Carr came to James' court in England, Overbury became not just his secretary, but his mentor and political advisor.

In 1607, during a tilting march, Carr broke his leg. The king was in attendance and noticed the injured young man, who then quickly became a favourite. Robert Cecil, Lord Salisbury, James' Chief Minister, advised the king to give Carr Sir Walter Raleigh's manor at Sherborne. At this time, Raleigh was in the Tower of London accused of treason after the Cobham Plot. His wife, Bess Throckmorton, was given a paltry sum in compensation for the loss of the manor.

By 1610, Carr's influence was enough for him to persuade James to dissolve parliament when some of its members had publicly attacked the king's favourites. The following year, Carr became Viscount Rochester and also a privy councillor.

All was going swimmingly until 1612, when Salisbury died. Until that time, he had held everything together, managing to suppress James' more extreme ideas from bearing fruit. However, when he died, Carr took over many of Salisbury's duties without having the wisdom of his predecessor to keep affairs on an even keel. At around the same time, the Howard Clan became the most powerful faction at court.[280]

Shortly after Salisbury's death, the heir to the throne, Prince Henry, also died. In very short order, these two powerful men who would have restrained James from giving his favourites so much power, especially where foreign policy was concerned, were no longer a voice of sanity at court. Indeed, the instant these two dissenting voices were silenced, James deprived his Privy Council of all consulting rights. This left it as a body with administrative responsibilities but no authority. Instead, James put all his trust in Robert Carr who, aided by Overbury, worked on government papers.

Unfortunately, Carr's only claim to anything was being the possessor of a handsome face. He alienated the House of Lords. The situation, already simmering, was made worse when James made Carr virtually Lord High Everything Else. It was not long before there was a groundswell of revolt in parliament. This dissatisfaction percolated down to the people, which only made the situation worse than anything that had happened during the Tudor dynasty.[281] If anyone wanted to see James, they had to get through Carr's ring of steel first. It will not come as a shock to know he became very rich, mostly from the bribes paid out for access to James. The king also continued to shower him with gifts.

The only fly in the lovers' ointment was Overbury's distrust of the Howard faction. This distrust increased when Carr fell in love with Frances Howard, daughter of the Duke of Norfolk and wife of the Earl of Essex. They had been married when he was 13 years-old and she 14. Somerset took his problem to James, who agreed to set up a commission to establish whether the Essex marriage was legitimate.[282]

Carr was riding high, which to anyone with two brains cells is a warning to be careful. The Howard faction, formerly such a formidable force in English politics, became little more than a sycophantic faction who went as far as to desert Catholicism, a central tenet of their family life during the Tudor era. They were so keen to obtain and retain every ounce of power they could, they entered into an agreement with Carr that he could marry the Countess of Essex. The only impediment, of course, was the existence of the Earl of Essex.

They all set about obtaining the divorce. It was noted that James himself was pruriently curious about the details. Using his influence, the divorce went through. All was sweetness and light. Not. Overbury was still a problem, but the Earl of Essex retired from court.[283]

The Howards then manipulated Overbury into what was perceived to be disrespect of the queen. They persuaded James to send him to the Tsar's court as an ambassador. Overbury had no intention of accepting and declined the offer. This was then blown up into an offence tantamount to treason, but all Overbury wanted was to stay close to his friend. Sadly, James was persuaded to put him in the Tower of London, where he died five months later. James then made Carr Earl of Somerset and the two lovebirds were married. Aaah!

In 1614, Carr, by then Lord Chamberlain, was supporting the Spanish party, while more experienced politicians wanted the king to strengthen links with Protestants in Europe. James continued to shower his favourite with gifts until a certain George Villiers was made the king's cupbearer. He caught the eye of the king who promptly fell out with Carr and wrote a letter detailing his complaints against him.

Carr might still have retained some of the king's favour, but in 1615, a huge weed floated into the happily married couple's garden of delight when it was revealed that in order to obtain her divorce, Frances had murdered Sir Thomas Overbury. James, in an act of self-preservation, insisted that the subsequent trial be conducted in the full glare of publicity. And it was.

At the subsequent trial, four people, including the Lieutenant of the Tower and one of Frances' waiting women, were hanged. Somerset and his wife were also brought to trial and condemned. Frances confessed her guilt but nobody has ever been able to establish the level of her husband's involvement in his friend's death.

James, understandably, and also in another act of self-preservation, sent repeated letters to Carr telling him to admit his guilt, and saying that if he did so, he would be pardoned. Why did the king do that? James is alleged to have said, 'It is easy to be seen that he would threaten me with laying an aspersion upon me of being, in some sort, accessory to his crime'.[284] Carr refused to admit anything.

Although both had been found guilty and condemned, their lives were spared. The scandal disgusted the country, especially the growing number of Puritans, when they realised that people like Carr had been showered by James with gifts and honours.

When George Villiers superseded Carr in James' affections, the Howard faction lost all credibility. They tried to entice James with another handsome youth, and 'washed his face every day with posset curd'. All their attempts came to nothing and very soon they had lost all their positions and influence at court.[285]

After being found guilty, Robert and Frances Carr were put into the Tower of London. Frances was pardoned immediately but not released until 1622. Somerset himself refused to give an inch and was not released until 1624. He briefly emerged in 1630, when he was prosecuted by the Star Chamber for giving the Earl of Clare information about a paper written by Sir Robert Dudley, advocating the establishment of an arbitrary government.

He died in 1645. He left one daughter, Anne, from his marriage to Frances. Anne later became the wife of the first Duke of Bedford.[286]

George Villiers, Duke of Buckingham

George Villiers came from relatively humble beginnings. He was born in Leicestershire around 1592, the second son of Sir George Villiers and his second wife, Mary Beaumont. Villiers first caught James' eye when he was made the king's cupbearer in 1614, at the age of 21. At that time, Robert Carr, Earl of Somerset was James' favourite, and a man cordially hated by everyone at court, but especially by Queen Anne. It appeared that the newcomer was a good bet to unseat the favourite. They were right.

John Oglander later observed that he 'never yet saw any fond husband make so much or so great dalliance over his beautiful spouse as I have seen King James over his favourites, especially the Duke of Buckingham'. Sir Edward Peyton is quoted as saying James would 'tumble and kiss' (Villiers) 'as a mistress'.

Villiers' father died when the younger George was a child. His mother then married Sir William Compton, but she remained a powerful influence in her son's life, ensuring that he learned the necessary accomplishments of a gentleman. She sent him to France for two or three years to attain the skills in riding and dancing. He was lauded with the 'daintinesse of his leg and foote'.

Jean MacIntyre claims that Villiers realised his influence would outlast James' life, so he made himself Prince Charles' – now heir after the death of Prince Henry – best friend. He also taught Charles that masques not only presented a higher reality, but could create reality.

Thus, when he became James' cupbearer in 1614, Villiers was not only an excellent dancer and experienced in the art of masques, but he was also handsome, witty and he amused the king.[287]

As part of his duties as a cupbearer, he not only had to ensure nobody poisoned the king's drinks, but he also had to chat with James and keep him entertained. This position was one of trust as well as importance.[288] By 1615, after the fall of Robert Carr, George Villiers was knighted and made a gentleman of the bedchamber. Not only did he soon replace Carr, but lands and wealth followed. His rise was meteoric.

There are, as with Esmé Stewart and Robert Carr, question marks over the nature of his relationship with James; however, in 1617, in a toast, James said

'I love the Earl of Buckingham more than any other man. Christ had his John and I have my George'.[289]

Buckingham had won his king's heart, but he alienated his fellow courtiers. However, his mother had taught him well for he was very well versed in the values and fashions of the time. He had learned French, dancing and fencing while in France, and had an accomplished academic background. We must not forget that James, too, loved literature and learning, so Buckingham was an ideal companion. In 1615, he was made Sir George Villiers; in 1616, he became the king's master of the horse; in 1617 the Earl of Buckingham, and in 1619 Lord High Admiral. But over all this lay the question, especially among his other courtiers, as to whether he was James' lover. Courtiers resented him even more when he began to enrich his relatives as well as himself.

The philosopher, Francis Bacon, hitched his star to Buckingham's wagon and was given the role of Lord Chancellor. Bacon used his position to give favours to Buckingham's allies. In time, parliament launched an enquiry into corruption, and Bacon was blamed. Buckingham distanced himself from the furore, for he was busy amassing wealth and power in Ireland, especially in the building and control of Irish estates.

Parliament, ever vigilant when it came to their own prerogatives, launched a parliamentary commission investigating abuses over monopolies and other financial shenanigans. Buckingham managed to extricate himself from that mess, too. He pretended to support the enquiry, but took advantage of the in-fighting within parliament to scupper it.

In May 1620, Buckingham married Katherine Manners, daughter of the Earl of Rutland. Her father was completely against the union, but they ignored him and enjoyed a very happy marriage, having four children. Buckingham continued to build his public profile; one could say he was an early supporter of self-promotion within the public sphere. What some would call a triumph of appearance over content.

To aid this, Buckingham commissioned portraits of himself and his family by Van Dyke and Rubens among others. Each succeeding portrait became more flamboyant. In the 1625 portrait by Michiel van Mierevald, Buckingham's jacket is emblazoned with pearls. Another portrait, by Van Dyke, shows Buckingham and his wife as Venus and Adonis – nice calves, shame about the face! This portrait, of course, portrays him in a heterosexual role, which could have been deduced from the fact he had four children, but it may well have been done to contradict the rumours of an affair with James.

In 1623, when James made him the Duke of Buckingham, George also became the only English duke who was not a member of the royal family. As ever, with an eye to the future, he danced alongside Prince Charles and the two became firm friends.

This new advancement made Buckingham even more unpopular with the English nobility. And then he ventured into the treacherous ground of foreign affairs, which, to be honest, he bungled. He did accompany Prince Charles to Madrid to arrange the marriage between the English heir and the Spanish king's daughter. Their main objective was an Anglo-Spanish alliance that would help put Frederick V, James' son-in-law, back on the throne of the Palatinate.

However, Buckingham's attitude, helped greatly by the fact the Spanish Infanta instantly disliked Charles, caused the whole venture to fail. So, they both came home and allied themselves with those parliamentarians who wanted war with Spain. If anything, this made Buckingham even more despised, something that was not improved when he then negotiated Charles' marriage to the French princess, Henrietta Maria, who was … a Catholic!

In 1625, James died, but Buckingham's position with Charles, now Charles I, was solid and unassailable. The duke set off on an ill-prepared land and sea campaign to Cadiz. Indeed, the whole thing had been so carelessly organised, it was called off and everybody recalled to England. The troops were either drunk or suffering from disease. This time, Buckingham could not side-step the responsibility and he was publicly blamed for the fiasco. So much so, parliament began impeachment proceedings against him.[290]

He managed to dodge that bullet by persuading Charles to dissolve parliament and it all came to nothing. In 1627, Buckingham then led an equally unsuccessful force to relieve La Rochelle. The city had, under the Edict of Nantes, gained the right of religious freedom. Cardinal Richelieu didn't agree with the Edict and lay siege to the city. Buckingham took around 7–8000 troops to oust the cardinal's forces. Richelieu then reinforced his troops. In the end Buckingham was forced to return to England with the loss of more than half his original forces.[291] He survived another attempt to impeach him, being once more saved by Charles. But, by now, Buckingham was public enemy number one.

On 23 August 1628, in Portsmouth, a soldier called John Felton stabbed Buckingham to death. Many people celebrated his demise, but Charles sincerely mourned the loss of his friend. He had Buckingham buried in the Henry VII Chapel in Westminster Abbey, but, because of the duke's unpopularity, the burial was secret and performed at night.[292]

The words 'Enigma of the World' were engraved on his tomb.[293]

Charles I

Charles I is seen as a bit of a Marmite monarch. Some see him as a slightly less-than-dashing cavalier out to stop all the Puritan killjoys making his people utterly miserable – or at least less miserable than they already were. Others see him as a diehard monarch set on enforcing his divine right to rule as king.

One would normally think the true answer lay in the middle somewhere. I believe had Charles not adhered to his father's arrogant certainty that his was the only opinion worth having, England would never have suffered the seventeenth-century civil war, but his attitude made his death inevitable; and die he did. On a scaffold outside Whitehall.

He wore two shirts as he walked across the park to his death on that cold January day, so that the crowds would not see him shiver and think him afraid. His final word to the people gathered to witness the execution of a king was 'Remember'.

Charles was the second son of James VI & I. Had his elder brother, Henry, not died in 1612, it is doubtful if the English Civil War would have happened. Their father, James, had an overweening, arrogant, superiority regarding his rights as a monarch. Until 1612, it was only Robert Cecil, Earl of Salisbury, and Prince Henry who managed to regulate James' more erratic notions. However, both these influences for moderation died in 1612. After that, James did as he pleased and if parliament didn't please him, he dissolved it.

Charles was born in Dunfermline Castle in 1600. He was a sickly child who was not well enough to move south with the rest of the family when James became king in 1603, and who was carried everywhere until he was 8 years old. He believed utterly in his father's notion of the divine right of kings. Even the imperious, vain and changeable Elizabeth I realised that sometimes the monarch had to be pragmatic. Charles' later intransigence led inevitably to a head-on collision with parliament and the Scottish Presbyterian element.

He became an accomplished scholar and physically stronger by dint of long hours practising riding, tennis and golf. In 1612, Henry, the brother Charles admired, died of typhoid. Shortly after, his sister, Elizabeth, married Frederick Elector of the Palatinate, a region of Germany. This affected Charles who became introverted and subdued, something that manifested in him appearing cold and aloof.[294]

He was careful not to criticise the louche court of his father, but he did distance himself from it, becoming close to his mother. When she died in 1619, he became even more lonely until his friendship with George Villiers blossomed. This tarred Charles with the same brush as Villiers, resulting in him being distrusted by the people and members of parliament, especially when Villiers brokered his marriage with the French, Catholic, Henrietta Maria.

In 1625, James died. Charles, completely misreading the room, promised freedom of worship for Catholics, including his wife. He also said she would be responsible for the education of their children to the age of 13. In other words, they would be reared as Catholics – another nail in Charles' coffin. Villiers and Henrietta Maria hated each other. Charles objected to her giving her French entourage plum jobs; he felt sidelined, so much so, in 1626, he expelled the entire French members of the court.[295]

The beginning of the erosion of Charles' relationship with parliament began in 1625 with the breaking of treaties with Spain. Spain did not react in a military fashion, but Charles demanded money 'to set out his fleet against an unknown enemy in a war that had not yet been declared'. Two members of parliament commented. Sir Francis Seymour said, 'We know not our enemy', while Simon Weston declared, 'Let us first desire to know our enemy before we agree to contribute to a war'.[296]

Parliament in general was hostile to him, believing all these shenanigans were a precursor to the restoration of a Catholic monarchy, which, in the 1680s is exactly what happened. Opprobrium heaped on Villiers' head, naturally percolated down to Charles, so from the beginning of his reign, his association with parliament was jaundiced and embittered. Indeed, Charles became the first king to be denied funds from tonnage and poundage duties that had been automatically given to every other monarch, simply because of the degree of hatred towards Villiers.

The king then decided to give Richard Montagu, who most people believed was anti-Calvinist, the post of royal chaplain. This first parliament, that should really have been a piece of cake for Charles, became known as the 'Useless Parliament'. Charles dissolved it. Before his next attempt, he made his most outspoken critics sheriffs in various counties. This meant they could not attend parliament, but all it achieved was to leave space for a new Leader of the House, Sir John Eliot, who was one of Villiers' most vociferous critics. So much so, Charles sent Eliot to the Tower. Parliament then refused to transact any business until Eliot was released. Charles dissolved parliament. You can see a trend building here can't you?

The king then went one better than his father. James had at least believed parliament had legal powers over him. Charles didn't. This came to a head in 1628 when parliament was called, but this time, the House of Lords that had always supported the monarch, supported the Commons. They refused to discuss any money for Charles until they had aired their grievances against him and his taxation policy. He was forced to sign the Petition of Rights, giving demarcation lines for the king and enforcing the rights of subjects. Parliament still didn't vote to give him any money.

When George Villiers was assassinated, the killer was imprisoned in the Tower of London, but he became a folk hero to Londoners. Charles locked himself in his bedchamber and wept.

Prominent MPs attacked various clerics, among them William Laud, Bishop of London and the aforementioned Richard Montagu. Laud also employed Roger Manwaring, who had been impeached for saying that refusing to obey the king was a crime against God. Charles' response was that religion was not the business of parliament. John Eliot and eight other MPs ended up in the Tower … and … Charles dissolved parliament.

You can see where this is going, can't you? Charles decided to dispense with parliament altogether. He used advisors to create a taxation system, and became the father of nine children, eight of them being born in this eleven-year period. His entire concentration was towards making a refined and formal court and doing as little work on his duties as king as he could get away with.

Without parliament to grant him money, Charles exploited the wealthy and raised unpopular taxes – a tautology if ever one existed. But he hid behind his advisors, so they became the ones criticised, not him. William Laud, by this time Archbishop of Canterbury, was harsh on Puritans and Presbyterians, but distrusted Catholics. The introduction of a new prayer book in Scotland led to riots in Edinburgh.

In 1640, out of necessity, Charles recalled parliament. It became known as the 'Short Parliament', mostly because the new Leader of the House, John Pym, said there would be no discussions about money until the members' grievances had been heard. Guess what? Charles dissolved parliament. This left him with no money, no unified religious policy and riots in London. Archbishop Laud was chased out of Lambeth Palace by the mob.

Charles could not reign without parliament, but, equally, he could not expect parliament to be anything other than hostile towards him. When the Scots invaded Northumberland and Charles was forced to sign the Treaty of Ripon saying they could stay in Northumberland and he would pay them, he realised he had no option but to recall parliament. This one became known as the 'Long Parliament'.[297]

Harbottle Grimston – what a fabulous name – said 'The Common-wealth hath been miserably torn and macerated'.[298] John Pym argued that the king had been misled by evil advisors. Laud and Wentworth, Charles' leading advisors ended up in the Tower, giving the king no option but to go along with parliament. His inability to be decisive exacerbated the situation. Parliament rescinded all Charles' taxation laws and it was decided that any taxes not raised by parliament were illegal. Furthermore, the members also voted to say that only parliament could dissolve itself. Laud and Wentworth were executed, and, by 1642, the king's stock in Westminster was at an all-time low. Anyone perceived to be of the royal party was under threat of violence. Even the queen was threatened with impeachment.

Charles ordered that the main agitators in both houses be arrested. Parliament refused point blank. The king then attempted to arrest six leading members, including Pym, but it backfired spectacularly when ordinary Londoners ran riot, dragging Catholics out of their houses and killing them.

Parliament then decreed it did not need the royal assent to pass laws. By this time even Charles realised he was onto a loser. He fled north, and tried to access the armoury at Hull, but was told to go forth and multiply, only in fewer words. He fled south to Nottingham and raised his standard, declaring that parliament was in rebellion. Parliament responded by declaring that anyone not supporting it would forfeit their property.

Many of the aristocracy joined Charles because they feared an uprising of the lower orders of society. Charles sent Henrietta Maria and his younger children abroad but kept Charles, Prince of Wales with him.

The first battle of the Civil War was Edgehill, near Oxford, in 1642. It was a stalemate with both sides claiming victory. Charles then marched towards London but Londoners came out in support of parliament, so he retreated to Oxford and set up court there. There were various skirmishes between the two sides, neither side gaining much ground.

In 1645 the New Model Army was formed. It was a professional body of men, promoted on merit not social standing. There followed a decisive victory for parliament at Naseby. Prince Charles fled to the continent and in 1646, King Charles surrendered. In 1647, he was handed over to the parliamentary commissioners and thus began the countdown to his execution. Initially, he was held at Hampton Court Palace, but he escaped and fled to the Isle of Wight under the mistaken impression the governor was sympathetic. He was imprisoned at Carisbrooke Castle, and escaped from there, too, but was quickly recaptured.

In late 1648, parliament voted to negotiate with Charles. One of the dissenting voices belonged to Oliver Cromwell, the leader of the New Model Army. Thomas Pride removed from parliament any member who did not support the army, this becoming known as 'Pride's Purge'. Those members left were called 'The Rump Parliament' and it was the Rump that brought charges of treason against the king. Three courts declared the charges illegal, so parliament formed a new court, the High Court of Justice to prosecute the king.

His trial began on 20 January 1649. Charles refused to acknowledge the validity of the court and when addressed replied, 'I would know by what power I am called hither, by what lawful authority'.

On 26 January the king was found guilty; fifty-nine commissioners signed his death warrant, his sentence being execution because he had used his power as king to follow his own wishes instead of what would be good for the country.

Charles I was executed on 30 January 1649. Among his last words were 'Liberty and freedom consists of having government, not having a share in government'.[299]

So why did it have to come to this? Clive Holmes maintains after Charles' clashes with parliament, that nobody on the parliamentary side could ever feel safe while he was alive. However, he goes on to argue that the king was negotiating with his enemies right up until mid-January 1649, but that he remained intransigent. That they then decided to go ahead with the trial has been regarded as *an extended negotiation*, the purpose being a settlement, not regicide. Since Charles completely refused to co-operate, he comes across not as a martyr, but as a politician who miscalculated and pushed his luck, never believing they would kill an anointed king.[300]

Clarendon, the historian of the English Civil Wars, wrote that the execution was 'hypocrisy of the deepest villainy and most bloody treasons that any nation was ever cursed with or under'. He believed there would be a European outcry. But although many words were spoken in criticism of the act, nothing actually happened. No country broke off relations with the new British Republic and neither did they acknowledge Charles II as king.[301]

Fun Fact

Charles I is known by several nicknames, such as the Martyr King, the White King and the Man of Blood depending on your point of view of his execution, his status as a saint in the Anglican Church and his actions during the Civil War.

Jane Whorwood

'You may freely trust Whorwood in anything that concerns my service, for I have had perfect trial of her friendship to me. I cannot be more confident of any.' Charles I to William Hopkins, Master of Newport Grammar School, 1648.

Jane Whorwood is generally presented as a dashing, daring, courageous woman who thought little of putting herself in danger if it meant she could help Charles I during the Civil War. And all of that is true. It is also true she made a very unhappy marriage to an abuser who moved his mistress into the marital home and beat Jane severely when she refused to countenance the interloper.

Jane was the sister of the Countess of Lanark and the stepdaughter of James Maxwell, one of the bedchamber grooms Charles was allowed to keep by his side during his captivity.[302] She was born in Westminster in 1612, her father being a Scottish courtier and her mother a laundress to Anne of Denmark, queen to James I.

Her father died in 1617 and her mother then married James Maxwell. In 1634, Jane married Brome Whorwood and by him she had four children, two of whom died in infancy, a son who died in a boating accident when he was 22, leaving only a daughter, Diana, who lived until 1701. Brome Whorwood fled to the Continent in 1642, staying there for three years before coming home. Jane lived at the family home, Holton House, on the outskirts of Oxford, but she spent most of her time travelling on spy duty for the king.

Most of her contacts were laundresses and merchants in a network that her mother and stepfather organised. Maxwell had been Black Rod in parliament in 1622, but when Charles I and parliament fell out in a big heap, he became one of the king's private financiers.

It seems clear that Jane enjoyed the precarious life of a spy, once smuggling gold worth £80,000 (roughly £16.5 million in 2024), in barrels of soap. This money helped Charles, Prince of Wales, and his mother, Henrietta Maria, to escape to the continent.

During the 1640s, Jane established a network of spies from London to Edinburgh, acting as an information conduit between the king's supporters and relaying messages from the king. At this time, she also hosted Thomas Fairfax, the parliamentarian commander at Holton. She helped organise Charles' escapes, including his final bid for freedom from Carisbrooke Castle, when she smuggled in acid to help cut through the bars of his prison. Charles' guards had been bribed to assist him in his escape, but they pocketed the money and betrayed him.

At that time, Jane was aboard a ship waiting to pick Charles up and take him to Holland. It was five weeks before she discovered he had been recaptured.[303] In 1647, she embezzled parliamentary funds, sending them to Charles, then at Hampton Court Palace, to fund his escape. This was not discovered until 1651, at which time she was imprisoned.[304]

No portraits of Jane have been identified, but she was described as 'tall, well-fashioned with a round visage and pock holes in her face'.[305] Letters between Jane and Charles while he was imprisoned in Carisbrooke Castle indicate that they were lovers in 1648, although all the letters from his supporters were in code and few of them survive.

Jane's husband, Brome, was violent towards her and after her son, also called Brome, died in 1657, she fled the marital home in fear of her life. The couple were formally separated in 1659.[306] He was regularly ordered to send her payments but refused point blank. 'If she were dying and a halfpenny would save her, I would not give a halfpenny', he said. Nice chap!

John Fox, in his biography of Jane Whorwood, claims the reason for no portrait of her being identified is that, unlike Jane Lane who helped Charles II after the Battle of Worcester, Jane Whorwood's attempts to help Charles I were all a failure. If you add to that the fact that conspirators are not only hidden but often hidden from each other, then this becomes understandable.[307] Indeed, in the past fifty years, it has only become known that husbands and wives working at Bletchley in the Second World War never spoke about their work there and had no idea of what the other was actually doing.

Jane was clearly a complex character and quite unsuited to the Stuart traditions of how a lady should behave. Her husband, three sisters and mother-in-law excluded her from their wills. She clashed with her in-laws because she was confident, strong-willed, rich and cultured. She also had red hair, part of her Scottish heritage, but generally held in dislike and suspicion by the English. William Seymour, Marquess of Hertford later said: 'Had the rest done their parts as carefully as Whorwood, the King would have been at large'.

Part of her training must have come from her stepfather. Jane saw what a skilled operator he was while negotiating his way through the maelstrom of court and parliament and rising up through the ranks as he did so.[308]

When Brome repeatedly refused to give Jane any money, she sank into poverty, despite the locals who knew the couple testifying to his brutish behaviour. She died in 'genteel poverty', Fox opining that she was possibly 'mentally damaged'. One wonders if that might have been from her active, perilous lifestyle or the beatings from her husband.[309] Brome Whorwood left Holton to his youngest daughter, Diana, and Jane stayed with her until her death in 1684.[310]

What is saddest of all though is that, after the restoration of Charles II, Jane's efforts on his father's behalf were completely ignored. The fact that we know so little about her is partly due to the new king's ingratitude, while the men who had worked for Charles I trumpeted their own 'heroic' actions, Jane's equally heroic actions were completely ignored. Fox likens writing her biography to 'attempting to restore a shattered vase from pieces, fragments and slivers … she becomes the disappearing rustle of a long skirt, a riding habit or a sea cloak'.

James Stanley, 7th Earl of Derby

Stanley was born on 31 January 1607, the eldest son of William Stanley, 6th Earl of Derby, his mother being daughter to Edward de Vere, 17th Earl of Oxford. Through his paternal grandmother, he was a descendant of Henry VIII's sister, Mary Tudor, and Charles Brandon, Duke of Suffolk.

Stanley was elected to parliament in 1625 and, on Charles I's coronation, created a Knight of the Bath. He served jointly with his father as Lord Lieutenant of Lancashire and Cheshire, and assisted in the administration of the Isle of Man, later becoming Lord Lieutenant of North Wales. In 1626, he married the granddaughter of William I of Orange, who was known as 'William the Silent'. The couple had six sons and four daughters.[311]

After his marriage he assumed most of his father's responsibilities. William handed over the financial control of his estates, reserving only £1000 pa (about £205,000 in 2024) for himself. The new earl used his wife's marriage portion to buy back holdings formerly held by the family that had either been sold or leased. He proved a reluctant magistrate, only rarely attending assizes or quarter-sessions. In 1626, he had a gross annual income of £5400 (about £1,112,000 in 2024). He was known to be a good landlord, not indulging in the practice of rack-renting that was so prevalent, but he could also be ruthless.[312]

In character he was a man of deep religious conviction and nobility. He was single-minded in his devotion to Charles I. The historian, Clarendon, described him as 'a man of great honour and clear courage'. He went on to say that Stanley's defects were 'the result of too little knowledge of the world'.[313] In religion he was a moderate, committed to maintaining the Church of England as it had been under James I.[314]

Stanley took no part in the dispute between Charles and parliament, generally preferring to stay on his country estates than be present at court. However, when the Civil War broke out in 1642, he dedicated himself to the royalist cause. In 1642, his father died and he became Earl of Derby.

He offered to raise troops and secure Lancashire, but Charles, not a natural solider, may have been envious, and ordered Stanley to join him in Nottingham where the king had raised his standard. Stanley was defeated at the battles of Chowbent and Lowton Moor, won the struggle for Preston but failed at Lancaster Castle. He was also defeated at the Battle of Whalley and then withdrew to York. So perhaps Charles did not have much to be jealous about.

After York, he travelled to the Isle of Man where he helped Prince Rupert, before taking Bolton in a bloody battle that later became known as the Bolton Massacre. He followed Prince Rupert to Marston Moor before returning to the Isle of Man, offering refuge to any royalists who were fleeing from the parliamentary forces. He was a strong administrator, but not always a just one. He maintained order and encouraged trade, but imprisoned those who spoke out against him, and abolished tenant rights, introducing leaseholds instead.

In 1649, after the execution of Charles I, Henry Ireton, one of the prominent parliamentarians, offered to make peace with Stanley, but he refused. Charles II made him a Knight of the Garter in 1651 after Stanley supported his invasion. During that, Stanley was defeated at the Battle of Wigan Lane, being badly wounded and barely escaping. He joined Charles II for the Battle of Worcester and accompanied him to Boscobel House.

Stanley was captured near Nantwich, court-martialled in Chester, and found guilty of treason because he associated with Charles II. One source says that Cromwell supported his appeal, while another says Cromwell was determined he be executed.

Stanley was executed at Bolton because of his part in the aforementioned massacre. He was beheaded at the Market Cross in Churchgate, Bolton.[315]

Undoubtedly, the Bolton Massacre was ultimately his undoing, so perhaps it is relevant to examine what happened. For Stanley, it was a fight in a muddy street that was not a battle but became depicted as a war crime. 'Nothing heard but kill dead, kill dead was the word in the town, with horsemen pursuing the poore amazed people, killing, stripping and spoiling all they could meet with' wrote an unknown contemporary chronicler.

What seems to have happened is that, smarting under his recent defeats, Stanley asked Prince Rupert to allow him to lead the assault. At that time Bolton was known as the most independent Puritan town in Lancashire.

It should have been a great victory; 600 prisoners and 50 officers were taken and it was so successful, in fact, that Stanley was the first in the royalist army to fight through the town's defences. Prince Rupert, however, was not impressed and sent him back to the Isle of Man.

In truth, it was a war crime. Royalist soldiers were allowed to run riot with wholesale theft, murder, extortion and rape. There are tales of violated women, and Captain Bootle, already a prisoner, being murdered by Stanley because he had once been his servant, so his death was seen as personal. However, it was Prince Rupert who gave the *no quarter* order, but it was Stanley who paid for it.[316]

As many as 1500 people were massacred and much of the town was destroyed. There is still a plaque outside 'Ye Old Man and Scythe' where Stanley was beheaded.[317] There was a rumour that Stanley was really a Catholic, which would have been like a red rag to a bull in such a Puritan outpost. However, the truth is that he pledged loyalty to the Church of England on the scaffold. His body was buried at Ormskirk. Stanley is also known as the 'martyr Earl of Derby'.[318]

Henry Jermyn

Jermyn was born in 1605 and was known as an English royalist, politician, diplomat, courtier and property developer. He was the fourth son, but only the second surviving son, of Sir Thomas Jermyn, vice-chancellor to Charles I.[319]

His education was mainly gained by foreign travel. He left England in 1618 for three years and in 1623 became a member of the Earl of Bristol's household when the latter was ambassador to Spain. Jermyn failed to recognise the Duke of Buckingham, who was, allegedly, not offended.

He was under the legal age when he first became an MP for Bodmin in 1625 and again in 1626. His youth and inexperience ensured that he contributed nothing to the Commons proceedings in either year.[320] In 1627, he became a gentleman usher in Queen Henrietta Maria's private household.[321] He was described as 'tall, broad-shouldered, elegant and refined', the poet and essayist Abraham Cowley saying he was 'a soul composed of the eagle and the dove'.

Jermyn attended Henrietta Maria when she came from France to marry Charles I and had already befriended her. He was described as 'handsome, discreet, a fluent French speaker and no lover of the Duke of Buckingham', which is not surprising when we consider the animosity between the duke and the queen.[322]

In 1627, the queen sent Jermyn to France to convey her sympathy to Louis XIII on the death of the Duchesse d'Orleans; whilst there he was mistaken as a peace envoy for a while because the Duke of Buckingham was also in Paris. By 1628, Jermyn was MP for Liverpool and vice-chamberlain to the queen. During the parliamentary recess, he travelled to Jersey to train the island's militia, but he remained close to Henrietta Maria.[323] In 1629, he was licensed to promote a treatment for sheep-rot, developed by Sir Robert Le Gris. For the next decade, Jermyn and his brother, Thomas, exploited their connections at court for monetary gain, although the monies gained were held in reversion until after the Restoration.[324]

In 1632, the queen sent him back to Paris to congratulate her mother on surviving a coach accident. The following year, Jermyn blotted his copybook. Buckingham's niece, Eleanor Villiers, one of the queen's ladies, became pregnant citing Jermyn as the father. He refused to marry her, citing that she had slept with two other men besides himself. For this, Charles banished him, but he was back within the year.[325]

By 1539, Henrietta Maria had made Jermyn her master of the horse. During the Short Parliament in 1640, he represented Corfe Castle, but by the time of the Long Parliament later that year, he was MP for Bury St Edmunds, alongside his brother, Thomas. He fled to France after the First Army Plot, which planned to use the military to subdue parliament, failed. Within two years he was with Henrietta Maria in France, helping her to raise loans to buy arms and recruit soldiers for the royalist cause. In 1643, he was made colonel of Henrietta Maria's bodyguard and the title of Baron Jermyn was conferred upon him. This was purely so that if he happened to fall into parliamentary hands, he would be beheaded, not hanged, drawn and quartered as a common traitor.[326] In 1643, Jermyn was accused by parliament of political crimes and 'too great an intimacy with the Queen'. Agents ransacked his Whitehall apartments trying to find proof of the assertion, but presumably found nothing to substantiate it.[327]

In 1645, he was made Governor of Jersey, but fell out with Edward Hyde, later to be one of Charles II's prominent courtiers, because Hyde brought Prince Charles to Jersey against Jermyn's advice.[328] He took little interest in Jersey and proposed selling it to France in return for military assistance to Charles I.[329] He stayed close to the queen and the royalist faction in France, but he distrusted Hyde's influence over the Prince of Wales.

Whilst in France, he became a substitute father to Prince Charles, administering the prince's finances and paying him an allowance out of his French pension. He appointed Charles' tutors and decided on the curriculum during his education.[330]

During the commonwealth, Charles II and his court lived in virtual poverty, but Jermyn, by dint of grants, lived in comparative luxury. After the Restoration, Jermyn was appointed to the Court of Chancery, which is when the monies held in reversion in the late 1620s were granted to him. He became Earl of St Albans and JP for Suffolk and Middlesex, but Hyde, by then the real power behind Charles II's throne, ensured Jermyn was not given a government post. Instead, in 1669, he was sent as ambassador to France and was privy to the Secret Treaty of Dover, which was an agreement that Anglo-French forces would assault the Dutch.

He was present, in 1669, at the deathbed of Henrietta Maria, and was executor of her will. He retained Charles II's good opinion, being made Lord Chamberlain and a Knight of the Garter in 1672, but in 1674, he left public office.[331]

Jermyn was a friend of the poet, Abraham Cowley, and Sir William Davenant, the poet and playwright. He was also addicted to gambling and known to be extremely handsome, although Britannia describes him as 'a man of dissolute morals'. It was a regular rumour that he had married Henrietta Maria after the death of Charles I, but this is generally believed to be false.[332] It was also rumoured that he fathered at least one of her children, possibly even the future Charles II. Nathaniel Angelo, a clergyman from Windsor stated that 'all the royal children were Jermyn's bastards'.[333]

Jermyn was also a great property developer. In 1662 he gained the leasehold of Pall Mall Field and built grand houses in what became known as St James's Square. Soon Jermyn Street and St Albans Street followed, and the entire area known as St James became filled with grand houses. He was nicknamed 'The Founder of the West End'. Later in the 1660s, he also developed the area called Soho Fields.

Jermyn never married and died in his house in St James's Square in 1684. He was described by John Evelyn as 'a prudent old courtier and much enriched since his majesty's return', and by Andrew Marvell as 'full of soup and gold'.[334]

He was buried with his ancestors at Rushbrook, his earldom passing to Charles Beauclerk, one of his illegitimate sons, who became the 1st Duke of St Albans.[335]

One story that has persisted is that when Charles I attended his wife's bedchamber to visit her, the attendant who lit his way was Jermyn's cousin, Tom Killigrew. Killigrew opened the queen's door only to see Jermyn and the queen sitting together on her bed. He immediately dropped the taper and made a great pantomime of scrabbling about on the floor trying to retrieve it and apologising. By the time he stood up, the queen had composed herself, and Jermyn had vanished. Later reports state that Killigrew was completely honest, so we will never know if the rumour was true.[336]

Interlude – (With No Fun or Ice Cream)

Since the subject of this book is favourites of the monarchy, strictly speaking, this section should not be here. However, the Britain to which Charles II was restored in May 1660, was very different from that over which his father and grandfather had reigned.

For that reason alone, it is logical to cover – briefly – what happened between January 1649 and May 1660.

Called 'The Commonwealth of England', the only time there has been a republic in Britain was this short period of eleven years. Throughout, there was fighting in Scotland and Ireland between parliament and the royalists.[337]

The prime mover we all remember is Oliver Cromwell. He has always been seen as a divisive character. Winston Churchill called him a military dictator; others believe him to have been a hero of liberty.

Cromwell was born in 1599 in Huntingdon. His great-great grandfather had married Katherine Cromwell, sister of Henry VIII's minster, Thomas Cromwell, who had obtained ex-monastic lands for the family. By 1628, Oliver was MP for Huntingdon, and in 1640, MP for Cambridge. He was a religious independent who believed his successes were due to divine providence.[338]

In 1645 he became a commander in the New Model Army and was prominent in defeating the royalist forces. He berated parliament for being reluctant to promote ordinary men of ability over gentlemen who only wanted to negotiate peace with the king. That said, during the late 1640s, he believed that Charles would eventually come to the negotiating table. But when the king kept escaping, Cromwell concentrated on hounding him to his death. In 1647, he was made Lieutenant-General of the army.[339]

In 1649, he was sent to Ireland to quell the royalist support. Drogheda refused to surrender to him, so he stormed it, putting the 3000 strong garrison to the sword. He then went on to do the same to Wexford, but this time he did not spare the civilian population. The following year, he won a decisive victory at the Battle of Dunbar and chased Charles II and a second Scottish army south as far as Worcester, scoring yet another victory in 1651.[340]

In 1653, Cromwell was made – or made himself – Lord Protector of a united 'Commonwealth of England, Ireland and Scotland'. For the next five years, the Protectorate ruled England, but when Oliver died in 1658, his son, Richard, became Lord Protector and was singularly useless. So, in 1659, The Protectorate Parliament was dissolved and the Rump Parliament restored to begin the process of restoring the monarchy.[341]

In theory, England should have been better governed under parliament and much more settled. So why did it all fall apart?

Because of disagreements, no stable government lasted longer than a few months, and little meaningful legislation was transacted. It was only because of Cromwell's strong character that parliament held together at all. From 1648 to 1653, the Rump Parliament was in charge.

There is a telling opinion by Blair Worden that 'Cromwell was very practised at not knowing'. So much so that in 1648, he made sure he was in the north of England, so that he remained officially ignorant of Pride's Purge. He timed his return to London, so he reached it on the evening that Pride arrested leading opponents in the Commons and was thus able to declare 'that he had not been acquainted with this design'. Well, derr …

Worden goes on to say that 'The Remonstrance', the document given to Oliver Cromwell in 1657 asking him to make himself king, was seen in Richard Cromwell's hands the day before, so there is little doubt he knew what was afoot, but maintained he had known nothing about it.[342]

After making himself Lord Protector, Oliver replaced the Privy Council with 'The English Council of State'. The monarchy and the House of Lords was abolished and not brought back until the Restoration. Most of the Rump Parliament had been made up of gentry, who were conservatives and less than a quarter of them were regicides.[343] Regicide was generally considered the worst of all crimes and England had suffered from the perceived murder of its monarch, one consequence being an open season declared on English shipping.

The main problem with the new system was that there were too many diverse opinions. From those who wanted to simply restore order to the land, to visionaries who wanted to make a land akin to heaven on earth and those who wanted to run England on the same model as ancient Rome. What they all got was everyone being persecuted by a revolutionary government that was determined to restrict individual and collective behaviour. Social legislation against swearing and drunkenness was passed. Theatres and play houses were closed. Strict Sunday observance became the order of the day and Christmas, Easter and Whitsuntide were banned.[344]

Parliament became regarded as an illegal, unconstitutional body, so when Cromwell dissolved the Rump Parliament and replaced it with the Barebones Parliament – don't you just love these nicknames? – there were hopes that things would improve. The Barebones assembly was ruled by Cromwell and the army, with a 'nominated assembly' run by the army.

Good things were put in place. The Church of England was retained, but bishops were outlawed. All court proceedings were held in English, not Latin. During the Protectorate, Cromwell and the army dismantled the 'English Council of State' and Cromwell chose his own council. He was given – or took, depending on your view – sweeping powers. He did try to unite England and Scotland with the 'Tender of Union', but it was not a great success. The Scottish parliament was – here's that word again – dissolved and thirty members given seats in the London parliament. It lasted until the Restoration.

Parliamentary members were freely elected but Cromwell considered they did not enact his policies efficiently, so then England was given direct military rule, known as 'Rule of the Major-Generals'. The country was split into ten areas, each ruled by a major-general, who had powers to raise taxes and keep the peace.

Parliament then decided it wanted to make the position of Lord Protector hereditary. One could say a bit like the monarchy, then! In 1657, they offered the post of 'king' to Cromwell but after considering it, he refused.[345] Officially, he said he could not accept a position he had spent so long fighting against, but some historians believe he thought the position of monarch was cursed by God and he would be cursed if he accepted it.[346]

In 1658, Cromwell fell ill with what has been thought to be malaria and an issue with kidney stones. He died, possibly of sepsis, in September 1658 and that night a huge storm swept England and Europe.[347] Cromwell, I feel, was a man with sound and fair principles who discovered he had to be a virtual dictator to get anything done. He aimed to heal and settle all the difficulties and ill-feeling engendered during the Civil War, but he achieved none of those things and, in fact, by the last year of his protectorship, the military opposition to civil and parliamentary life had crippled his regime.[348]

Oliver's son, Richard, was ousted after a year and the Rump Parliament was returned. George Monck, 1st Duke of Albemarle, who had fought on both sides during the Civil Wars, was at that time in Scotland. He marched to London, assessed the situation and began secretly negotiating with Charles II. Charles then issued the 'Declaration of Breda', in which he accepted the crown of England. The Rump Parliament became the Convention Parliament, which decided that Charles II had been the monarch since the execution of his father in 1649. Charles entered London on his thirtieth birthday, 29 May 1660, to rapturous acclaim from the ordinary people. That day was afterwards known as 'Oak Apple Day'.[349]

Cromwell was buried in Westminster Abbey, but not for long. On 30 January 1661, the twelfth anniversary of the execution of Charles I, his body was exhumed, as were those of John Bradshaw and Henry Ireton. Cromwell's body was hanged in chains at Tyburn and then beheaded before, allegedly, being thrown into a pit. His head was put on a pole outside Westminster Hall where it stayed until 1685. At some point, it was buried beneath the floor of the antechapel at Sidney Sussex College in Cambridge.[350]

Fun Fact

It is not such a fun fact that there was little merriment and joy during the 1650s in England. The authorities tried to ban Christmas, especially in Puritan strongholds, tearing down decorations, arresting people who congregated in churches on 25 December and locking churches so worshippers couldn't get in. Officially, pubs were also closed but a few bribes soon sorted that. Imagine the scene. It is Christmas Day and the church is locked. Never mind, lads, let's go and open up the pub.

Charles II

The return of Charles II to England on his thirtieth birthday marked what everyone hoped would be a peaceful restoration of the monarchy after eleven years of a republic many found hateful and repressive. The huge query in the minds of those in power, and those who had invited him back after the bolognaise Richard Cromwell made of things following his father's death, was what sort of monarch would Charles be? Only time would tell.

The future Charles II was born on 29 May 1630. By the time he was 10 years old, he had two younger brothers and three younger sisters, as well as an extended family that included the children of the assassinated Duke of Buckingham. And in a case of déjà vu all over again, the younger Charles became as close to the young Duke of Buckingham as their respective fathers had been to each other.

William Cavendish, Earl of Newcastle was chosen to be Charles' tutor; an inspired choice in hindsight. He instilled a preference for the practical and pragmatic over academic theorising. In addition, he taught Charles to fence, dance, hunt, and to take an interest in engineering and science. Cavendish was so successful that Charles didn't really listen when his chaplain tried taking him down the academic route. In character, this Prince of Wales turned out to be superficially interested in many things but not invested enough to study any of them in depth. In one way, he was more like his grandfather, James I, in his interests, but unlike James in that he was fundamentally idle and not interested in any kind of extended study.

This emphasis on the practical over the academic probably stemmed from Cavendish's belief that any problems the young Charles would encounter in the ensuing years and when he ascended the throne, would be better resolved by a practical approach. Unlike the education of Charles I, Cavendish also tutored his charge to put little emphasis on religion, because, as the 'hourly history' puts it, 'monarchs who place too much emphasis on gaining a spiritual throne, risk losing their earthly ones'.[351] On wonders if Cavendish was far-sighted or just had a crystal ball to hand.

The hoo-hah with the Short and Long Parliaments bore out Cavendish's view. The young prince was forced to witness his father's powerlessness to prevent the execution of his friend, Strafford, on a trumped-up charge, and caused purely because Charles I had interfered in religious policy. It must have been a salutary lesson.

By 1645, Prince Charles was in command of part of the royalist army, covering south-west England. His next few years, away from his parents, began the legend of the licentious man, whose nickname would match that of a very fertile and successful stud stallion called 'Old Rowley'.

Charles was very charismatic. He adored women and they seem to have adored him. Even as a penniless exile, he was never short of company in bed. When Charles I thought his son to be in danger – from the parliamentarians, not women – he ordered him to go first to the Scilly Isles and then to Jersey.

By this time, the prince was over six feet tall (about 185 cms) and physically attractive as well as physically active – ahem! He was a doer rather than a thinker, which made him as unlike his father and grandfather as it was possible to be. Although possibly not completely accurate, this general view of him as a dashing, courageous cavalier stood him in good stead with his future subjects, who were pre-disposed to like him. But then who wouldn't be after the fun-averse Puritans?

When the Scots handed Charles I over to the parliamentary forces, it became clear that this new republic was intent on executing its monarch. In the British Library (Harley MS 6988) is a blank sheet of paper. The only marks on it are at the bottom. They are Prince Charles' signature and his royal seal. With the sheet went a message to Cromwell that he could name his own terms if he would spare the king's life. Cromwell ignored it.[352]

Charles II was proclaimed king of England, Scotland and Ireland, but, unsurprisingly, parliament did not recognise him. At that time, the young king was in Europe. Three months after his father's execution, Lucy Walter bore him a son, James. Young James would be the first of eight illegitimate children by different women. Charles accepted all of them; he liked children. He gave them titles, some of which are still around today.

The best thing Charles did when he fled England was to take Edward Hyde with him. Hyde would later become Earl of Clarendon and he became utterly loyal to his new master. We will see later how that panned out.

The new king's biggest problem was the decision to ally himself with either the Irish Catholics or the Scottish Presbyterians. The former were too closely linked to their first loyalty to the Pope and the concept of the divine right of kings. There was a danger of making the Pope too powerful a force in England. For once, Charles dithered but in the end, he issued the Declaration of Breda in which he agreed to make Protestantism the state religion of England, Scotland and Ireland. This was, at best, making the most pragmatic decision possible, but, unlike his father, the younger Charles was not particularly religious.

He landed in Scotland in 1650 and was crowned king at Scone on 1 January 1651. After which, he led a Scottish army to England to regain his throne. However, a victory for Cromwell's forces at Worcester soon put paid to that. From the top of the tower of Worcester Cathedral, he watched his forces being routed. He allegedly escaped Worcester by climbing down a rope from what is now a restaurant called King Charles House, and escaping to Boscobel. He fled across England and escaped to his mother in Paris, but by 1654, France was making conciliatory noises to the English government, so Charles, along with Edward Hyde, fled first to Belgium and then Germany.

Nicole Greenspan points out the issues Charles suffered during his exile, not least of which was the problem of allegiance. In England, at least by the authorities, royalism was considered a *malignancy* and the relationship between Charles and his court in exile was in direct correlation with the likelihood of the exiled king regaining his kingdom. Loyalty to God, the Church, the monarch, the government (i.e. parliament) were frequently in conflict, especially in Scotland and Ireland. How could the exile command loyalty in that case? Especially when he was almost penniless and his 'court' was in Europe.[353]

The 1650s must have been depressing for him. European powers were cosying up to England and Charles was living on charitable donations. Until 1658, when Oliver Cromwell died and his son, Richard, became Lord Protector. By the time it became clear Richard didn't have the wherewithal to protect a dead slug, England's government was out of control. There were no funds to pay state officers or judges, and the English fleet refused to carry on without wages.

Only at that point did George Monck march down to London and start the process of changing the balance of power. Soon European monarchies were warming to the idea of an England with a restored monarchy and welcomed Charles to their courts. I wonder what his true state of mind was at this sudden renewal of adulation. I suspect a hardy sprig of cynicism had grown in the preceding eleven years, and this volte-face only made it increase.

In April 1660, Charles moved his court to Breda in the Dutch Republic and waited. Parliament was split between those who didn't mind having a king back, but it had to be a king with defined restrictions, and those who were happy to have a king back period! Monck purged parliament of those who wanted restrictions, at the same time obtaining from the army a promise that whatever parliament decided, it would accept.

Charles wrote another Declaration of Breda, although it is much more likely that Hyde wrote it. This one promised to act with parliament, restore harmony to the country, and pay the army. It was a brilliant stratagem. Everyone assumed that because Charles said nothing about vengeance against those who had executed his father, they had nothing to fear. Phew. Parliament smiled, voted to restore the monarchy with no restrictions, and invited their king home.

His response was that he and the army had agreed to be bound by parliament's decisions, but he would accept no other preconditions being put on his return. There would, he said, be no royal vengeance, but that some in England 'needed to be subdued by force rather than wooed by kindness'. If nothing else, this was a timely reminder about how much power would be in his hands.

Charles II landed at Dover on 25 May 1660, but refused to set foot on English soil until he had met and embraced George Monck. He agreed to uphold the law and the Protestant religion. And bided his time.[354]

New regalia had to be made for Charles' coronation, since the previous royal crown etc., had been melted down. This was later the subject of one of Arthur Conan Doyle's Sherlock Holmes stories, *The Musgrave Ritual.*

Charles was crowned on 23rd April 1661, probably chosen because it is St George's Day. The new king proved to have a flair for public spectacle, and was often seen enjoying himself at the races.[355]

In fact, he preferred racing at Newmarket and enjoying himself to attending to state business. Besides, he had Hyde for that. He believed in the beneficial effects of physical exercise – I'm saying nothing! He absented himself from official meetings or Privy Council meetings whenever he could, although he was very interested in the navy. He proved to have a short attention span and people learned that if they wanted him to listen, they had to keep what they said to the pertinent facts.

Charles seems to have had trust issues – well, there's a surprise. He tended to believe that any advice given was forwarded to advance the advisor more than it being the right course of action. He was inconsistent and would often do what his friends advised rather than his councillors, especially if their advice proved inconvenient. His actions proved him to be fickle.

Edward Hyde was his most powerful minister and George Monck his Lord-Lieutenant of Ireland. And then a big weed, provoking a scandal, blew into the royal garden. His younger brother, James, had an affair with Hyde's daughter, Anne, and became pregnant. Charles arranged a secret marriage but it inevitably led to claims of cronyism. Many demanded the marriage be annulled. Charles refused and made Hyde Earl of Clarendon because, quite frankly, he was too useful to antagonise.

Things had calmed down some by the time of the king's first parliament. Three issues were to be decided. Firstly, pardons for treason against those rebels who had aligned themselves against Charles I; secondly the issue of royal and crown lands that had been sold off; and lastly, the creation of a national Church.

This is where those who had heaved a sigh of relief when Charles had conveniently omitted to say anything about vengeance had relaxed too soon. He was adamant that no mercy to the regicides would be shown, by which he meant those who had signed his father's death warrant could expect only the full rigour of the law. He did sign the Act of Indemnity and Oblivion, which granted immunity except for murder, piracy and regicide.

This is not the place to go into Charles' revenge on his father's killers, but for those interested in the details, I heartily recommend *The King's Revenge* by Walsh and Jordan and *Killers of the King* by Charles Spencer, both of which are in the Select Bibliography at the end of this book.

As far as the crown and royal lands issue was concerned, restoration was ordered for all those except the ones that had been sold. Those royalists who had lost lands because they supported Charles I were left to sort out their own restorations. This led to accusations that the new king was treating his enemies better than his friends, but it was a pragmatic decision for a monarch still feeling his way back to power. He did create a commission to oversee compensation.

Charles really disliked Presbyterianism. He felt a Church without bishops was akin to a realm without a king, but he was fine with the Church of England, with ordained clergy who were loyal to the crown.

The Cavalier Parliament in 1661 created the Clarendon Code, which made the Anglican Prayer Book statutory liturgy for all worship in England. It banned the gathering of more than five people who did not follow it, and was targeted against the Presbyterians. By the end of Charles' second parliament, he was granted a generous allowance, and those regicides caught so far had been given a fair trial and executed.[356]

In 1662, Charles married Katherine of Braganza, daughter of the king of Portugal, but she proved unable to give him a child and since he was seeding children hither and yon except in his own marriage bed, this was a problem. His reasons for the match were that the Spanish empire was crumbling. Portugal had gained independence from Spain, and Charles was always close to the French, but he needed allies to fight the commercial war with the Dutch. The other – huge – reason for the match with Katherine was that she brought a dowry of 300,000 Portuguese crowns (worth approximately £46.1 million in 2024). She also brought the cities of Bombay and Tangiers.[357] Charles supported Prince William of Orange and when the latter came to power in the Netherlands, Charles believed everyone would ally themselves against Spain. It didn't quite turn out like that. Charles' war with the Dutch was only partially successful and then, in 1665, plague broke out in London.

By September 1665, 7000 people a week were dying. Charles moved his court to Oxford. He was still spending lavishly and taxation was very high to pay for the Dutch war. His popularity was low. He was rescued in part by the Great Fire of London in 1666, mostly because the Lord Mayor was dithering about how to put it out. Charles and his brother, James took charge. They organised bucket chains and used gunpowder from the Tower to blow houses up to create fire breaks. For a short while, Charles became popular again, mostly because he was the hero of the hour, and the xenophobic populace blamed the French for setting the fire.

However – you just knew there had to be a however – this was only the calm before the storm. And it will come as no surprise to learn that the issue was religion, plus problems over the succession. Shades of Elizabeth I, but a tad more complicated. At least Charles had his brother, James, Duke of York to fall back on since he and Katherine had produced no heirs.

The situation was not helped by Barbara Villiers, Lady Castlemaine, his 'maîtresse en titre', who joined with her relative, George Villiers, to oust Edward Hyde, the man who had given Charles decades of faithful service and sound advice. They succeeded in getting Hyde impeached and exiled. And Charles – the self-serving rat – didn't lift a finger to save this loyal councillor and grandfather of his nieces.

Public opinion also turned against the king because of his immoral lifestyle. The whole thing exploded when Charles entered into a secret negotiation with Louis XIV, using Charles' younger sister, Henriette, known as Minette, as a go-between. In 1670, Charles signed a secret treaty in Dover. It promised French finance, arms and soldiers to help him force England to become a Catholic country. One has to remember here that when Charles I married Henrietta Maria, one of the tenets of their marriage agreement was that the children would be brought up for their first thirteen years as Catholics.

Part of the deal was that Charles had to openly convert to Catholicism. However, later in 1670, Minette died. She was a particular favourite of her eldest brother and he was heartbroken. The idea regarding his conversion also died.

But affairs with France were not over. In 1672/3, Louis paid Charles enough for the king to issue a Declaration of Indulgence regarding religion, which only goes to show how much religion didn't mean to him. Echoes of the formerly-Protestant Henri IV of France saying Paris was worth a Mass. The Declaration stated that Catholics could worship in the privacy of their own homes. Part of the thinking behind this was that his brain-dead brother who had obviously inherited their father's inability to read people or situations correctly, had become a Catholic.

The situation only lasted as long as Charles had money because when he went cap in hand to parliament for funds, he had to withdraw the Declaration of Indulgence. Worse still, he had to agree to the Test Act, which banned Catholics from holding any kind of public office. This resulted in brother James being forced to resign as admiral of the English fleet.

Then the French connection became public. James, having lost his wife, Anne Hyde, to breast cancer, married the Catholic Mary of Modena. Match that with the 'childless' Charles, and the country believed it was heading into a Catholic monarchy. Anti-Catholic feeling was at an all-time high and the king's popularity was at an all-time low.[358]

In 1675, with the aid of Louise de Kérouaille, one of his mistresses, Charles was alerted to the activities of the French astronomer, Sieur St Pierre, who was working on a system to determine longitude and latitude using the moon and stars. Charles became so interested, he formed the Royal Observatory, employing John Flamsteed as 'astronomical observator', so as to forward the research into an investigation that would perfect the art of navigation at sea.[359]

In other ways, with all the kerfuffle about Popery and the king's unpopularity, Charles really wasn't having the best of times. A sliver of light appeared when Sir Thomas Osborne, later Earl of Danby, succeeded Edward Hyde as Lord Chancellor. Just as efficient as Hyde, Osborne soon had the royal finances on a more secure footing.

Until 1678, that is, when a certain Titus Oates spread rumours that led to the incident known as the 'Popish Plot'. The plan was that Charles would be assassinated and Catholic James would be put on the throne. Then documents were found – to add verisimilitude to an otherwise …well, you know the rest of the sentence. These were, allegedly, correspondence between James and Louis XIV's confessor.

But conspiracy theories do not need verisimilitude, or at least not much, to make them credible. The anti-Catholic mobs exploded onto the streets. Catholics were banned from London; some priests and laymen were executed; and there was a movement to expel Queen Katherine from Whitehall. That last one failed in the House of Lords.

Then Charles' former ambassador to France, Ralph Montagu, let slip that Osborne had been negotiating with Louis for enough money to free the king from any parliamentary control. This led to a bill to exclude James from the succession because he was a Catholic. It was passed by 79 votes.

But Charles was having none of it. He would not allow any interference in the matter of the succession. The issue split the House of Commons into something approaching the beginning of the two-party system we have today. The Tories supported the king. The Whigs wanted James excluded. Rumours abounded that Charles had married Lucy Walter while in exile, which made James Scott, Earl of Monmouth, their son, a very popular figurehead. There was significant lobbying to have him legitimised.

Charles refused. He prorogued parliament seven times in the 1679/80 period to prevent any debate on the matter. In November 1680, a second exclusion bill was defeated, and Charles, in common with his predecessors, dissolved parliament. There was a new parliament after fresh elections in 1681. He dissolved that, too. Instead, he summoned the Scottish parliament, which passed legislation stating that exclusion was illegal. The Act of Succession stated that the succession was determined solely by blood proximity to the monarch and it was not the business of parliament to interfere or change that.

For the final five years of the reign, any Whigs holding public office were painted by the Tories as republican rebels and sacked. In 1683, the Rye House Plot aimed at assassinating both Charles and James on their way home from the races at Newmarket, made the king's popularity soar again. His purse also soared after he received the revenue on overseas trade levies.

On 2 February 1685, Charles suddenly fell ill. It is not known if he suffered a stroke or had kidney disease, but he died four days later, having converted to Catholicism. His had been a life of struggle, but, unlike his two predecessors, he did triumph over parliament.

Through all his adult years, in exile and then as king, Charles showed a politically-deft hand in getting what he wanted, using his charm to lull hostile adversaries into a sense of false security, outmanoeuvring them at every turn and steering his ship of state with an understanding of authority through some very rough waters, while never losing sight of his objectives, possibly because his principles were flexible. He also excelled at bluffing and would have made a formidable poker player.

Dilettante he was, certainly. But a skilful one whose reign, in comparison to those of his grandfather and father, and soon his brother, was a point of calm in an often antagonistic and hysterical world.

John Wilmot, Earl of Rochester

We have a pretty, witty, King
Whose word no man relies on.
He never said a foolish thing,
And never did a wise one.
John Wilmot, Earl of Rochester.

John Wilmot was, appropriately as it turned out, born on 1 April, April Fools' Day, in 1647; a man who wasted an exceptional brain by becoming a dissolute public disgrace.

He was a poet and courtier who reacted against 'spiritual authoritarianism'; in other words, rigid rules such as strict Church attendance, low threshold of openness or tolerance, a religion that is conventional, not questioned or self-questioning.

Andrew Marvell considered Wilmot the best English satirist. His poetry was censored in the nineteenth century, but revived by people like Graham Greene in the twentieth. Wilmot was born in Ditchley in Oxfordshire. His father, Henry, had been created Earl of Rochester for his services to Charles II in exile. It was Henry who organised the young king's escape after the Battle of Worcester in 1651. Henry died in 1658 and John inherited the title.

The young John was educated at Burford Grammar School and then attended Wadham College, Oxford in 1660, at the age of 13. This is allegedly where he first discovered his sexual appetite and spent the rest of his life satisfying it. In 1661, Edward Hyde, Earl of Clarendon, the newly elected chancellor, gave Wilmot an honorary MA. Charles gave him a pension of £500 pa (£78,683 in 2024) in gratitude to his father's action in saving his life. He sent Wilmot on a three-year trip to France and Italy, allowing him to immerse himself in European arts and literature, but with the emphasis on French culture.

At Christmas 1664, Rochester made his formal debut at court. Charles tried to broker a marriage with Elizabeth Malet, a wealthy heiress. Her family blocked it, not wanting their daughter to marry a penniless youngster, even one who was an earl. So Rochester attempted to abduct her. Samuel Pepys in his diary for May 1665 says '… Lord Rochester's running away on Friday night last with Mrs Mallet [*sic*], the great beauty and fortune of the North … by coach; and was at Charing Cross seized by both horse and footmen, and forcibly taken from him'.[360]

Charles was furious with Rochester and stuck him in the Tower for three weeks, only releasing him when the 'penitent' wrote a grovelling letter of apology. In the winter of 1665, Rochester enlisted in the navy during the Second Anglo-Dutch War. He proved to have outstanding courage, so Charles appointed him as a gentleman of the bedchamber on a pension of £1000 pa. In the summer of 1666, Rochester returned to the navy, covering himself in glory by rowing between English ships under heavy fire to deliver messages to the rest of the fleet.

Upon his return to England, he again paid court to Elizabeth Malet, only this time with more success since they eloped as far as Knightsbridge Chapel and were married. The couple had four children, three girls and one boy who died at the age of 10. In 1667, still seven months under the minimum age for entry to the House of Lords, Charles gave Rochester special licence to take his seat there, mostly because he needed all the supporters he could muster.

It is virtually certain that Nell Gwyn was first Rochester's lover and then his lifelong friend; helping to bolster his influence with the king. He seemed to live a double life; that of the quiet gentleman on his country estates and the riotous way of life at court, following the example of the king. Rochester became one of a group known for drunkenness, extravagant behaviour and 'witty' conversation. Andrew Marvell named them 'The Merry Gang'.

Gilbert Burnet, the Scottish philosopher and historian, said of Rochester, 'for five years together, he was continually drunk … not perfectly master of himself … that led him to do many wild and unaccountable things'.

In 1669, Rochester blotted his copybook again, this time whilst Charles was dining with the Dutch ambassador. The earl indulged in a bout of fisticuffs with Tom Killegrew, an action for which Charles banned him from court, but he soon recalled him.

By 1673, he was training Elizabeth Berry, who went on to become the most famous actress of the age. She was also his mistress and bore him a daughter. This was the year the Duke of Buckingham finally lost the king's favour and this rebounded onto Rochester. His revenge was to write a scathing poem saying that Charles was more obsessed with sex than the safety of his realm. He then made the mistake of accidentally showing it to the king who was, let's say, less than chuffed. One rhyming couplet ran:

> Restless he rolls about from whore to whore,
> A Merry Monarch, scandalous and poor.[361]

Rochester was exiled from court, but two months later he was back and Charles made him Ranger of Woodstock Park.[362]

By 1675, Rochester and his merry gang were rakes around town. They scandalised society but Charles always saved them from arrest. Rochester was as big a hell-raiser as the others but Alexander Larman describes him as having 'something of the angel undefaced'. He was a leading figure at court and some believe Charles saw him as a surrogate son, partly because of his father's support of the exiled king and his own courageous actions in the navy. Others, of course, thought differently. Samuel Pepys stated, 'it was to the King's everlasting shame to have so idle a rogue his companion'.

As the years of debauchery from the time he was 13, of sexual activities with every rank of woman from street whores upwards took their toll, Rochester was still able to inspire utter loyalty in his friends. He seemed to have an inbuilt decency of character saying later in his life that 'he should do nothing to the hurt of any other in his pursuits'.

And then came the action Charles found it difficult to forgive. In 1675, at a court banquet, Rochester – by this time, unsurprisingly, three sheets to the wind – together with his group, rampaged into the Privy Gardens at Whitehall. This garden had been lovingly put together with many of Charles' treasures, one of his most cherished being a sundial constructed by Francis Hall at the University of Liege.

Unfortunately, to Rochester's drunken eye, the sundial became the object of his anger, mostly because of its phallic shape. He attacked it with his sword, shouting, 'What! Dost thou stand here for f*** time?' Charles' pride and joy was destroyed. Everyone was shocked into sobriety and fled. Most escaped, but Rochester was not one of them.

Charles was so incandescent, he immediately left court. Nobody knew where the king had gone for ten days. He was eventually discovered on the royal yacht. Henry Savile tried to intercede for Rochester, who had himself left court. He was stripped of his titles, only temporarily, but informed that on his death, the title of Ranger of Woodstock Park would go to his uncle, not his son.[363]

He fell into disfavour again the following year when one of his companions was killed in an incident with the Watch. Strangely for someone who had showed such courage under fire, Rochester allegedly fled the scene.

Under the pseudonym Dr Bendo, he set up a clinic to help 'barren women'. Gilbert Burnet opined that his limited success was due to Rochester impregnating the few who did end up pregnant.

By the age of 33, Rochester was dying from several forms of venereal diseases and the effects of years of alcohol misuse. There are also suggestions he suffered from renal failure due to Bright's Disease, a form of chronic nephritis.

The aforementioned Gilbert Burnet, who later became Bishop of Salisbury, attended Rochester in his last illness. When Burnet left his side, the earl said 'Has my friend left me? Then I shall die shortly'. Which he did, so very quietly and 'without a shudder or a sound'.

Burnet later wrote that Rochester had converted to the Anglican church on his deathbed. The truth of this has been questioned but Graham Greene, in his biography on Rochester, calls Burnet's book 'convincing'.

When Charles II read the 'pretty, witty king' verse, he is alleged to have replied, 'That's true, for my words are my own, but my actions are those of my ministers'.

Most of Rochester's poetry was not published under his name until after his death, and because it is likely most of his poems appeared in manuscript form, it is thought a lot of them did not survive. Burnet later alleged that while on his deathbed, Rochester ordered that all of his 'lewd' writings were to be destroyed.

He became the model for rake-like heroes in the period, including Thomas Shadwell's *The Libertine*. Early in the twenty-first century, Stephen Jeffreys wrote a play about Rochester, also called *The Libertine*, which was made into a film in 2004, starring Johnny Depp. A century after Rochester's death, his reputation was in tatters. Samuel Johnson called him a worthless, dissolute, rake. Not until the twentieth century did that reputation recover somewhat. Ezra Pound thought Rochester's poetry equal to or better than that of Pope or Milton.[364]

Interestingly, Murray Pittock wrote a thought-provoking paper on *John Wilmot and Mr Rochester*, in which he avers the 1847 publication of *Jane Eyre* led its author, Charlotte Bronte, to choose the name Rochester for her hero deliberately.

Pittock cites Mr Rochester's Christian imagery to describe erotic feelings. He puts Rochester's right to 'get pleasure out of life' as 'an inspiration rather than a temptation'. More talk of passion is variously described as heaven and hell. It is an intriguing read examining how the life of John Wilmot, probably taken from Burnet's *Life and Death of John, Earl of Rochester*, affected Bronte's view of her hero.[365]

Louise de Kérouaille, Duchess of Portsmouth

Louise was born in 1649, the daughter of Count Guillaume de Penancoët, Siegneur de Kérouaille, a noble family from Brittany. She was introduced into Henriette, Duchesse d'Orleans' household. Henriette (Minette) was Charles II's younger and very much beloved sister. Louise's family originally hoped that their daughter would catch the eye of Louis XIV and become his mistress, but what actually happened is that when Minette came over to Dover in 1670 to discuss the secret treaty with her brother, Charles noticed Louise. When Minette suddenly died later that year, Charles appointed Louise as lady-in-waiting to Katherine of Braganza.

She treated the queen very respectfully and the two formed a friendly relationship, partly because Louise, like Katherine, was a Catholic. When she caught Charles' eye, the French ambassador and Henry, first Earl of Arlington, encouraged the relationship.

Outwardly, Louise appeared languid and indifferent, lacking any kind of ambition. In reality, this was a front. She made Charles wait – not something he was used to – before eventually succumbing.[366]

During the English Civil Wars, Louise's family had taken in fugitive royalists, which stood her in good stead. In 1671, Arlington arranged a 'gathering' where she was put directly into Charles' path and they began their relationship. By this time, Barbara Palmer, Lady Castlemaine, was on her way out of favour, and Charles unceremoniously dumped Nell Gwyn, temporarily. Louise became his favourite.

She bore him a son in 1672 and was made Baroness Petersfield, Countess of Fareham and Duchess of Portsmouth for life. Her son was created Duke of Richmond in 1675, the title still held by his descendants today. As well as Duke of Richmond, he was created Duke of Lennox and Earl of Darnley. All these titles had Barbara and Nell spitting feathers because they had, ineffectively, been pushing for titles for their sons by Charles for years.

Louise was very extravagant, but not in a pushy way. She preferred turning on the waterworks to storming about losing her temper when she wanted something, in marked contrast to Barbara and Nell, Louise was gentler and less demanding in her treatment of the king. Charles paid all her bills without turning a hair. She knew the art of gentle persuasion and was a sensitive, deferential and polished aristocrat, who knew the strength of tears as a weapon.

She tried to goad Nell Gwyn in court. On one occasion as they met, Louise said:

'Why, Nellie, you are grown rich, I believe by your dress. Why, woman, you are fine enough to be a queen.'

Nell's response was instant:

'You are entirely right, Madam. And I am whore enough to be a duchess.'

Strangely enough, the two became friends and played cards or took afternoon tea together, but Nell never stopped teasing her. Barbara tried to upstage Louise by wearing excessive jewellery or ensuring that more horses pulled her carriage than pulled Louise's. Finding this strategy did not work, Barbara descended into brash coarseness, whereas Louise always presented herself as refined and sophisticated. That said, she was always devastated when Charles' eye roved, whereas Barbara raged and had an affairs of her own, and Nell simply ignored it. When Charles abandoned her for Hortense Mancini, Louise took to her bed and wept. Nell nicknamed her 'Weeping Willow'. After Hortense fell into disfavour, Louise was back in the sunshine of the king's eye and stayed there until he died.

In 1674, Charles gave her venereal disease – there's a surprise. He sent her a pearl necklace and a diamond with a combined worth of £10,000 (£1,605,000 in 2024). No wonder he was always short of money.

The writer, John Evelyn, described Louise's living quarters as 'a splendid Appartement at Whitehall, luxuriously furnished, and with ten times the richnesse and glory beyond the Queenes'.

In 1680, a pamphlet, articles of 'Treason and Other High-Crimes and Misdemeanours Against the Dutches [*sic*] of Portsmouth' was published alleging that she:

- Laboured to subvert the Government of Church and State.
- Plotted to introduce Popery and Tyranny in the Three Kingdoms.
- 'Nourished, fomented and maintained that fatal and destructive Correspondency and Alliance' between England and France.

It all came to nought, but in 1682, she had a brief affair with Philippe de Vendome, at which point Charles *persuaded* him to return to France and forgave her. He was furious at her betrayal – really! He had obviously never heard the phrase about sauce, goose and gander, which originated around 1670.[367]

By 1681, Louise's annual income was £136,000 (£24,385,000 in 2024). The French gave her gifts on the understanding that she would champion her native land with the English king. On one occasion, Louis gave her a pair of earrings, allegedly worth £18,000 (£3,227,000 in 2024). Sadly, I can find no image of them, but if they did exist is it likely they were broken up when Louise fell into penury in later life.

John Wilmot, Earl of Rochester referred to Louise in his *Satire on Charles II* as Carwell, an Anglicised form of her name. She helped engineer his permanent banishment from court. The English cordially hated her, because she was Catholic, but mostly because she was French. Nell Gwyn called her *Squintabella* and, when mistaken for Louise in her carriage in the streets of London, had to show herself to the crowd with the words, 'Pray good people, be civil. I am the Protestant Whore'.

Louise was astute enough to understand what made Charles tick and what drove him. For this, she retained his affection until he died. During the Popish Plot, Louise was protected by Katherine. Charles thought the world of her, nicknaming her 'Fubbs', a comment on her plumpness. He even named the royal yacht *HMY Fubbs*.

Louise was probably the most proactive person persuading Charles to convert to Catholicism on his deathbed. One of his final admonitions to his brother, James, was 'do well by Portsmouth'. Certainly after his death, Louise fell quickly out of favour. She retired to France, leaving many of her possessions behind in the mistaken view that she would be able to come back and recover them. She did attend the coronation of George I in 1714.[368]

After her return to France, all her pensions and those of her son, were lost. Louis XIV granted her pensions but her standard of living was a shadow of what it had been. In 1692, a particularly bad winter forced her to witness the poverty of her tenants. She wrote to the controller-general of finance asking him to reduce taxation and to make ex-soldiers exempt from paying any tax.

In 1698, Louise returned to England to beg William III to reinstate her pensions. He gave her a promise of £1000 (about £145,000 in 2024). Back in France, she faced multiple lawsuits, but continued to spend lavishly with no money to pay for any of it. She sold off some of her lands and after Louis XIV's death in 1721, she was granted an annuity of £24,000 (about £4,341,000 in 2024). Her son died in 1723 from a combination of debauchery and alcohol. Louise's final ten years were spent doing good works – building a hospital, refurbishing a local church, and giving money to charitable causes.

Despite living in debt during her last years, Louise received a pension and protection from Louis XIV and after him the French regent, Philippe II. She died in Paris in 1734, aged 85.[369]

Many historians believe Louise was the love of Charles' life. He had a full-length portrait of her in his bedchamber and through all his political strife, she remained his closest confidante. Her descendants have titles spanning England, Scotland and France. One of those descendants was Diana, late Princess of Wales. Which means that another of her descendants will sit on the British throne.

Thomas Osborne, Earl of Danby, later, 1st Duke of Leeds

Osborne was descended from an apprentice in London who, in 1559, leapt into the Thames, rescuing his master's daughter and then marrying her. That fortunate man went on to become Sir Edward Osborne and later, Lord Mayor of London in 1583.

Thomas Osborne was born in 1632. In 1638, his elder brother died when the roof collapsed on him. Thomas survived, allegedly because he was searching for his cat at the time. In 1647, he succeeded to the baronetcy and the estates.[370]

Thomas' father worked for the royalist cause, and after his death, his son travelled extensively in Europe. By the time of the Restoration, he had an estate worth less than £1200 pa (about £202,696 in 2024) and debts of around £10,000 (about £1,689,000 in 2024). He attempted to solve his financial problems by becoming Sheriff of Yorkshire, but when he wished to serve a second term, he fell foul of Edward Hyde, Earl of Clarendon, who had other plans, including excise farms. Osborne tendered for one of the farms, and lost. He became one of Clarendon's bitterest enemies.

As a member of parliament, he sat on several committees and is on record as speaking in the House thirty-three times. However, his true skill was in lobbying. He joined forces with the Duke of Buckingham, who also hated Clarendon.

There was a hitch in his career when he wounded his opponent in a duel, but while he had to lie low for a time, his personal stock rose because of it.

Osborne helped draw up the address of thanks after Clarendon's fall and was active in bringing a public accounts bill to inquire into juror restraints, miscarriages during the Dutch wars and charges against a man called Mordaunt, who was one of Clarendon's allies. When challenged, he said he was a spokesman for 'the four hundred of the House of Commons thought by the Chancellor useless and inconsiderable'. Burnet described him as 'a very plausible speaker but too copious'. Osborne also had a hand in drawing up reasons for proceeding against Clarendon and was named to the committee considering the earl's banishment.

In 1668, with the help of Buckingham, Osborne was one of the Irish Commission finding grounds to dismiss Ormonde, and in the following year he was appointed to be treasurer of the navy, initially sharing that post with Sir Thomas Littleton.

By 1669, he was making overtures to Clarendon's supporters and seeking a stable royalist majority in parliament for foreign policies, especially those regarding France and religion. By this time, Osborne and Buckingham were growing apart, especially on the subject of religious toleration. He supported the renewal of the Conventicles Act, something that brought him membership of the cabinet council, and ready access to the royal court.

In 1673, he gave the vote of thanks for Charles' Declaration of Indulgence, but helped draft the address for the suppression of Popery, one of the results of which was the resignation of James, Duke of York as Admiral of the Fleet. The Lord Treasurer, Thomas Clifford, also had to resign, and Osborne succeeded him, shortly after being created Earl of Danby in 1674.

He based his ministry on 'sound churchmanship, sound finance and the Protestant interest'. He was successful because he started 'counting heads', royal patronage and a form of the modern parliamentary whip tradition. He actively interfered in by-elections to ensure that his preferred candidate won and became so unpopular that in 1675, there was a move to impeach him. It collapsed. His problem was that he was very plain speaking, which did not go down well. He spoke to Charles II on the subject of the Duke of Buckingham's unbusinesslike behaviour, in terms that we would say today was 'calling a spade a spade'.[371]

He certainly improved the royal finances and ensured salaries and pensions were paid regularly. In the House, he preferred quantity to quality in his parliamentary colleagues, mostly because they had little understanding of what was being debated, so voted the way he wanted them to.[372]

In 1677, he was made Lord-Lieutenant of the West Riding of Yorkshire and awarded the Noble Order of the Garter.

He was a very able politician, needing to strengthen the royal authority. He was a member of the established Church and an enemy of Catholics, dissenters and anybody who supported religious toleration. Osborne is often credited with inventing 'Parliamentary Management' to create an organised government lobby, something he regarded as necessary to royal policy. 'Nothing is more necessary than for the world to see that he (the King) will reward and punish.' That said, he opposed the Royal Declaration of Indulgence and urged rigid enforcement against Catholics. He also conducted the Compton Census, that asked for returns from every diocese stating the number of dissenters, both Catholic and Protestant, in order to prove their insignificance, and thus ease Charles' conscience. In 1676, he also moved to suppress coffee houses. He failed. He brought in a bill in 1677 to ensure that, in the case of a Catholic succession, any royal children would be brought up by Protestant bishops. He failed in that, too.

He was keen to increase English trade abroad by making the Dutch allies, in preference to the French. In 1674, he stopped the war with the Dutch Republic and remained on friendly terms with William of Orange, being prominent in negotiating the latter's marriage to Princess Mary, James, Duke of York's elder daughter. This laid the foundations for the Glorious Revolution in 1688 and the Act of Settlement in 1701.

His aims were directly opposed to the secret 1670 Treaty of Dover, but he did agree in 1676 to a treaty which netted Charles £100,000 pa (almost £20 million in 2024) and pushed a bill through parliament for war against France. In all things, Osborne was faithful to what he saw as the national interest. He was, of course, bound to fall foul of Charles eventually. And this is where his lack of personal charisma played a large part because he was unable to rely on anyone's support.

Pepys claimed Osborne was 'one of a broken sort of people that have not much to lose and therefore will venture all'.[373]

Osborne maintained his power by jealousy and corruption, actively excluding men of ability from high office. Burnet called him 'the most hated minister that had ever been about the King'. He had none of those amiable virtues that counter any faults. John Evelyn called him 'a man of excellent natural parts but nothing of generosity or gratefulness'. The Earl of Shaftesbury opined that Osborne was 'proud, ambitious, revengeful, false, prodigal and covetous to the highest degree'.

In the late 1670s, Osborne was impeached and imprisoned in the Tower of London for five years until James II ascended the throne. In 1688, he was one of the 'Immortal Seven' who invited William of Orange to depose James, his father-in-law and bring the Protestant religion back to England.

In 1694, Osborne was created Duke of Leeds. He led the government in the 1690s for a few years but was compelled to retire from public office in 1699, although he remained active – sometimes obnoxiously – in politics. One instance is when he supported a motion that stated the Church of England was in danger. Thomas Wharton, 1st Marquess of Wharton spoke against the motion. Osborne rudely reminded him he, Wharton, had once used a church pulpit as a lavatory.

In 1711, at the age of 80, he competed for the post of Lord Privy Seal but failed to get it. He died in 1712 and was buried in the Osborne family chapel in All Hallows Church in Harthill in South Yorkshire.[374]

James II

To be pedantic, James' proper designation is James VII and II because at this point, England and Scotland were separate nations.

James had none of his father's or elder brother, Charles' charisma; instead he inherited all of his father's lack of judgement and obstinacy, and certainly none of his elder brother's political shrewdness. He was born at St James's Palace in 1633, the second surviving son of Charles I and Queen Henrietta Maria and educated with Charles, George and Francis, sons of the assassinated Duke of Buckingham.

At the age of 3, James was appointed Lord High Admiral, but this was, unsurprisingly, only an honorary position, not formally confirmed until James was an adult. Likewise, although he was designated as Duke of York at his birth, this title was not settled on him officially until 1644.

During the Civil War, both James and brother Charles barely escaped capture by the parliamentary forces after the defeat at Edgehill. James ended up in the royal enclave at Oxford, and had a Master of Arts conferred upon him at the age of 9 – yes, really and he was also made colonel of a volunteer foot regiment; all those with a volunteer foot step forward.

After Charles I surrendered to parliament in 1646, James and his younger siblings were held in St James's Palace in London. However, his father ordered him to escape in 1648 after parliament had debated making James the king. Helped by a royalist spy, Joseph Bampfield, he escaped across the channel to The Hague.

Things deteriorated for James after his father's execution and his elder brother's defeat at Worcester. He sought asylum in France and served with honour in the French army, having been given command of a captured Irish regiment in 1652 and made Lieutenant-General in 1654.

In 1657, he was expelled from France after his brother, Charles, signed a treaty with Spain. Initially, James disagreed with Charles' decision but he ended up leading six British volunteer regiments against his former French comrades.

In 1660, he returned to England with Charles for the Restoration. Since Charles was only 30 years old, James was not seriously considered as heir-presumptive, but he was created Duke of Albany. He was close to Edward Hyde, later Earl of Clarendon, and had become close to the latter's daughter, Anne Hyde, whom he seduced in 1659 by promising to marry her. In 1660, to most people's dismay, Anne became pregnant. They were even more dismayed when James secretly married her. The child, a boy called Charles, died in early infancy, as did the following five children.

However, two daughters, Mary and Anne, survived and caused their father much anguish in later years. James was a fond father, playing with his children, unlike the normal royal tradition. His wife was devoted to him until her death in 1671, even though he was an unfaithful husband. He was known for not requiring a high standard of beauty in his conquests, unlike his brother. Gilbert Burnet wrote 'his mistresses must have been given to him by his priests as a penance'.

As well as having his appointment as Lord High Admiral confirmed, James was also made Warden of the Cinque Ports and Governor of Portsmouth. He precipitated the Third Anglo-Dutch War by sending the navy to attack forts in Africa, in order to facilitate the English slave trade. In 1644, Charles gave him Dutch territory captured in America. New Amsterdam was renamed New York in James' honour and the Dutch Fort Orange, on the Hudson river, was renamed Albany.

In retaliation, the Dutch sailed up the Thames in 1677 and attacked the English fleet at Medway, causing James to supervise fortifications along the south coast.

However, where James really shone was during the Great Fire of London. 'The Duke of York hath won the hearts of the people with his continual and indefatigable pains day and night in helping to quench the fire' wrote one witness in a letter.

In 1672, Charles formed the Royal African Company, who exercised martial law in West Africa to help the English trade in gold, silver and African slaves, some being branded DY for the Duke of York. Later the historian, William Pettigrew, would write: 'the Royal African Company shipped more enslaved African women, men and children to the Americas than any other single institution during the entire period of the trans-Atlantic slave trade'.[375] According to the BBC World Service 'Story of Africa', King Tegbesu — now known as Benin — made around £250,000 a year from selling people into slavery from 1750. It is only slightly heartening to know that it was the British who led the movement to abolish slavery in 1783.

During his time in France, and as a child under the guidance of his mother, James had, of course, been exposed to Roman Catholicism. He secretly converted in the late 1660s, but, in 1673, when the Test Act became law, he was forced to resign as Lord High Admiral, and his conversion became public. However, Charles II decreed that James' daughters, Mary and Anne, must be brought up as Protestants. That said, he allowed James to marry an Italian Catholic princess, Mary of Modena.

In 1677, Charles arranged the marriage of James' elder daughter, Mary, to William II, Prince of Orange – Charles' and James' nephew. James was reluctant to give his consent but did so eventually.[376]

The knowledge that James had converted to Catholicism created a well of hysteria, which led to the Titus Oates affair and the fabrication of the Popish Plot to assassinate Charles and replace him with James.[377] That this was widely believed, gives an idea of the attitude to Catholicism over a century after the reign of Mary Tudor, by now known as 'Bloody Mary'.

So tremendous was the furore, Lord Shaftesbury created the Exclusion Crisis, a plot to disbar James from the succession and replace him with Charles' illegitimate son, the Duke of Monmouth. The clamour caused Charles to dissolve three parliaments. By 1680, public feeling was such that Charles told James to leave England. He went, initially, to Brussels, but then to Scotland where he lived in Holyrood House in Edinburgh. James was even less popular when *HMS Gloucester* ran aground onto a sandbank, leading to much loss of life. This was attributed to the fact that James had argued with the pilot and then delayed abandoning ship.

Things turned round a little in 1683 when the Rye House plot to assassinate both Charles and James was made public. The plotters' plans backfired and the brothers rode on a – temporary – wave of sympathy. The Duke of Monmouth, one of the conspirators, let the cat out of the bag, forcing him to flee and Essex to commit suicide sooner than be brought to justice. During the wave of sympathy, Charles made James a member of the Privy Council.

In 1685, Charles died and James succeeded him. The 'Loyal Parliament' voted the new king a generous income and he did work much harder at being king than Charles had ever done. It is a shame that the first English dictionary did not come out until 1755, because it would have done James a favour to learn the definition of *compromise*.

He made no concessions, so Monmouth's Rebellion in Somerset and Argyll's in Scotland were not a surprise. Both rebellions were crushed viciously. Argyll was taken prisoner and executed, since he was already under sentence of death. Monmouth attempted to escape but was captured and later executed in the Tower of London. It was Judge Jeffreys, whose name has come down through history as a ferocious and cold-blooded monster, who sentenced most of the rebels to death or transportation at what later became known as the 'Bloody Assizes'.[378]

In response, James enlarged his army, causing more disquiet because it was not normal to keep a standing army in peacetime. If you add that he also gave the command of several regiments to Catholics, the level of public alarm can be imagined. Parliament objected, so James prorogued it, meaning he did not dissolve it, but merely ended that session and never called another.

In 1686, two papers written by Charles II stating arguments for Catholicism over Protestantism were published. By James. One could be gracious and call this move unwise, but why not say it as it was and call it unbelievably stupid? He went further, trying to repeal the Penal Laws that confirmed the state religion was Protestantism. He wrote to the Scottish Privy Council asking for toleration for Catholics, but not for Presbyterians. James also allowed Catholics to hold high office and received the Papal Nuncio, something that had not happened since the reign of Mary Tudor.

By now James was haemorrhaging support – there's a surprise. So he dismissed judges who disagreed with him, and also Heneage Finch, the Solicitor-General. In 1687, he issued the Declaration of Indulgence for Catholics and Protestant dissenters and went further the following year by decreeing it should be read aloud from every pulpit in the Anglican Church, thus alienating the bishops. James then tried to force a president on Magdalen College, Oxford, in violation of the Fellows' rights to choose their president. He insulted people left, right and centre, pushing his Catholic agenda, completely unable to see the disaster he was creating. When he reiterated the order for the Declaration of Indulgence to be read in Anglican churches, seven bishops, including the Archbishop of Canterbury, refused. He had them arrested and tried for seditious libel.

But one of the final nails in James' coffin came when Mary of Modena, his queen, gave birth to a Catholic son. This opened up a can of worms that could never be closed. There was even a scandal that the baby had died at birth and been replaced with a live boy child ferried into the queen's bedchamber in a warming pan. The country had had enough. The century-old spectre of fire for heretics was well and truly alight.[379]

In November 1688, seven Protestant nobles invited William of Orange to come to England with an army. W.A. Speck is of the opinion that this was not a spontaneous uprising against James and that he was not sent packing by the majority of his subjects.[380] It is true that Danby later regretted his part in the Glorious Revolution. Danby's son wrote in 1715: 'I can take God to witness that I had not a thought when I engaged in it (and I am sure my father neither) that the prince of Orange's landing would end in deposing the King'.

William Gee, however, was among those who had decided 'they would never lay down arms 'til they had made the Prince of Orange King'.

Most of those who rose against James simply wanted to use Orange to persuade James to change his ways. In this writer's opinion, they had two chances of that – fat and none! However, other historians are adamant that William of

Orange's plans had been put in place for a very long time, probably, one would think, at around the time he married James' daughter, Mary.[381]

In November 1688, William of Orange landed. Many army officers, including John Churchill, defected, as did James' younger daughter, Anne. James tried to flee to France, throwing the Great Seal of the Realm into the Thames. He was captured, but William allowed him to escape, probably not wanting his father-in-law to become a religious martyr. James fled to the court of Louis XIV.

In January 1689, William summoned the 'Convention Parliament' to decide how to deal with the situation. Parliament decided that since James had fled and disposed of the Great Seal, he had abdicated. James' daughter, Mary, was declared queen, to rule jointly with William. There then followed a Declaration of Rights, listing James' abuses of his power. That led to the Bill of Rights that declared no monarch could be a Catholic and no monarch could marry a Catholic. This later led to the Act of Settlement in 1701, the first tenet of which is that the monarch cannot be or marry a Roman Catholic.

In March 1689, James landed with French troops in Ireland in an attempt to regain his kingdom. The Irish Parliament supported him, but in July 1689 he was defeated at the Battle of the Boyne with William in charge of the English troops. James fled. Again. And who can blame him?

Louis allowed him to live at the royal chateau of Saint-Germain-en-Laye. Some of James' supporters attempted to assassinate William, but that made James even more unpopular in England. Louis attempted to persuade James to become king of Poland, but he refused. Then, in 1697, Louis made his peace with William and left James to his own devices.

The exiled king spent his remaining years as a penitent. He wrote a memorandum to his son on how to rule England. Perhaps it would have been more accurately titled how *not* to rule England, especially as it said that the majority of major office holders should be Catholic. Honestly, how many times does a person need to stick his head in an anthill before realising it isn't the best idea he has ever had?

James died in 1701 of a brain haemorrhage – probably from underuse! His heart was put in a silver casket and given to a convent in Chaillot; his brain in a casket ended up at the Scots College in Paris. Bizarrely, the flesh of his right arm – don't ask, I have no idea – was given to the Augustinian nuns in Paris. The rest of him was put in a triple sarcophagus in a side chapel of St Edmund's chapel in the Church of the Benedictines, Rue St. Jacques, Paris. Lights around it were kept lit until the French Revolution, when his sarcophagus was raided.[382]

However, when all is said and done, James' lasting legacy to Britain is the absolute knowledge that parliament rules the realm and the monarch does not.

Katherine Sedley, *suo jure* – in her own right – Countess of Dorchester

Katherine was born in December 1657, the daughter of the Restoration poet, Sir Charles Sedley. She grew up 'notoriously plain', because she had dark hair and she was slim, unlike the prevailing fashion which was for women to be blonde and voluptuous.

Her father was a notorious rake and her mother ended up in a psychiatric hospital, at which point, dad brought his common-law wife into the house and threw Katherine out. However, she went into service with Mary of Modena after her marriage to James, Duke of York, who made Katherine his mistress.[383]

She was very ugly by seventeenth-century standards, and wondered how she had become the mistress of the Duke of York: 'it cannot be because of my beauty for he must see I have none. And it cannot be my wit for he has not enough to know I have any'.[384]

After James came to the throne in 1685, he was pressed by his confessor and some of his councillors to end his relationship with Katherine. Queen Mary of Modena had always been against her husband's adultery, but was more upset that Katherine was a staunch Protestant. This alarm was echoed by his Catholic advisors, since they believed James, being an equally staunch Catholic, was inviting serious issues on the religious front when that situation was already difficult.[385]

While acknowledging the religious opinion of his confessor, he was quick to tell his councillors 'not to meddle in things that in no way related to them' and added he had no idea they had all entered the priesthood, which was very witty coming from a man said to have no sense of humour.[386]

In 1686, James created Katherine Countess of Dorchester for life; the degree of ill feeling towards her, especially as she was known to love making fun of people, heightened. Mary of Modena was incandescent and caused Katherine to be threatened with the loss of her pension, so she agreed to go and live in Ireland.[387]

In 1696, she married Sir David Colyer, who later became Earl of Portmore. Their son inherited the earldom from his father. Following the Glorious Revolution in 1688/9 and after William and Mary took the throne jointly, Mary II refused to receive Katherine at court because of her adultery with James. Katherine responded by asking why Mary was any different from her, since while Katherine had broken the adultery commandment, Mary had broken the commandment about honouring her father, so she was no better than Katherine was.[388]

Katherine was renowned for her earthy sense of humour and being unladylike. After James lost the throne, she talked her way out of prison. She also wrote to her sons: 'if anybody calls either of you the son of a whore, you must bear it, for you are so. But if they call you bastards, fight till you die, for you are an honest man's sons'.[389]

When George I came to the throne, Katherine was invited to his coronation. There she encountered Louise de Kérouaille, Charles II's mistress, and Elizabeth Hamilton, Countess of Orkney, mistress to William III. She said, 'God! Who should have thought that we three whores should meet here?' Also at George's coronation, the Archbishop of Canterbury enacted the ritual question asking if the people accepted their new king. Katherine, seeing how many soldiers were in attendance asked, 'Does the old fool think that anyone will say no?'

She gave James a daughter, Lady Katherine Darnley, who features in the ancestry of the Mitford sisters. She was also the grandmother of Erasmus Darwin's wife. Erasmus was the grandfather of Charles Darwin.

Katherine died in 1717 in Bath. She later became a prominent character in Walter Colyton's *A Tale of 1688*, which contains a discussion about her time as James' mistress, referred to by her as 'splendid slavery'. Her companion calls it a 'strange slavery to have royalty at your feet, a Countess' coronet upon your head and the whole court at your disposal'.[390]

After her death, Katherine's body was transferred to the Portmore vault in the old church at Weybridge.[391]

John Drummond, Earl of Melfort

John Drummond was born into a Scottish noble family in 1649, but not at Drummond Castle, the family home, which was, at that point, occupied by the New Model Army.

In 1670, he married Sophie Maitland, a Scottish heiress. They had six children in the next ten years, at which point, Sophie died. Later, after John joined James in exile, his properties were confiscated but Sophie's estates were passed to their surviving children in 1688. The children used the surname Lundin and had virtually no contact with their father.

After Sophie's death, John married Euphemia Wallace and had another seven children, who were, for the most part, brought up in France. John's son, who became the second Earl of Melfort, took part in the 1715 Jacobite uprising, and his grandsons were senior officers in the French Royal Écossais Regiment.

By 1673, John was the representative of the Crown in Scotland and was given a commission in the Foot Guards. By 1679, he was Deputy Governor of Edinburgh Castle and the following year was made Lieutenant-General and Master of Ordnance. James, having been given a lot of power in Scotland by his elder brother, Charles II, was made High Commissioner to the Parliament of Scotland in 1681. This enabled him to create a power base with Catholics and led to the Test Act in Scotland, requiring unconditional loyalty to the monarch 'regardless of religion', but with a qualifier to uphold the Protestant religion.[392]

Further honours followed for Drummond including the post of Treasurer Depute of Scotland in 1682, and two years later joint Secretary of State for Scotland with his elder brother, James Drummond being made Lord Chancellor. This ensured both brothers were perfectly situated to influence James when Charles II died in 1685.

When James succeeded to the throne, John and James, Duke of Perth, converted to Catholicism and became close to the new king. They both urged James not to compromise on his religious policies – as if James needed any encouragement on that front.

Initially, James was supported by the people, who assumed he would not try to weaken the Protestant Church in England or Scotland, but by 1685, John and James were more or less ruling Scotland, even though they spent most of their time in London. They fed James misinformation about the true state of affairs, to suit their own agenda.

The fact that they had converted to Catholicism led them to support James in policies that were, at best ill-timed, and at worst undermined what support James did have. The truth was that the king's policies destabilised Scotland, but of course, Drummond never told him that. This situation was exacerbated when the Scottish Parliament was suspended and Queensberry forced to resign because he did not support tolerance for Catholics or Protestant dissenters.[393]

In 1686, John Drummond was created Earl of Melfort and given a place on the Privy Council in England. The earldom was created in the peerage in Scotland and outlawed by William III in 1694, and in 1695, Drummond was attainted by Act of Parliament and stripped of his honours.[394]

His appointment to the Privy Council caused much antagonism, especially among the Tories because it meant James' closest advisor was isolated from the mainstream and filling the king's head with misinformation. Drummond was also unpopular for driving the creation of the Order of the Thistle, which rewarded Scottish Catholics as well as the Earl of Arran, who was sympathetic to them. The earl was later imprisoned in the Tower of London by William III, and died after fighting a duel in 1715.

In the early part of James' reign, many were prepared to put up with his Catholicism because they feared another civil war. By 1688, that had swung 180 degrees to the opinion that the only thing stopping another civil war would be for James to be deposed. James fled. Drummond went with him.[395]

He urged James to leave by telling him that William's reign would be a very short disaster, since he would never be able to satisfy his Orange followers, and that Louis XIV would soon reinstate James.[396]

It is true that some Jacobites were disillusioned with William's rule, especially after the Presbyterians in Scotland had declared for William. This led Drummond's elder brother, James, to be imprisoned. King James asked Viscount Dundee, who had a lot of influence with the Highland clans, for help, but although their actions were initially successful, Dundee died, and the Highlanders became disunited.[397]

Those who remained loyal landed with James in Ireland. Here, Drummond proved to be unpopular with virtually everybody. He mismanaged the military so badly that he was blamed for the failure of the Siege of Derry and the defeat at Newtownbutler in 1689. So strong was the view of Drummond as an incompetent commander, he received threats to his life. He asked James to be allowed to return to France, and left Ireland.[398]

Even in exile, from the relative safety of France, Drummond continued to press for an invasion and, eventually, the French agreed. Of course, he had to draft another uncompromising Jacobite declaration as a forerunner, one that was published by James in 1692 saying that once he was restored to his kingdom, there would be no pardons for anybody who had been disloyal. Good move. Not! This lost James support from both French and English Jacobites.[399]

It did not help that the French fleet was destroyed by bad weather and the combined Anglo/Dutch fleet at Cape La Hogue later in 1692.[400] Those who had remained loyal to James were infuriated when a letter, drafted by Drummond, but read out in the Scottish Parliament as a letter from James, demanded obedience on an *or else* basis. The letter caused public fury in Scotland, which only proved James consistently learned absolutely nothing from his life experiences.

Drummond was forced to resign his post in the exiled court in 1694, and given the post of ambassador to Rome. He failed to persuade the Pope to support James and one wonders if he was given the job just to get him out of the way. His career was over, but after James died in 1701, Drummond wrote a letter to his elder brother, James, that somehow was 'misdirected' and landed in London. The contents caused him to be accused of treason.[401]

After James' death, Louis XIV granted Drummond the honours William had taken from him, but they were as if he were a French peer —Duc de Melfort. They were not recognised by successive English and then British governments.

Drummond died in 1714 and was buried in the Church of Saint-Sulpice in Paris. History, in general, has not been kind to him, and one can understand, given his incompetence and intransigence, why. One historian said his career was 'based on flattery, officiousness and subservience to James' exalted conception of prerogative'.

John Miller's book does not mince words about Drummond: 'He was a brazen liar, insufferably vain and v indictive [*sic*] who insisted on handling all business himself while lacking the memory or application to execute it properly. His main objective was to perpetuate his own influence and to this end he flattered and encouraged James' misconceptions and slighted all criticism, however constructive'.

'He has a blind complaisance for whatever he sees that the King wants', wrote d'Avaux. 'What Lord Melfort tells him always seems to him so good and so well considered that he does not consider the representations of others. Melfort played on James' stubbornness and flattered him even when he was wrong. This made James believe that Lord Melfort is almost the only man who advises him well and loves his interests; and Melfort, to confirm the King in this opinion, makes him distrust everyone'.[402]

To Drummond's credit, however, is his astute creation of two art collections. The first, in England, he was forced to leave behind when he fled. The second, in France, was later sold by his second wife, Euphemia, who lived to the grand old age of 90![403]

Richard Talbot, Earl of Tyrconnel

Richard Talbot was born in 1630/31, probably in Dublin. He was one of sixteen children and the youngest of eight sons. The Talbot family was descended from a Norman family who settled in Leinster in the twelfth century, and were, and remained, a Catholic family.

Very little is known about his upbringing. We do know that three of his brothers entered the Church in Europe, and a little about another brother, Peter.

Talbot was taller and stronger than was usual of the period, described as 'one of the tallest men in England and possessed of a fine and brilliant exterior'. In other words, he was considered extremely handsome. However, he was also extremely short-tempered and was known to snatch his wig from his head and throw it on the floor, or, occasionally on the fire. He also had a reputation for duelling, becoming known as 'Fighting Dick Talbot'.

He began his military career in the Confederate Wars that followed the 1641 Irish Rebellion. He was a cavalry cornet, which has nothing to do with the musical instrument, but was a junior rank in the cavalry. When, in 1647, Parliamentary forces defeated the Irish at Dungan's Hill, most of the survivors were butchered, but Talbot, possibly because of his young age, was ransomed.

In 1649, he was part of the royalist force besieged in Drogheda. He only survived because he was so badly injured he was thought to be dead. However, possibly helped by a parliamentary soldier, he was disguised as a woman, and escaped. He fled from Ireland, and eventually turned up with many other exiles in Madrid.

In 1655, a royalist agent called Daniel O'Neill took Talbot to meet Charles II, then in exile. Talbot volunteered to go to England and assassinate Oliver Cromwell. However, details of the plot were leaked and Talbot ended up being arrested. He was detained, but then released, only to be arrested a few months later when another would-be assassin, James Halsall, was caught.

Talbot was questioned at Whitehall, with Oliver Cromwell being present. Cromwell, allegedly, claimed kinship with him, asking why he had wanted to kill him when he, Cromwell 'never prejudiced him in his life'. Talbot's brother, Peter, said this story was untrue and that, in hearing of it 'nothing made me laugh more'.

Talbot was threatened with torture and sent to the Tower of London. However, in keeping with his character, he spent the only money he had left buying alcohol and plying Cromwell's servants with it until they were completely drunk, before climbing down a rope and escaping. He was quite good at getting out of these scrapes, wasn't he? Some of the old-guard royalists declared he had given Cromwell information and been allowed to escape. I prefer the 'getting the servants drunk' version.[404]

In 1656, in the pivotal moment of his life, he was introduced to James, Duke of York. Padraig Lenihan in his book on Talbot, *The Last Cavalier*, states, 'When young Dick Talbot elbowed his way into the little court of the exiled James Duke of York in 1657 he began the relationship that would structure his entire life and career'.[405]

They developed an instant, lifelong friendship that never faltered. James appointed Talbot to be a gentleman of the bedchamber, and put him in charge of James' own regiment. This was against the advice of the Duke of Ormond, another of the old guard, who considered Talbot to be unreliable in his actions and his adherence to Catholicism. However, he acquitted himself well in Flanders and at the Siege of Dunkirk in 1658.

When Charles II was restored to the thrones of England and Scotland, Talbot was confirmed in his position as gentleman of the bedchamber and sent on diplomatic missions. The 1662 Act of Settlement was passed and Talbot became a 'land agent' for royalists wanting a reversal of Cromwell's land settlement in Ireland. He acted for James and other court figures, and the following year began a campaign for Catholic landowners to have their forfeited estates returned, and any new cases to be presented in a new act of parliament. He clashed with the Duke of Ormond again and ended up being sent to the Tower for a month by Charles.

Talbot spent the following years cementing his place in James' entourage and building links with upcoming men in an effort to oust the old guard. He was a divisive figure at court, being very domineering and having 'strong opinions expressed with much swearing'.

In 1669, he married Katherine Baynton and the couple had two daughters before she died in 1679. I do not imagine her husband was an easy man to live with. The same year as their marriage, the Duke of Ormond was dismissed, and Charles began to ease the restrictions on Catholics. By 1670, Talbot was representing himself as an 'agent general' for Irish Catholics lobbying for the land question to be reopened. Initially, things seemed to be going well, but the movement collapsed in 1673 when the English Parliament made counter-moves against the Catholics.

The situation worsened when the Test Act was passed and James resigned, thus telling everyone he had converted to Catholicism. He could no longer protect Talbot, who was effectively barred from court for the next decade. He spent time on his estates in Yorkshire and at Luttrellstown in County Dublin, planning out a new garden.[406]

In 1679, after the Popish Plot, Talbot fled to France. His brother, Peter, was not so lucky and was arrested, dying in prison in 1680. In France, and by now widowed, Talbot met an old flame, Frances Jennings, sister of Sarah Churchill, the future Duchess of Marlborough, who would cause so much trouble in William and Mary's reign by fomenting discord between the joint monarchs and Mary's sister, Anne. Talbot and Frances were married in 1681, and she gave him another daughter.

After the Rye House Plot in 1683, Talbot returned to London. Charles II issued a warrant stating that he could live in Ireland, keep horses and arms, and move about freely. All this was helped enormously by the fact that James was, once more, in the ascendant and his status as heir to the throne confirmed.

1685 was an important year. Charles II died, so England lost a politically astute king who knew when to compromise and work his way through the political minefield. James ascended the throne. Unlike his elder brother, he was pig-headed and refused to compromise on anything. However, initially, all seemed hopeful and the rebellions by the Duke of Monmouth in England and the Duke of Argyll in Scotland were quashed very quickly.

James created Talbot Baron of Talbotstown, Viscount Baltinglass and Earl of Tyrconnel, the latter for the second time. He was sent to Ireland as Commander-in-Chief of the Irish army and began to accelerate the recruitment of Catholics to the army. So much so, that by 1686, two-thirds of the army was Catholic and forty per cent of the officers were, too.

At the time Clarendon, James' father-in-law, was viceroy in Ireland. He was very concerned about Talbot's focus on promoting Catholics, saying, 'the Irish talk of nothing now, but recovering their lands and bringing the English under their subjection'.[407] Despite this, Talbot continued to push for the improvement of the legal status of Irish Catholics, although James was not so keen. However in 1686, Catholics were appointed to the Irish Privy Council and one Catholic judge to each of the three common law courts. Talbot continued to push for the Irish land question on behalf of Catholics. James was more than reluctant to do this since English Catholics had written to him urging him not to offend the Protestants.

Clarendon continued to find Talbot a thorn in his side in Ireland. 'Whether my lord Tyrconnel will continue to be so terrible as he is at present, nothing but time will determine.' It would not be a problem for long, however, as in 1687, Talbot was made Deputy of Ireland and Clarendon dismissed. James gave Talbot strict orders that he was not to dismiss anyone on the grounds of their religion, and he also vetoed a statutory solution to the land question, softening the blow with a nebulous possibility that he might, at some time in the future, in the fullness of time, when the time was right etc., allow the question to be discussed in parliament. James did his best to clip Talbot's wings by making him deputy under Thomas Sheridan, who became chief secretary.

However, Talbot, being Talbot, pushed ahead filling posts in every administrative department with Catholics, except the Irish treasury, which remained in Protestant hands. By making new borough charters, he also made the local administrations Catholic controlled, in readiness for a future parliamentary sitting.

By 1688, Talbot was in his late fifties. He had no son, just daughters who were Protestant. Where the fly emerged from the ointment was when it became clear his Catholic reforms had been enacted so quickly, he destabilised all of James' dominions. If these things could happen in Ireland that fast, it could spread to England, Scotland and Wales.

Two things hastened the demise of James' reign. First, was the birth of a healthy boy to his Catholic queen, bringing back the spectre of Catholic oppression à la Mary Tudor. The second was James' stupidity in the matter of the seven bishops, who were imprisoned. These events destroyed his political authority.

Talbot recognised this and warned his friend that there was a plot afoot in Holland. Initially, James refused to believe him. When he realised it was true, he ordered Talbot to send 2500 Irish troops to England, including their crack regiment, the Foot Guards. While obeying, Talbot realised it was leaving Ireland massively vulnerable, but the troops were better employed keeping England and Scotland safe.[408]

Talbot then faced a series of challenges. Many Protestants had fled to Ulster or England. Despite attempting to control this with his Catholic army units, they failed at Enniskillen and Derry. He then considered negotiating with William of Orange on the understanding that Catholics were given a guarantee that they would retain their positions in the army and government. William, much more enlightened than most, believed religion had nothing to do with monarchy and was quite amenable to the idea. However, Talbot changed his mind and did not open negotiations.

At the beginning of 1689, he issued warrants to massively expand the Irish army by some 40,000 troops, despite there being very little money to pay them and having very few experienced commanders to lead them.

James landed in Kinsale in March 1689 intending to use Ireland as a base. He met Talbot and created him Duke of Tyrconnel and Marquess of Tyrconnel. Talbot was concentrating on preparing for a sitting of the Irish Parliament to raise taxes for James and pass a new Act of Settlement. Just as events came to the boil, he fell seriously ill, not returning to his duties until August, five months later. In the interim, parliament refused to raise taxes or enact Talbot's proposals for a change to the Act of Settlement.

By July 1689, James' forces were suffering reverses all over the place, including a threat from the English to march on Dublin. Talbot argued against defending Dublin, advising James, 'I am not for venturing the loss of all to preserve a pace which you must lose as soon as the battle is lost'. Instead, he urged James to flee to France and the two sides retired for the winter.

During the ensuing Battle of the Boyne, Talbot's cavalry was one of the few Jacobite regiments to mount fierce resistance to William's forces. After the defeat, he emerged as leader of the 'Peace Party', opposed by Patrick Sarsfield's 'War Party'. Talbot argued for a settlement with William, but sailed to James in France urging him to lengthen the war in order to negotiate a better peace.

Talbot fell sick in Brittany, not returning to Ireland until 1691, when he received a welcome from troops weary of war. He was replaced as Lord Deputy by Charles Chalmot de Saint-Ruhe, a French officer. He travelled to Athlone where he was treated with utter contempt, so he went back to Limerick and was thus blameless for the defeats at Athlone and Aughrim, where Saint-Ruhe was killed. He tried to re-establish his authority at Limerick but died of apoplexy after a 'merry dinner' with Saint-Ruhe's deputy.

Talbot made a lot of enemies in his lifetime, but there is very little left of any contemporary correspondence. This has led to opinions of him being based on papers left by his enemies, so he did get a negative press. One historian called him 'a figure midway between a buffoon and a villain'.[409]

The historian, Macauley, wrote a history of England that became very popular in the nineteenth century. He called Talbot a 'foul-mouthed thug, brazen liar, childish braggart, shameless pimp'. In *The Irish Times* in 1958, J. P. Kenyon referred to Talbot as a 'bogtrotter' who spoke for 'the rapacious, ignorant, anarchic forces of Irish Catholicism at the lowest stage of civilisation in Western Europe'. Don't you just love historians who demonstrate their impartiality!

More recently, Talbot has received a more sympathetic press. Padraig Lenihan says: 'Talbot could have lived uneventfully and comfortably but he was driven (and that is not too strong a word) to use his high connections to redress a communal and national grievance by blocking, subverting, or unravelling Cromwell's punitive land confiscations and thereby restoring Irish Catholics to their rightful place in their own country'.[410]

What is also true, and must be considered is that Talbot's perceived vices were typical of those of the Stuart court he inhabited.

William III and Mary II

Jonathan Keates, in his biography of William and Mary, states that many British people believe our democracy came from the Greeks. He argues that, in real terms, it came from William III. His predecessor and father-in-law, James II, had, with tunnel-visioned determination, tried to return the country to Roman Catholicism, and had, in consequence, kick-started the Glorious Revolution of 1688.

When James fled – effectively abdicating, according to parliament – the throne was offered initially to Mary, his daughter, and William's wife. However, William would not countenance that at all, and Mary was not keen to become queen anyway. A compromise was reached whereby, for the first and only time in British history, the country has had joint monarchs.

Where does the democracy bit come in, I hear you ask? The system of government Britain enjoys comes, in the main, from William's clear-sighted realisation that, in order to rule, he needed to compromise. In discussions with parliament, he agreed to restrictions on the power of the monarch that would have had his predecessors spinning in their graves. It was tacitly agreed that parliament would run the country and the monarch would not.[411]

So how did a Dutch prince come to rule England? Princess Mary, daughter of Charles I was married to Prince Willem of Orange-Nassau at the age of 9. This was an expedient/diplomatic marriage designed to have an English alliance with a Protestant state to help Charles' struggle with parliament. I use the term English, not British, because until the Act of Union in 1707, the English and Scottish nations were not a union. Sorry Wales, you just get clumped in with England.

The Dutch were happy with the marriage because they saw it as a lever to detach England from Spanish influence. The Spanish had, until about sixty years previously, ruled over the Dutch provinces. The one person not happy with the marriage was Princess Mary. She was a typical spoiled Stuart brat, always standing on her dignity as a princess of England, daughter and granddaughter of a king, tactless, and high-handed. It is an understatement to say she did not get on with her mother-in-law, Amalia, who had started life as a lady-in-waiting to the queen of Bohemia.

They loathed each other. A successful social climber with all the power on the one hand and a haughty, entitled, harridan, and no power on the other. It didn't help that Amalia saw Mary as nothing more than the means to get a male heir for Orange. In 1650, Mary became pregnant. A month before her child was born, her husband died of smallpox.

The child, a boy, was born on 4 November and christened William Henry. A child of state from the instant he emerged from the womb, William never really had a childhood. To make things worse, he was born with a spinal deformity and had lifelong asthma, which worsened as he grew older. That said, he had his mother's dark eyes and sensual mouth, but they were mixed with a hook nose and a pale complexion.[412]

It did not help family relations when his mother wanted to name him Charles after her father and brother. She lost. The Supreme Court of Holland ruled that William's guardianship should be between his mother, his paternal grandmother, Amalia, and Frederick William, Elector of Brandenburg. However, Mary showed absolutely no interest in his early years and the child was brought up mainly by governesses. Because he was seen as the leader of the Orange Party, William was brought up a Calvinist. In 1659, he began studies at the University of Leiden, and although, officially, he was never enrolled as a student, he stayed for seven years.

In 1660, his often-absent mother died at Whitehall of smallpox. Before her death, she asked her brother, Charles, newly crowned as Charles II, to look after William's interests. At this time the States of Holland controlled William's education. Charles more or less told them to take a running jump, which they did in 1661. The boy's education then became a bone of contention between the 'Oranges' and the pro-republicans.

De Witt, a leading republican, took over William's education, teaching him state affairs and playing real tennis with him. Cromwell had insisted, in the Treaty of Westminster in 1654, that became part of the Dutch Act of Seclusion, that Princes of Orange were excluded from the office of Stadtholder, the governor of the Dutch states. Both Mary and Amalia tried to get this law reversed, because they wanted the position for William. They failed.

After a lot of to-ing and fro-ing, De Witt had to give way when, in 1670, William was admitted to the Council of State, with full voting rights. He also obtained permission to travel to England, to persuade Charles II to repay a debt owed to the House of Orange. Charles was unable to pay, so William simply reduced the debt. While in London, he had issues with the lax and immoral behaviour of Charles and his brother, James.

There was still a lot of debate about making William Captain-General of the Dutch army, but he was given the appointment on his twenty-second birthday. He then wrote to Charles II asking him to put pressure on the Dutch government to appoint him as Stadtholder, in return for his support. Charles ignored the letter. 1672 saw disaster for the Dutch provinces when they were invaded by France, England and Cologne. Louis XIV began trying to extract money from the Dutch. De Witt became very unpopular.

In July 1672, William was finally appointed Stadtholder. He received an offer from Charles II to surrender to England and France and become Sovereign Prince of Holland. William refused, saying 'there is one way to avoid this; die defending it in the last ditch'. This was a reference to the fact that the Dutch waterline had been flooded and the French army were blocked.

Charles II tried to wriggle out of his responsibility for the war by writing a letter declaring he had no option because of De Witt's aggressive tactics. Both De Witt and his brother were murdered and William wasted no time in replacing the Dutch regents with his supporters.

He allied himself with Spain, Brandenburg and the Holy Roman Emperor, Leo I, and then began to force his enemies to withdraw. This included the bombastic and arrogant Louis XIV, who had had visions of ruling the whole of Europe.

In 1674, William was appointed Hereditary Stadtholder. He was also offered other honours, but refused them. 1676 brought another French offensive, which, of course, Louis was certain he would win. However, all it did was make the Dutch/Spanish accord stronger. What changed the balance of everything was when William married Mary, the elder daughter of James, Duke of York and Anne Hyde. The French decided to sign a peace treaty, but Louis, forever after, saw William as 'my mortal enemy', and William was determined Louis would never have universal kingship over Europe.

Louis retaliated by revoking the Edict of Nantes, sending many Huguenot refugees flooding into Holland. William was now a strong candidate for the English throne, especially if, as seemed likely, Catholic James was excluded.[413]

Let us now turn to Mary for a while.

Mary was born in St James's Palace in April 1662, and named after her paternal great-great-grandmother, Mary, Queen of Scots. For most of her life, since Charles II had no legitimate children, she was second in line to the English throne after her father, James, Duke of York. Charles insisted Mary and her younger sister, Anne, were baptised as Anglicans.

The two sisters were mainly brought up at Richmond Palace by Lady Frances Villiers. Their education consisted of music, dancing, drawing, French and religious instruction. Mary is known to have written passionate letters to Frances Apsley, who became uncomfortable with the intensity of Mary's friendship and cooled it a little. That intense friendships between high-born women were common occurrence in the seventeenth century is confirmed in the Alpennia blog: 'underlying it is the firm principle of 17th century social politics that women's best and most lasting relationships were not with men, but with their female friends'.[414]

At the age of 15, Mary was betrothed to William. Charles II had wanted her to marry the French Dauphin, but parliamentary pressure held sway and William was chosen instead. James was totally against the marriage initially, but Lord Danby persuaded him to agree, which he reluctantly did. Charles agreed because he thought a Protestant marriage would make Catholic James more popular in England. It didn't, of course, and nobody with two brain cells to rub together would ever have thought it would.

As a prize for agreeing to the marriage, James was given the unenviable honour of telling the prospective bride. Mary wept all that afternoon and all the following day. In November 1677, the couple were married in St James's Palace, and then left for Holland. They had a very rough sea crossing, could not land in ice-bound Rotterdam, and had to walk through frosty countryside until coaches could pick them up. In December 1677, William and Mary made their formal entry via a procession to The Hague.

Mary, unlike some of her relations, was very personable. She decided she had to make the best of things and, in consequence, became very popular with her new subjects. She became not only devoted to her new country but also to her husband, a difficult task because William had never been taught – and never learned – to court popularity.

She became pregnant but suffered a miscarriage, something some historians believe may have stopped her having further children, which is a shame because she would have made a wonderful mother. She was also ill during 1678–80 and was extremely unhappy at being childless.[415]

Princesses were, of course, expected to produce children, but in this Mary had proved a single failure. It is known she suffered at least two miscarriages, and after that William apparently saw no reason to support his wife or even try for another child. Instead, he turned to Elizabeth Villiers, one of Mary's ladies-in-waiting, who was known as Squinting Betty.[416]

In May 1684, the Duke of Monmouth was living in the Netherlands. William was probably already planning to become the king of England, and he did not believe Monmouth had enough support to supplant him. Meanwhile, after a rocky start, William and Mary, obviously helped by the Protestant element, became close to each other. Mary, allegedly whilst playing cards in 1685, was told of her uncle's death, that her father was now king of England and that she was now heir-presumptive.

When Monmouth left the Netherlands, William informed James of the fact, and also sent English regiments back to England. Monmouth was defeated. Louis XIV then tried to bolster James by invading Orange and increasing his persecution of the Huguenots. But it was James who really dropped a clanger. He needed his daughter and her Protestant husband to be at odds with each other. He ordered Mary's English staff to inform her that William had a mistress, Elizabeth Villiers by name. A distraught Mary waited outside Villiers' room and caught William leaving it. However, William denied adultery, possibly telling Mary that Villiers was passing on spy intelligence. That's one phrase for it, I suppose. Mary half believed him, dismissed her staff and packed them all back to England.[417] She tried to put up with the situation, but it pained her deeply, until she upbraided her husband, who banished Villiers. For a while. It was not long before his mistress returned, however, and Mary simply learned to put up with the state of affairs, so to speak.

In 1685, William decided to try and appease James while not upsetting the Protestants. He wrote an open letter to the English people saying he disapproved of James' Catholicism. English politicians began urging him to invade. In truth, nothing much happened until James' queen, Mary of Modena, gave birth to a healthy boy in June 1688. Everyone knew he would be brought up a Catholic and the spectre of religious persecution raised its head so seriously that pleas to William to invade increased. William always referred to the child as 'the pretended Prince of Wales'.

Mary suffered agonies of guilt over the split between her father and her husband, but, being a steadfast Anglican, she decided that William had acted by necessity 'to save the Church and the State'. In 1688, William landed at Brixham, stating 'the liberties of England and the Protestant religion, I will maintain'.[418]

James' support dwindled; he fled, was captured and then allowed to escape to France. William was the last person to successfully invade England using armed force. A still guilt-ridden Mary was ordered by him to appear cheerful. Sarah Churchill, whose raison-d'être was to foment as much trouble for people as she could, criticised the new queen as being *cold* towards her father.

Initially, parliament tried to make Mary sole queen. However, William wasn't having that and Mary, believing wives should defer to their husbands, stated she had no desire to reign. She declared her opinion 'knowing my heart is not made for a kingdom and my inclination leads me to a retired, quiet life'.[419] But they couldn't ignore her completely. James was deemed to have abdicated. The throne was vacant. Parliament offered it to William and Mary as joint sovereigns – 'the sole and full exercise of the regal power … executed by the said Prince of Orange in the names of the said Prince and Princess during their joint lives'. This declaration was later extended to exclude not only James and his heirs, other than Anne, the Protestant sister of the new queen, but all Catholics. 'It hath been found by experience that it is inconsistent with the safety and welfare of this Protestant kingdom to be governed by a papist prince.'

Neither William nor Mary enjoyed their coronation. Mary declared it to be 'all vanity' and William considered it 'popish'. And it was just as well they were joint monarchs because William spent most summers in Europe on campaign, leaving Mary to rule with a council of nine members. She hated it, but stepped up to the plate every time.

While they had been crowned in England, Scotland was another matter. Reading the runes correctly, William sent a conciliatory letter to the Estates of Scotland. Perfectly in keeping with his character, James sent arrogant, intransigent orders. Support rose for the new monarchs and in April 1689, Scotland declared that William and Mary were their monarchs.

Where William really scored was agreeing to the Bill of Rights, which not only complained about James' actions, but put many restrictions on the power of the monarchy. It was also agreed that if William and Mary had no children, the throne would pass to Anne and any children William might have if Mary died and he remarried. But Catholics and those who married Catholics were excluded.

So, the nations on the British mainland were sorted. But there was still Ireland. The Battle of the Boyne fixed that. William tried to balance policy between the Whigs and the Tories. When the Whigs expected to dominate following elections, he began to favour the Tories, but when they didn't support him, he turned to the Whigs. It was a Whig government that created the Bank of England.[420]

To those who were unsure how the *joint* part of joint monarchy would work, Mary soon reassured them. Abel Boyer summed up her contribution. 'While he went abroad, as the arbiter of Europe to wage a just war, she stayed at home to maintain peace and administer justice; he was to oppose and conquer enemies, she to maintain and gain friends.'[421]

From 1688–1697, William continued to go on campaign, fighting in Europe each summer. He left Mary, with his advice, and she proved to be more than competent. She refrained from interfering in politics, but stepped in when her uncle, Henry Hyde, plotted to restore James to the throne. She did the same thing in 1692, when John Churchill, whose wife was the prima donna in Princess Anne's court, was dismissed for plotting against William.

In fact, 1692 was a dismal year for Mary. She fell ill with a fever, and missed attending church for the first time in years. She also missed visiting her sister, Anne, who was going through a very difficult labour, resulting in the child dying. Mary visited her but instead of offering her sister a shoulder upon which to cry – and who could know better than she how it felt to lose a child – Mary upbraided Anne about the degree of power Sarah Churchill exercised in her circle. The two sisters never saw each other again.

Mary was always expected to outlive her asthmatic husband and obese, frequently ill, sister. She was tall, around 5' 11" (about 180 cms). She was fit, walked regularly between Whitehall and Kensington, prayed twice a day and was seen as strong. Depicted by Jacobites as an unfaithful daughter, who had destroyed her father for her own gain, she was, in fact, modest and diffident. Often seen as being under William's thumb, she proved to be capable and confident.[422]

William and Mary shared a love of making homes – notably Kensington Palace at that time, in a small village outside London. William is also credited as reviving a love of gardening in England through projects he oversaw at Hampton Court Palace and Kensington, developing new hybrids.[423]

It was a continuing sadness to Mary that her husband was unfaithful to her. She wrote a letter in 1694 saying that continual worry had destroyed her looks, that she was only 32, but wondering if her husband would continue to love her. When a ruby dropped out of a ring William had given her after their wedding, it seemed like an ill omen. On 19 December, Mary was suffering from a heavy cold when she saw a rash on her arms. She instantly realised she had smallpox. In a typical Mary gesture, she ordered all her servants who had not had the disease to leave Kensington immediately.

She shut herself in her private rooms, sorted her papers, burning many letters from James and William and giving instructions about how her debts were to be paid. When she had done that, she sent for her husband, who was at Whitehall. To him she had written a special letter. It was destroyed, but we do know that in it she accused him of sacrificing her happiness by his relationship with Squinting Betty, and compromising his ultimate salvation.

Only then did she go to bed and allow the doctors in. The minute William realised the truth, he collapsed sobbing and refusing all consolation. He spoke to Burnet: 'There is no hope for the queen. From being the happiest, I am now the miserablest [*sic*] creature upon earth. I have never known one single fault in her.'

Mary faced her death serenely. She told the Archbishop of Canterbury that she 'had nothing to do, but to look up to God, and submit to his will'. Mary II died in the early morning of 28 December 1694. William retreated from public view and sent Squinting Betty packing. Mary was buried in Westminster Abbey in March 1695 to the accompaniment of Henry Purcell's *Thou Knowest, Lord, the Secrets of our Heart*.[424]

William's closeness to Bentinck and van Keppel led to accusations of homosexuality, especially as he now had no mistress. These close friendships aroused jealousy at court, leading to a 1696 plot to kill William and put James back on the throne. It failed but led to a surge of support for William. The ringleader, John Fenwick, was beheaded. In 1697, Louis XIV finally recognised William as king of England, and his support for James tailed off. That, however, was changed when Charles II of Spain died leaving all his territories to Louis' grandson. At that point, Louis recognised James and Mary of Modena's son as the *de jure King of England* – king by right. All this kerfuffle led to the War of the Spanish Succession (1701–1714).

In 1700, the only surviving son of Princess Anne, Prince William, Duke of Gloucester, who, after the shock of Mary's early death, became a favourite of the king, died of hydrocephalus – water on the brain. He was only 11 years old and the Protestant heir after Anne.[425]

To settle the question about the succession, the Act of Settlement in 1701 declared that after Anne and any children she might yet have, the throne would pass to the Electress Sophia of Hanover, a granddaughter of James I, and her Protestant heirs. Catholics were, once more, debarred from the throne.

Early in 1702, while out riding, William fell from his horse, which stumbled into a molehill. He broke his collarbone, but developed pneumonia. For years afterwards, Jacobites raised a glass to 'the little gentleman in black velvet'.[426]

When William realised he was dying, he showed 'a clear and full presence of mind and a wonderful tranquillity'. He sent for Bentinck, pressed his friend's hand to his heart, sighed, and died. While his body was being prepared for burial, a ring containing a lock of Mary's hair was found tied around his arm.[427]

History has not always been kind to William III. He brought to the monarchy one feature of life in Holland – that of tolerance towards other faiths. In working with all religions, he shaped a new kind of state in which religious differences were not a basis for exile, persecution, martyrdom or a cause for civil war. What changed was the understanding of the monarch's role in Britain. Dour, possibly charmless he might have been, but his legacy for Britain is still a huge part of the national psyche.

Hans Willem Bentinck

Bentinck was born in July 1649 in Diepenheim, Holland. He came from a noble family. As a child, he was appointed page of honour and chamberlain to the future William III. When William fell ill with smallpox in 1675, Bentinck slept in his master's bed to help the sick man 'absorb animal spirits' from his healthy body.[428] This devotion was the beginning of a lifelong, close friendship, but not as some have suggested, a homosexual one. William did not have the time or the inclination for affairs because of his burden of work on state matters.[429]

In 1677, William sent Bentinck to the English court to enlist help for the Dutch against Louis XIV, and also to negotiate the marriage between William and the elder daughter of James, Duke of York, Princess Mary. When the newly-married couple returned to Holland, Bentinck accompanied them, as did the sisters, Elizabeth and Anne Villiers. Within months, Bentinck and Anne were married. They had seven children before her death in 1688.[430]

In the early 1680s, Bentinck travelled to England on William's behalf, in a diplomatic role. When William began preparing to invade England in 1688, Bentinck went to the German princes to ask for support for the enterprise, or, failing that, their neutrality. He was prominent in the plans for invasion, supervising the arrangements, raising money, hiring transport, and preparation work on the landing sites, as well as organising a massive propaganda campaign.

After the Glorious Revolution, in 1689, Bentinck was given many honours: Viscount Woodstock, Baron Cirencester and the second incarnation of Earl of Portland. When James landed in Ireland in an effort to regain his throne, Bentinck commanded a cavalry unit at the Battle of the Boyne. He was wounded in the Battle of Landen and also present at the Siege of Namur in 1695, but his main role remained that of a diplomat.

In 1690, he mediated between William and the burgomasters of Amsterdam. Five years later, he became enmeshed in a corruption scandal involving the East India Company whose board had been heavily involved in bribery and corruption. Bentinck was cleared. When George Barclay led an unsuccessful Jacobite plot to assassinate William, Bentinck was informed of the conspiracy and was instrumental in thwarting it. The ramifications led to the House of Commons swearing a loyalty oath to William, saying his escape had been divine providence.[431]

Bentinck was also involved in the negotiations for the Peace of Ryswick, that ended the Nine Years' War between France and the 'Grand Alliance', consisting of the Dutch Republic, England and the Hapsburgs. He negotiated the partition of the Spanish monarchy with Louis XIV, and signed two partition treaties on William's behalf.

In the meantime, Bentinck had become very jealous of Arnold van Keppel, and, in 1699, he resigned all his household offices, but retained William's friendship and goodwill. The king still sent his friend on diplomatic missions. However, as a foreigner, he was extremely unpopular in England. William gave him 135,000 acres in Ireland, but when he also attempted to give Bentinck a gift of Crown land in Wales, parliament stopped it.

In 1701, he was impeached for his role in the aforementioned partition treaties, but the case against him fell apart. He attended William on the latter's deathbed and was, thereafter, occasionally employed by Queen Anne. As a princess, Anne had told Bentinck to 'check the insolence of Elizabeth Villiers to the Princess of Orange', which was a bit rich, since Bentinck was married to Elizabeth's sister at the time.[432]

Bentinck died in 1709 at his house, Bulstrode Park in Buckinghamshire, and was succeeded by his eldest son, Henry. His fortune was estimated at £850,000 (approximately £128,400,000 in 2024).[433]

Philippe d'Orléans called Bentinck the politest man in Europe, recounting that when they approached a door, Orléans gestured Bentinck should go first, at which point, he thanked him before going through the door.[434]

Rosenheim, in a review of two biographies of Bentinck, highlights that he was an 'Anglo-Dutch favourite' emphasising William's view of a dual responsibility to England and to Europe and that Bentinck was an internationalist. He was seen, despite the enormous influence he had over the king, as executing William's policy, not making it, and viewing politics on an international level. His resignation in 1699, possibly before he could be pushed out of office, ensured that he retained not only William's friendship, but also his wealth and possessions.[435]

Arnold Joost van Keppel: First Earl of Albemarle

Van Keppel was born in 1670, in the De Voorst country house in the Dutch republic, the house being financed by William III. Van Keppel was an heir, part of the junior branch of an ancient family in Gelderland.

He became a page of honour to the future William III in his mid-teens, possibly in 1685, and certainly accompanied him to England in the 1688 Glorious Revolution. The two were close, leading, yet again, to rumours of homosexuality, but no evidence that William indulged in a sexual relation with either Bentinck or van Keppel has ever been discovered, and one can safely assume, that such information would have been assiduously pursued.

Van Keppel is alleged to have come to William's attention when he broke his leg in a hunting accident and made little of the injury. In 1692, he began to receive lands from William, which provoked further speculation about their relationship. In 1695, van Keppel was made groom of the bedchamber and master of the robes. The following year, he was created Viscount Bury and Baron Ashford before being created first Earl of Albemarle in 1697.

Two years later, he was given command of the First Life Guards.[436] He used his influence with William to persuade him to offer John Churchill the post of governor of Prince William, Duke of Gloucester. Churchill was at that time out of favour with William. The king felt threatened by Churchill as a military commander. In addition, he was at odds with Princess Anne, Gloucester's mother, because of the malign influence exercised over the princess by Churchill's wife, Sarah. However, once William realised Churchill was not a threat to him, he offered the post, which improved his relationship with Princess Anne. Churchill, had, of course, been the princess' first choice of governor to her son. Or, more likely, it was Sarah Churchill's choice. This improved Churchill's standing with William, who took him back into his favour.[437]

In 1700, William gave van Keppel lands in Ireland, but parliament forced the king to cancel the grant, so William gave his favourite £50,000 instead (almost £8,681,000 in 2024). William also created van Keppel a Knight of the Garter. He served with both English and Dutch troops, becoming colonel of several regiments, as well as being made governor of 's-Hertogenbosch, a city in The Netherlands.

Van Keppel was both handsome and charismatic, so it is not surprising that Bentinck became very jealous of him and his influence over William.[438] In truth, William found him better company than Bentinck because the latter was so busy with affairs of state and that was all he wanted to discuss with the king. Van Keppel was given honours in Holland, being made Knight of Zutphen, Knight of Holland and West Friesland and Lord van der Voost. In 1702, he was sent to The Netherlands to arrange the next summer campaign. He arrived back in England in time to be at William's deathbed. William gave him the keys to his cabinet, containing the king's private papers, with the words 'You will know what to do with them'.[439]

William bequeathed van Keppel £200,000 (around £39,391,000 in 2024) and the lordship of Bredevoort. He retired to Holland and, as a noble, took his seat in the States General, also becoming a general of cavalry.[440]

In 1705, he visited England and Queen Anne, before going to the University of Cambridge to be given an honorary degree as a doctor of law.[441]

He was present at the battles of Ramillies in 1706 and Oudenaarde in 1708, as well as distinguishing himself at the Siege of Lille. He proved himself to be an able commander under John Churchill, by then Duke of Marlborough, but was defeated at the Battle of Denain in 1712 and taken prisoner. He died in 1718, aged 48, being succeeded by his son, William Anne, one of two children from his marriage to Gertrude, daughter of Major-General Scravenmore.[442]

Following the death of Queen Anne in 1714, van Keppel was sent by the States General to Hanover to congratulate George I, who held him in high regard. He was buried in The Hague.[443]

An interesting fact is that Charles III's queen, Camilla, is descended from van Keppel.

Elizabeth Villiers

Elizabeth was another member of the ubiquitous Villiers family that seems to have almost haunted the Stuart dynasty since George, later first Duke of Buckingham, caught the eye of James I. Elizabeth was first cousin to Barbara Villiers, later Lady Castlemaine and one of Charles II's mistresses.

Elizabeth's parents were asked by Charles II to bring up James' two daughters, Mary and Anne, ensuring that the girls remained Anglicans. Charles, as we have already seen, was very aware of public opinion. He remained determined that nothing would stand in the way of Mary's position as heir to the throne after James and, if the worst happened, which it did, her position as the only Protestant heir. Having spent most of their childhood with the Villiers family, it must have been some solace to the shocked Mary when she was married to William of Orange, that Elizabeth, Anne, and Katherine were able to accompany her when she travelled to The Hague. In common with Mary, Elizabeth developed a deep friendship with Frances Apsley, who we shall meet later. Elizabeth was no beauty, having a cast in one eye that some have attributed to her being short-sighted. This led to her nickname of Squinting Betty.[444] She was also described as 'ungainly, had a passable figure and a long, white, neck'. Dean Swift was much more pointed: 'the good lady squints like a dragon'.[445]

However, despite all this, she attracted William of Orange. Initially, she tried to deflect him by encouraging a Scots mercenary called Captain Wauchop, but William dismissed him and Elizabeth yielded to the inevitable. By 1679, their relationship was the talk of Paris, and most other places. The only person who didn't know was Mary.

And that is when Dr Covell, Mary's chaplain, and her old nanny, Mrs Trelawney, told the British ambassador. He lost no time in running and telling Mary the true situation. In public. Mary was mortified and humiliated, so waited outside Elizabeth's bedchamber and caught William emerging from it. He was furious. She was distraught. They avoided each other for several days. William dismissed Dr Covell and insisted the ambassador was recalled.[446]

Elizabeth was initially expelled, but she soon returned to The Hague. Most historians now agree that her relationship with William was less to do with the physical and more to do with their intellectual connection.[447]

What had initiated Elizabeth's return was a plea from her father to William and Mary, that gossip and rumour was rife in England, and if she were allowed to return to the Dutch court, it would die down. After her return, Mary refused to receive her. Elizabeth went to live with her sister, Katherine, who had married and settled in The Hague. Bentinck, married to the other Villiers sister, Anne, forbade his wife to socialise with Elizabeth.

After the Glorious Revolution, when William and Mary spent a lot of their time at Kensington Palace, Elizabeth lived nearby. Although the affair with William continued, both parties were very discreet.[448]

In 1694, Mary died, and only then did William realise the depth of his feeling for his queen, and the depth of her anguish at his affair with Elizabeth. He dismissed her. That same year, there was an alleged duel between John Law and Edward 'Beau' Wilson, in the course of which Wilson died. It is believed that Law challenged him after being encouraged by Elizabeth, possibly because Wilson was attempting to blackmail her. Law was tried and sentenced to death. The sentence was commuted to a fine because it was only manslaughter. Only?! Wilson's brother appealed this light sentence and had Law imprisoned. However, he escaped and fled to Amsterdam.[449] A year later, Elizabeth married George Hamilton, Brigadier-General of the Royal Scots. William soon created him Earl of Orkney, Viscount Kirkwall, and Lord Dechmont. He was also appointed as Governor of Virginia, an extremely lucrative post. Lucrative enough for him to pay for a deputy to be installed so George never actually had to go there.[450]

In 1695, William also settled part of James II's confiscated Irish estates on Elizabeth. Parliament revoke the grant in 1700.[451]

The couple had a very happy marriage, with three daughters, Anne, Frances, and Henrietta. Elizabeth remained in the royal sphere, entertaining both George I and George II at Clivedon in Buckinghamshire. Interestingly, Clivedon was at the centre of the Profumo scandal in the early 1960s that toppled Harold Macmillan's government.

In 1727, at the age of 70, Elizabeth attended George II's coronation, but she was still the object of ridicule. Mary Wortley Montague described her as 'a mixture of fat and wrinkles … with a considerable pair of bubbys a good deal withered …a great belly that preceded her'.

Elizabeth died at her house in Albemarle Street in 1733 and is buried in Taplow, Buckinghamshire.[452]

Frances Apsley

To be honest, not a great deal is known about Frances Apsley, but she had a significant effect upon the young Mary II and her sister, later Queen Anne.

She was born around 1653 and came from a family with a long history of service to the Crown. She was described as tall and thin with a horsy face. The future Sarah Churchill, then Jennings, referred to Frances as 'The Nag's Head'.

But she was high-spirited and creative, which is probably what drew Mary to her. Soon she was seeing Mary on a daily basis.

Frances' father was Treasurer and Receiver-General to James, Duke of York, and James' spokesman in the House of Commons. He fought as a royalist during the Civil War and was a close political ally of Edward Hyde, Earl of Clarendon, James' father-in-law. He also kept James' finances in order.

Frances' mother served Anne Hyde until the latter's death in 1671. She obtained bedchamber places for both her daughters, Isabella and Frances, and encouraged the correspondence between Frances and Mary and Frances and Anne. She believed, in the common opinion of the day, that these attachments were light and ephemeral; a kind of game of courtly love that meant nothing.

But it is the letters that Mary and Anne wrote to Frances that have come down to us. And I am taking much of this section from Molly McClain's examination of the letters, specifically between Frances and Mary.

In 1675, Mary began their correspondence. She wrote the first of over eighty passionate letters to Frances. In them, she portrayed herself as the neglected but loving wife, calling Frances her 'dearest, dearest, dearest, dearest, dear husband'. In common with her sister, Anne, Mary adopted pen names from seventeenth-century dramas, both girls competing for Frances' affection.

Mary's letters speak of seduction and betrayal, stating that when Frances leaves court, she will forget Mary. In that era, same-sex, erotic relationships were considered to be court entertainment. Mary had been brought up on the fringes of court life. Her main activities were playing cards, gossiping, reading contemporary plays, and attending the theatre and it is the literature of the day that Mary used to inspire her letters.

They have been viewed by historians as lesbianism, or play-acting by girls learning the tenets of love to prepare themselves for relationships with their future husbands. In the letters Mary and Anne wrote to Frances, they both present themselves as dutiful wives. Mary's letters are filled with utterances in terms of marital love and devotion. She called Frances 'Aurelia', drawn from a contemporary drama by Philip Massinger's *The Maid of Honour*.

For this 15-year-old princess, with her head full of courtly love and all the other conventions, the reality of marriage to William must have come as an enormous shock. He came late to his marriage bed on the night of the wedding, having been gambling, and then immediately undressed down to his woollen underwear and climbed into bed. Unsurprisingly, Mary's letters to Frances continued after her marriage. In one she says, 'though I have played the whore a little, I love you of all things in the world'. At this point, Mary was pregnant with the child she would miscarry. To Frances, she called the child she carried a bastard and declared that Frances had been cuckolded by William. However, after Mary's marriage, Frances tried to distance herself. Letters frequently went unanswered or contained sharp replies. What was clear was that Frances was much more clear-sighted about the real situation than the deluded princess. After Mary and William married, the tone of Frances' letters become more formal. By 1682, Frances herself was on the verge of marriage to Sir Benjamin Bathurst and didn't tell Mary, who upbraided her for having to find out from strangers.

So the question is, were Frances' letters more to do with political ambition than true feelings for Mary? What is known is that after William and Mary became joint monarchs, Frances made no attempt to continue the friendship. She was modest and private. She never wrote memoirs, probably in an effort to protect her erstwhile friend.[453] Frances died in 1727.

Queen Anne

Queen Anne was a much better monarch than many historians – until recently – have given her credit for.

Anne was more than aware that the previous fifty years of strife needed a figurehead of stability and throughout her frequently-ill life, she fought to do just that. R. O. Bucholz sums it up by focusing on Anne as a symbol of national unity through the use of 'royal ritual and symbol'.

She made full use of the trappings of ceremony previously associated with the Tudor monarchs and often echoed the sentiments of Elizabeth I to demonstrate her *Englishness*, as well as showing a feminine vulnerability to arouse loyalty and valour in her male courtiers.

Anne was known to be fanatical about protocols and courtly rituals and customs. Jonathan Swift wrote that she would 'observe her domestics of either sex who came into her presence, whether a ruffle, a periwig or the lining of a coat, were unsuitable upon certain times'. Bucholz links this determination for ceremony and ritual to the slights she received at the hands of William and Mary, and so sought redress as queen. She also used royal ceremony and court etiquette as a weapon to display her favouritism or otherwise to individuals.[454]

The future Queen Anne was born in 1665, the second surviving daughter of James, Duke of York and Anne Hyde. She was a product of her family history… 'bred in a civilisation deeply scarred by turmoil and in an age in which the past was a frail and uncertain guide to the future'.[455] James had given a verbal promise to Anne Hyde that he would marry her. Enough for Anne to be 'visibly pregnant' when Charles II made his entry into London in 1660. The daughter of Edward Hyde, future Earl of Clarendon, Anne was fit to be a mistress but not a royal wife. That James married her speaks of his integrity, but also his lack of foresight and demonstrated his father's stubbornness.[456] And we all know where that landed Charles I, don't we.

Princess Anne was born at St James's Palace, London on 6 February 1665 and immediately christened into the Church of England. From that point, she vanished into the obscurity of the nursery at Richmond Palace and the employees there became her family, not her parents. Anne's wet nurse, Martha Farthing, was given a pension of £300 when Anne became queen in 1702, and Martha's daughter, Margery, was regarded as her foster sister.

She inherited ill health from her parents, suffering all her life from defluxion, in other words, a copious discharge from the eyes. She was near-sighted, which had the result that all her life she preferred a closed circle of people around her. At the age of 2, she was sent to her paternal grandmother, Henrietta Maria, in France and put under the care of a French eye specialist, but with little improvement. And, showing her inherited stubbornness, Anne was unwilling ever to admit to her physical infirmities. However, her time in France shaped her openness to continental ideas and people and this was reflected in her later household, which included a Huguenot, a Dutch lady of the bedchamber and several Danish servants.[457]

Whilst still young, Anne lost her mother, grandmother and aunt, which made her feel insecure and uncertain for most of her life. Unlike her Tudor forebears, her education was abysmal, majoring on sewing, embroidery and domestic skills with very little history or geography. And, bearing in mind their position – not to mention the lack of surviving children in the royal family and the huge number of miscarriages and stillbirths – there was virtually no legal or constitutional learning. Neither Mary, her elder sister, nor Anne, ever came to understand the intricacies of English grammar or spelling. However, Anne did receive religious instruction in the tenets of the Church of England, despite her father's disapproval.[458]

In 1677, Mary married William of Orange and went off to The Hague. At the time, Anne was ill with smallpox and could not attend the wedding. She survived, but her governess, Lady Frances Villiers, who also caught it, did not. In 1679, Anne visited her father, James and his new wife, Mary of Modena in Brussels where they had relocated because of the strength of anti-Papist feeling in England. She returned with them and went to stay in Holyrood Palace in Edinburgh, but after that, she never left England.[459]

The year 1682 proved an embarrassing year for Anne, due to John Sheffield, Lord Mulgrave, eighteen years her senior, who wrote some letters to her. The whole thing blew up into an overblown scandal with rumours that Mulgrave had seduced the princess. He was banned from court, but the whole furore hastened negotiations for Anne's marriage.[460]

The negotiations were initially for her to marry George of Hanover, but eventually, the Lutheran George of Denmark was chosen. Her uncle, Lawrence Hyde and Robert Spencer, second Earl of Sunderland negotiated the marriage and it was eventually announced. William of Orange took offence that he had not been consulted or even notified of the betrothal.[461] He was also concerned that it would reduce his influence with the English court. Anne and George became a devoted couple despite many setbacks and griefs.

In 1685, James attempted to get Anne to baptise her daughter as a Catholic. She refused point blank, writing afterwards, 'the doctrine of the Church of Rome is wicked and dangerous' in a letter to her sister, Mary. Early in 1687, Anne miscarried yet again. George caught smallpox, as did their two young daughters, who both died. Later in 1687, she miscarried again.[462]

However, during that year, with Mary living in Holland, Anne became the figurehead for the Protestants. Just in time, too, because the following year, Mary of Modena gave birth to a healthy boy who was, of course, baptised as a Catholic. The phrase 'cat amongst the pigeons' comes to mind! At the time, Anne was in Bath and so not present at the birth, which was one of the foundations of the later bedpan baby rumour.

Happiness was just around the corner for Anne and George when, in 1689, she gave birth to a boy, Prince William of Gloucester, who, although sickly, lived. But it was now that the lives of William and Mary, who had just been crowned as joint monarchs, and Anne and George, became more difficult. To be fair, this was mostly because of Anne's close friendship with Sarah Churchill, who dominated the insecure, unconfident princess, and was cordially hated by her sister and brother-in-law. Despite that, William made Sarah's husband, John, Earl of Marlborough. Anne asked William for Richmond Palace, which he refused. She also asked for George to be given a position in the army. William refused that, too. In fact, during the 1690s, the couple suffered financial difficulties, mainly due to William's treatment of them. He put a restriction on their Danish properties, which meant their income was much reduced. However, Anne applied to parliament for money, and, despite William's opposition, parliament awarded her an annual grant of £50,000. It was a public defeat for William and Mary and did not go down well.[463] What a shame. How sad. Never mind.

When it became clear that Sarah Churchill held sway in Anne's circle, William dismissed John Churchill, but Anne refused to dismiss Sarah. It was around this time that Anne became Mrs Morley – although she seldom spelled it correctly – and Sarah became Mrs Freeman in their correspondence. William III became Caliban! He was so angry, he dismissed Sarah from the royal household and Anne moved to Syon House. William stripped her of her guard of honour and courtiers were forbidden to visit her. However, in 1694, Queen Mary died, which shocked everyone because she had always been much healthier than either her husband or sister. The net result was that William and Anne were publicly reconciled because she was now heir apparent. Her honours were restored and she moved into St James's Palace. William also gave his sister-in-law Mary's jewels, but he would not allow her any say in government or make her regent when he was absent from England.[464]

In 1697, Sarah took a decision she would come to regret. She found a place for her first cousin, Abigail Hill, as a woman of the bedchamber. Women of the Bedchamber performed menial tasks, and were different from ladies of the bedchamber in that they performed tasks that no lady of the peerage would be expected to undertake. Anne found Abigail to be gentle in her treatment. She insisted Abigail remain a 'woman' of the bedchamber instead of the more usual 'lady', someone highborn who could not be expected to perform lowly tasks. Edward Gregg refers to Sarah's later writings about Abigail as 'a classic of polished malice'.[465]

In 1700, Anne underwent her final pregnancy, which ended in a stillbirth and, incredibly sadly, William of Gloucester died soon after his eleventh birthday. Anne had had 17 pregnancies, 12 of which ended as miscarriages or stillbirths. Five children were born alive, but all, save William, died in infancy. Various theories as to why she lost so many children have ranged from lupus, through an auto-immune disease to Pelvic Inflammatory Disease. A recent theory has been forwarded by Professor Alice Roberts that Anne suffered from APS (Antiphospholipid Syndrome), also known as 'sticky blood', which attacks the proteins in the blood causing clotting.

Anne also suffered from gout and was usually carried in a sedan chair or pushed in a wheelchair. She was intrepid in her one-horse chaise, being described as 'furiously like Jehu and a mighty hunter like Nimrod'.[466]

In 1702, William died and, at last, Anne ascended the throne. She was a moderate Tory whose politicians shared her Anglican religious views. Her reign was to confirm England as a two-party state, the Whigs and the Tories. And since Sarah Churchill was an ardent Whig, who believed all Tories were closet Jacobites, the scene was set for plenty of strife. The political system at that time was very different from today, even though there were only two political parties – Whigs and Tories. Members of each party would be asked by the monarch to take on certain roles in government and the monarch was able to dismiss a minister from office.

Anne's coronation was a rushed affair, taking place on 23 April, St George's Day, just over a month after William's death. She said: 'there is not anything you can expect or desire from me which I shall not be ready to do for the happiness and prosperity of England'. She immediately made her husband Lord High Admiral, controller of the Royal Navy. Churchill became Duke of Marlborough and Captain-General of the army. Sarah was awarded the roles of groom of the stole and mistress of the robes. The Churchill star was definitely in the ascendant.[467]

The War of the Spanish Succession began in 1702 when Charles II of Spain died childless. It rumbled on until 1714, thus encompassing the whole of Anne's reign, and was all about who should now control the Spanish empire. The Tories were against the war, the Whigs in favour of it, but, after Churchill's victory at Blenheim in 1704, the war became more popular. Anne herself became a patron of the arts. She awarded the composer, Handel, an annual pension of £200 and knighted Sir Isaac Newton in Cambridge.

However, in 1703, a huge weed flew into Sarah Churchill's garden when she was suddenly summoned to Cambridge because her son, Lord Blandford, had caught smallpox and died. His parents, stunned by their son's death, went to St Albans. The loss almost turned Sarah's head. When she finally returned to court, she was more presumptuous than ever. The fracture in the relationship of the queen and her hitherto favourite that had begun with Sarah's almost violent partisanship for the Whigs against Anne's more moderate favouritism for the Tories, widened. Sarah, utterly confident to the point of extreme arrogance about her power over the queen, spent more and more time away from court. This hurt Anne very deeply and she began to see the Churchills in a more political light.[468] When Sarah once more lectured Anne that Tories were Jacobites, Anne responded with the words 'when you have had a few yeares [*sic*] more experience of that sort of people you are now so partiall to, you will find they are not what they would be thought to be'.[469] It was both a warning and a portent. This was the beginning of Sarah's constant complaint that Anne had changed towards her and Anne's response that she had not.

In 1706, Godolphin and the Churchills forced Anne to accept the Earl of Sunderland as a secretary of state. He was Sarah's son-in-law, and Anne disliked him intensely. She had hated his parents, but in 1702, Sunderland had been vociferous in his opposition to Prince George being able to sit in parliament and Anne never forgave him. Churchill's victory over Anne did strengthen the Whigs in parliament, but it certainly weakened their influence with the queen. In secret, she turned for private advice to Robert Harley.

The year 1707 was a momentous time for the country, because the Act of Union made England and Scotland one nation – Wales had always been considered part of England. The new nation was called Great Britain.[470] However, it was also an important year because of the Bishopric Crisis. The immediate cause was Anne's insistence that two Tory clerics be appointed to the bishoprics of Exeter and Chester, in direct opposition to the Whigs led by Godolphin. Still smarting from her defeat over Sunderland, Anne was determined not to give in to bullying again. The Whigs were incensed that their choices for the vacant sees had not been automatically endorsed by the queen. But the crisis definitely marked the end of Anne's friendship with Sarah and her influence over Godolphin and Churchill. In Anne's view, she was happier with Sarah's husband because he appeared to be closer to the Tories and had close personal friends in Henry St John and Sir Simon Harcourt.[471]

As Sarah's influence declined, Abigail's grew. Now married to Samuel Masham, Abigail was an intermediary between Anne and Robert Harley. In 1708, Godolphin and Churchill again forced Anne's hand, threatening to resign if she did not. Unwillingly, she dismissed Harley. This was also the year Anne vetoed the Scottish Militia Bill – the last British sovereign to veto a parliamentary bill. This was because her half-brother, James Francis Edward Stewart, was looking to land in Scotland and make a bid for the throne. In the event, he was unable to land, but the threat of a Catholic monarch frightened the people.[472]

Anne was also sick to death of Sarah's insatiable demands for money for the building of Blenheim Palace. After the great victory at Blenheim, Anne agreed to fund some of the cost. The Duke of Marlborough added £60,000 (over £11.5 million in 2024) to that when building commenced in 1705. However – wherever Sarah was involved, the word *however* seems to raise its head – her arguments with the architect Vanbrugh added hugely to the cost. Parliament also voted to give money towards the building but no precise sum was ever stated and nor was any thought given to inflation and the extras Sarah kept demanding. Anne grew increasingly disinclined to pay for it and after 1712, stopped paying anything and so did parliament. All work stopped. By that time, the palace had already cost £220,000 (over £38.5 million in 2024) and there was an outstanding bill to workmen for £45,000 (almost £8 million in 2024).[473]

Sarah, incensed that she had only just discovered how much influence Abigail Masham appeared to have gained over the queen, brought a poem to court insinuating that the two were lesbian lovers and all because Anne had given Abigail the rooms at Kensington Palace Sarah was wont to use when she did come to court. Modern historians are now in agreement that Anne regarded Abigail as nothing more than a devoted servant, but the queen never forgave Sarah for the insult.[474]

In 1708, another blow to the queen was the death of her beloved husband at Windsor. And here, Sarah made her final and worst mistake. She hurried Anne from the death chamber, removing a portrait of George and refusing to let Anne have it back, saying it was better not to look on that sort of thing. She completely took over, instructing Anne what to do, not allowing her an instant to grieve and ignoring her feelings, believing they were down to Abigail Masham's influence. The Whigs used George's death to strengthen their hold on power. His demise isolated Anne, especially since Sarah continued to criticise the widow's feelings of grief, being unsympathetic and scornful of them.[475] She continually wrote letters to the queen criticising everything. Anne fell back on her habit of finding a form of words and repeating them ad infinitum. Two such were: 'Whatever you have to say you may put in writing' and 'You said you desired no answer and I shall give you none'. Needless to say, this only increased Sarah's rage, being unable to believe she did not still have power over the queen.

A victory at Oudenarde had been won by Churchill's troops, but at a high cost to British troops. At the thanksgiving service at St Paul's, it was only as the queen and Sarah climbed up the steps to the cathedral that Sarah noticed Anne was not wearing the jewels she had put out for her. A public quarrel ensued during which Sarah was heard to tell the queen to 'be quiet.' Anne was mortified, and decided she no longer needed Churchill. However, he came to her and asked to be made Captain-General of the army for life.

Information as to specifics are sketchy because he destroyed all the relevant papers, but his demand alienated Anne. She believed it to be outside the constitution and requiring an act of parliament. Alarm bells rang, especially when Churchill pursued the subject with her. She put a warning shot across his bows when she dismissed his favourite commander, General George Montgomery who had been convicted of rape, if only to demonstrate that she, the queen, was head of the armed forces of Great Britain.[476]

When Henry Sacheverell preached a sermon against the Whigs, they howled for him to be impeached. But the tide was turning and there were riots supporting him. He was put on trial and sentenced to a mere three years' suspension of his preaching rights.

In 1710, Queen Anne hit back. Both she and Harley wanted peace and an end to the war. The dukes of Shrewsbury, Somerset and Argyll all supported Harley and of these three heavyweights, Shrewsbury was the real big gun. Anne dismissed Sunderland and then Godolphin. The Tories won a majority and Harley agreed that Philip of Anjou should have Spain in return for commercial concessions.

The following year, Sarah was forced to resign. Abigail Masham was made Keeper of the Privy Purse. Anne and Sarah had one final meeting, but we only have Sarah's account of what was said.[477] Anne was asked to create twelve new peers, and in amongst the winners was Abigail's husband, Samuel Masham. Anne was more worried that his new rank would lose her a good servant in Abigail, which supports the view that the queen regarded Abigail as such, and by this time, Anne was in fact closer to the Duchess of Somerset, who had replaced Sarah as favourite.[478] The Duke of Marlborough was dismissed as Captain-General.[479]

By this time, Anne was growing increasingly infirm. In the Treaty of Utrecht, Louis XIV recognised the Hanoverian succession in England, but Harley played a double game. He, along with Bolingbroke entered into secret negotiations to put the exiled James, Anne's half-brother, on the throne when Anne died and have another Stuart restoration. At the same time, he sent his cousin, Thomas Harley secretly to Hanover, to reassure Sophia about the succession. Bolingbroke had to force Thomas to travel after he had dallied in London for six weeks. Robert

Harley also attempted to make James convert to the Church of England, but failed. Then at the end of January, there was a run on the Bank of England.[480]

In July 1714, Anne dismissed Harley complaining that he was always drunk and disrespectful when he came to see her. On 30 July, the anniversary of the death of her son, William, Duke of Gloucester, the queen suffered a stroke. It was clear she would not recover and Shrewsbury was quickly sworn in as Treasurer.

On 1 August 1714, Queen Anne died at around 7:45 am. She was 49 years old. Her doctor, John Arbuthnot said, 'I believe sleep was never more welcome to a weary traveller than death was to her'.[481] Anne had made two wills, but horrified at the thought of death, she had signed neither of them and so died intestate. The sole bequest her successor, George I, made was a gift of £2000 (around £330,400 in 2024) to the poor.

What was her legacy? Edward Gregg who has, according to most historians, written the definitive biography of her, states that the standard picture of Anne as a 'weak, irresolute woman beset by bedchamber quarrels' was largely due to the malicious pen of Sarah, Duchess of Marlborough, who believed that with the names Morley and Freeman, she had equality with the monarch. But the only person deceived by this was Sarah because Anne never forgot who she was and her rights as sovereign. Her education and upbringing was not one befitting her station, but her ardent belief in the Church of England doctrine and her determination to protect the Protestant faith was her great strength. No political executions took place in her reign. Under her, the two-party state came into being and despite having to swim with the tide, she was never the tool of either political party and was, in that sense at least, a constitutional monarch.[482]

Her personal life was one filled with much sadness. The loss of all her children, followed by her husband; the ups and downs of politics and those wishing to use her for their own ends meant she frequently had to chart a very careful course to maintain some kind of equilibrium in a changing age. She reigned over twelve turbulent years, but her determination to preserve the Protestant religion, her almost constant ill health and compelling her ministers to do as she wished earned enough respect for that period in British history to be called after her.

In his paper on the reign of Queen Anne, Radice quotes Professor Clark … 'the central figure is a homely queen with beautiful hands and a musical voice "entirely English" as she calls herself in contradistinction to Dutch William'. Radice goes on to say that 'on all important occasions, her views and prejudices were those of her people'.[483]

She was buried in the Henry VII chapel alongside her husband and her children. It is somehow fitting that this book, which began with the reign of Henry VII should have that link to the last monarch of the Stuart era, and the final section of the book.

Abigail Masham (née Hill)

Abigail Hill was born around 1670, the daughter of a London merchant, Francis Hill and his wife, Elizabeth, aunt to the future Sarah Churchill, Duchess of Marlborough. Francis' speculations beggared the family, forcing Abigail to become a servant in the house of Sir John Rivers of Kent.

Hearing that the family had fallen on hard times, Sarah Churchill took Abigail into her own household, possibly embarrassed that such close relations were so impoverished, but also, perhaps thinking of Abigail as a potential servant in the then Princess Anne's household, to keep an eye on events when Sarah was away, as she increasingly was.[484]

In 1697, Anne discovered that Sir Benjamin Bathurst had been selling offices in her household. Sarah used that to persuade Anne to take Abigail on as a woman of the bedchamber. Despite Abigail's future elevations socially, Sarah always referred to her as a *woman* of the bedchamber. Apart from this, we know very little about Abigail between 1697 and 1707.[485]

By way of contradiction, Lydiard Park tells us that from 1700, Abigail was Mistress of the Maids on £500 a year (about £87,000 in 2024) in Princess Anne's household and puts her appointment as woman of the bedchamber in 1702.[486] I tend to favour Gregg's timeline since his biography is regarded as definitive.

From around 1704, when Anne was wearying of Sarah's continual political lectures and her frequent absences from court, Abigail, with her gentle and unassuming nature, began to supplant her cousin. Sarah always claimed this to be ingratitude on Abigail's part.

By 1705, Abigail was allegedly whispering Tory sweet-nothings into the queen's ear. Certainly she was regarded as second only to Sarah in influencing Anne. Then Sarah, who was still unaware of the viper in her nest, suggested that the queen should also take Abigail's sister, Alice, into her household. Anne replied that when there was a vacancy, she would, but in the meantime, proposed a pension to Alice Hill of £200 a year (about £40,624 in 2024). Sarah reduced that to £150 for life, which is possibly a reason Abigail turned for help to her second cousin, Robert Harley.

The following two years saw further changes in the queen's life. In 1706, Samuel Masham became a groom of the bedchamber to Prince George, Anne's husband. Possibly encouraged by Harley, the friendship between Samuel and Abigail grew. Anne, ever a romantic soul, encouraged the relationship, but was adamant it must be kept secret. By 1707, Anne had become, politically at least, increasingly isolated. Her beloved husband who had always supported her was stricken with frequent asthmatic attacks, forcing Anne to rely more and more on her closest household staff. Abigail's influence increased. Anne, too, was having health issues and relied more and more on Abigail who proved to be an excellent, caring nurse. At this point, Anne took Alice Hill into her household saying that Abigail was overworked. Sarah Churchill wrote a letter saying Anne's favouritism of Abigail could hurt her royal reputation. Anne responded by telling Sarah that, as groom of the stole, it was her duty to introduce Alice into the household.

Later that month, Sarah discovered that Abigail and Samuel had been secretly married, and that Anne had not only been present at the wedding ceremony, but had given the couple £2000 (about £406,243 in 2024) as a wedding present. She wrote one of her famous letters to the queen asking why she had not been told, only to receive a reply that said, 'I have a hundred times bid Masham tell it to you, and she would not'. This cemented the breach between Sarah and Abigail. The crises in government and the bishopric affair also widened the gap between Sarah and the queen, especially as Sarah took every opportunity to attack Abigail, including the accusation that she had taken bribes. Anne ignored the letter. That did not stop Sarah writing them, the constant demands being that the Queen must dismiss Abigail and Robert Harley. Anne stopped replying to any letters.[487]

Descriptions of Abigail vary according to the political/personal agenda of the person uttering them. Sarah called her 'hideously ugly'. Arthur Maynwaring, a journalist and self-styled secretary to Sarah Churchill said Abigail was an 'ugly hag with a frightful face and stinking breath'. One of Harley's supporters, Sir William Legge, First Earl of Dartmouth said she was 'exceeding mean and vulgar in her manners, of a very unequal temper, childishly exceptious [prone to taking exception] and raising objections and passionate'.

Even her good friend, Jonathan Swift, said that she was 'not very handsome, adding that she was of plain understanding, of great truth and sincerity … of an honest boldness and courage superior to her sex, firm and disinterested in her friendship and full of love, duty and veneration for the Queen, her mistress'.[488] I am not sure if that does not come under the heading of praising with faint damns.

In 1708, Sarah paid herself £12,000 (about £2, 272,000 in 2024) from the Privy Purse, allegedly in honour of a debt dating from 1702 of a promised pension from Anne. Then Sarah discovered that Abigail had been using 'her' rooms at Kensington Palace'. Maynwaring gave her fatal advice, which, being Sarah, she took. He probably wrote the poem accusing Anne and Abigail of being lesbians. The first verse runs:

> When as Queen Anne of great renown
> Great Britain's Sceptre sway'd
> Besides the Church, she dearly loved
> A Dirty Chamber-Maid.

Anne refused to respond to it, but she never forgave Sarah. Then came the incident at St Paul's thanksgiving service for victory at Oudenarde. Sarah interpreted Anne not wearing the jewels she had specifically put out for her as a direct result of Abigail's malign influence and told the queen to be quiet. The truth was probably that Anne, coming from Windsor, where her husband's health daily grew worse, was simply too tired from the journey to put them on. Jean Plaidy in her fictional account, *The Queen's Favourite* posits that Anne was so distressed by the numbers of her troops slain on the battlefield, she did not think wearing masses of jewels appropriate.

Whatever the truth of it, Sarah, as per usual, reverted to her pen. 'Your Majesty chose a very wrong day to mortify me, when you were just going to return thanks for a victory obtained by Lord Marlborough.'

This time, Anne responded. 'After the commands you gave me on the thanksgiving day of not answering you, I shou'd not have troubled you with these lines, but to return the Duke of Marlborough's letter safe into your hands, for the same reason, do not say anything to that, nor to yours which enclosed it.'[489] Had Sarah used her two brain cells to good effect, she would have read the warning in between the lines. But that would have been completely out of character, so she didn't.

In 1710, Samuel was promoted to Brigadier-General in the army and made the MP for Ilchester. Things were certainly looking up for the Mashams, and continued to do so when, having been forced to make twelve new peers, Samuel was made Baron Masham of Otes (the family seat of the Masham family). However, Anne only agreed to his elevation so long as Abigail stayed as her personal dresser, something a peeress would not do. Abigail was happy to remain in Anne's service.[490]

In 1710, Anne also sent an order to John Churchill to appoint John Hill, Abigail's brother, to the vacant colonelcy of the recently deceased Earl of Essex's regiment. Churchill ignored her. He and Sarah went to Windsor Lodge and he did not attend the usual Sunday cabinet meeting, believing his absence would disrupt it. It didn't and Anne was adamant that Hill was awarded his colonelcy. At this point, Maynwaring advised Churchill and Godolphin to force Abigail's dismissal, suggesting a petition to parliament to force the issue. Anne was outraged at direct governmental interference in her household affairs. The government backed down. Churchill threatened to 'retire' if Hill was given the colonelcy. This time Anne backed down. She had nothing to lose by doing so, since she kept Abigail, who knew she had tried to get the honour for John Hill, so nothing changed for Anne. But it was far from a victory for Churchill.[491]

In 1711, Samuel was made Comptroller of the Household, replacing Francis Godolphin, but by now, Anne was missing Abigail, who kept vanishing to have babies. In all, she had six pregnancies and four surviving children. At a time when the political playing field was chaotic, the Tories needed her to be with the queen all the time, but Abigail insisted on rushing to the bedside of her eldest son when he fell ill in 1713. Jonathan Swift wrote: 'she is so excessively fond it makes me mad; she should never leave the queen, but leave every thing to stick to what is so much the interest of the Publick as well as her own. This I tell her but I talk to the Winds'.[492]

Abigail fell out with Robert Harley in 1713, criticising him to Anne, who finally dismissed him. When Anne died in August 1714, there is no mention of Abigail in the reports of the queen's final illness or death. Swift was told that 'Poor Lady Masham is almost dead with Grief'.[493]

After Anne's death, Abigail went to Langley Marsh near Windsor where she and Samuel had a house, and then at the manor in Otes, where in 1734, Abigail died. She is buried at All Saints, High Laver, in Essex.[494]

Robert Harley

Robert Harley was born in Bow Street, London, the son of Sir Edward Harley of Herefordshire. He was educated at Shilton, near Burford in Oxfordshire, a school that produced many legal luminaries. He entered the Middle Temple in 1682, but was never called to the bar. His father was wrongly imprisoned on suspicion of being a supporter of the Monmouth Rebellion in 1685, but soon released.

During the Glorious Revolution, Harley acted as an agent for his father, promoting William of Orange and raising a troop of horse for William when he landed. During the ensuing struggle, he took Worcester for William before obtaining a commission as a major of militia foot in Herefordshire.

In 1689, he was elected to the rotten borough of Tregony in Cornwall, whilst acting as High Sheriff for Herefordshire. The following year he was elected to the Welsh constituency of Radnor, which he continued to represent until 1711. He was attentive to public business and to the form of ceremonial in the House of Commons.[495] Harley came from a Presbyterian nonconformist family that suffered under the post-Restoration laws, being banned from holding public office.[496] So it is not surprising he supported the Toleration Bill and helped defeat the bill put forward to put James II's son on the throne.

Harley was active in parliament, initially as a Whig, but when he became disillusioned with them, he defected to the Tories. His maiden speech majored on the unjust persecution of those who had followed the Duke of Monmouth, stating that these injustices must be remedied. Not a popular point of view.

He believed that English troops were being lost because of their (foreign) commanders and put forward a motion, later passed, that future foot regiments should be manned by Englishmen. He also opposed the Abjuration Bill that would have seen the followers of James II accused of treason.

In 1693, he actively supported the Triennial Bill that limited governments to three years in power, something that William had promised in 1688. But he was also concerned enough for the agricultural community's wellbeing to found the Land Bank, which did for agricultural affairs what the Bank of England did for monied ones. By 1698, Harley was the leader of a combined Whig-Tory opposition to the junto known as the New Country Party. He also began to associate with Godolphin and gained through him a path to the then Princess Anne.

Harley refused appointments in 1698 and 1700 because he did not want to serve with the Whigs. At this time, William was anxious about the succession, determined it should go to the Hanoverian branch, making Sophia of Hanover the heir should Anne not have further children. By this time, Prince William of Gloucester had died and it was fairly clear that Anne would not produce an heir.

To this end, William summoned Harley and asked him to help get a bill passed in parliament to that effect. Harley agreed to help and also persuaded William to accept further limits on monarchical power. The bill was passed and William approved Harley's appointment as Speaker of the Commons, a post he held from 1701–1705, overseeing the Act of Settlement banning Catholics or anyone married to a Catholic from becoming monarch. From 1704–1708, he combined his duties as Speaker with those of the Secretary of State, Northern Department.[497]

Harley was the first to capitalise on the possibilities of the post-1688 ruling that the monarch had to ask parliament each year for money to fund the following year.[498] He was certainly an early proponent of political 'spin' and was very careful about how he managed the media. He employed Daniel Defoe as a political writer, and also Jonathan Swift.

By 1706, Harley was working with Godolphin and Marlborough, but all was not harmonious. At the height of the issue over Sunderland being given a government post, Godolphin became suspicious that someone was tattling about him to Queen Anne.[499] And he was right. Sarah Churchill, Duchess of Marlborough, a fanatical Whig and becoming daily more estranged as favourite from the queen, told Godolphin that the, 'somebody artfull that takes pains to mislead Mrs Morley' was close to Anne. It was, of course, Harley, who, using his distant relationship to Abigail Masham, was engaged in the double objectives of gaining the mind and the affection of the queen by telling her 'reasonable men needed to be drawn away from violent Tories'.[500]

Sarah, as we have seen, finally worked out that Abigail had – in her eyes – supplanted her in Anne's affections and was actively working against her. Gregg asserts, with logic, that this was rubbish and Sarah was wrong. It was impossible for Abigail to establish Harley in Anne's affections, because the queen saw her purely as an excellent nurse and servant.[501] It didn't stop Abigail from trying, though. However, both Godolphin and Sarah were convinced Harley was the source of Anne's intransigence over Sunderland.

Finally, in 1708, Anne was forced to dismiss Harley and Bolingbroke when Godolphin and Marlborough told her they would not work with them. It did not help that a Scottish spy called William Gregg, a very low-paid, impoverished clerk in Harley's office, was caught giving state documents to the French. Defoe had warned Harley that his security was very lax but Harley disregarded him. Gregg was executed in 1708.

Harley was out but certainly not down. He kept in touch with Abigail who had now married Samuel Masham. There is no doubt that Harley used her without conscience to influence people whenever he could. The most startling example was the Sacheverell affair in 1709.[502]

After the Sunderland debacle, Anne was determined on payback. In 1710, she knew she could not dismiss Marlborough, but she certainly sacked his relations and Godolphin. Harley was back.

During the 1710–11 period, Harley was Chancellor of the Exchequer. His aim was for moderate politics. Angus McInnes examines his political standpoint. There is little doubt Harley was a divisive figure, but did he keep to his moderate principles, or was he a master-manipulator with an eye on self-advancement?

McInnes avers that he did keep shifting his viewpoint and changing his 'political coat' through the 1690s and as far as 1708. He kept falling out with Henry St John, Viscount Bolingbroke, who wrote a letter to Sir William Windham and said of Harley, 'whether this man ever had any determined views besides those of raiding his own family is, I believe, a problematical question in the world. My opinion is he never had any other'. McInnes goes on to say that Harley's own words do not speak about power-seeking or political preferment. He uses phrases such as, 'the dangers to the Constitution', 'the ancient liberties of England', and 'the good of this poor nation'. A closer study reveals that his views lost him quite as much power and influence as they gained. The 1708 break with the Marlborough/Godolphin junto sent him into political ignominy and disgrace. He knew that it would, but it didn't stop him. So that does not chime with Bolingbroke's opinion.

Instead, his actions speak of his desire for moderation in politics and gaining the support of moderates on both sides of the political divide. He said, 'I have no partiality to one side more than another'. He believed there was no difference between a 'mad Tory and a mad Whig' and that both were equally obnoxious.

His view was that extremity in politics was not good for the country and the only way to go was by 'avoiding madness on both sides'. He also believed party politics was detrimental to the authority of the Crown; that non-party government could only work if the Crown was free to choose its own ministers from both political parties, or from none. He saw Anne as a well-intentioned monarch.[503]

However, back in 1711, Harley was battling, but his bacon was saved by an attempt on his life by a French clergyman nicknamed the Marquis de Guiscard. During an interrogation before the Privy Council, Guiscard stabbed Harley. The knife is thought to have become stuck in Harley's ornate waistcoat. He had been in ill health and this only exacerbated public concern for him, but he ensured he made hay while the political sun shone on the incident. There was national rejoicing when he recovered. Guiscard was immediately attacked by several members of the Privy Council who, in the heat of the moment, forgot the perpetrator would need to be interrogated further. Unfortunately for them, he was fatally wounded, probably by James Butler, 2nd Duke of Ormonde. He lingered in Newgate for a week and then died.

Harley's biggest problem after his recovery was the crisis in public finance caused by the war in France. Lord Halifax wrote to Harley on the day that the new Treasury board met: 'Your great abilities and your knowledge of the Revenue, will soon make you master of all the business, but how you will restore credit, and find money for the demands that will be upon you exceeds my capacity'. And sort it, Harley did. He created the South Sea Company, which was initially successful until it went sour in 1720, by which time it was no concern of Harley's.

From 1711–1714, Harley was Lord High Treasurer, having been created Baron Harley of Wigmore, Earl of Oxford and Earl Mortimer. He claimed a distant family connection to the previous earls of Oxford, the De Veres. In 1712, he was made a Knight of the Garter and in November of that year, the Bandbox Plot tried to kill him again. This time, it was a very quick intervention by Jonathan Swift – aptly named in this instance – who saw a thread hanging from a package posted to Harley, immediately cut it and defused the loaded and cocked pistols. Possibly the first parcel bomb!

In 1713, Harley signed the Treaty of Utrecht, causing Anne to create twelve new peers, called Harley's Dozen, but this time also marked the complete breakdown of his relationship with Bolingbroke who was very resentful he hadn't been given an earldom. Harley had also fallen foul of Abigail, and Samuel – one of the new peers – also deserted him for Bolingbroke, as did Queen Anne. The main problem, which nobody cared about much, was that Harley's daughter had recently died, and he had, to use a modern phrase 'taken to the bottle'.

Four days before the queen died, Harley resigned. George I, the new monarch, was disgusted with Harley's involvement with the Treaty of Utrecht. In 1715, George impeached Harley and sent him to the Tower. It didn't help that Harley had been actively plotting with Catholic James. He was accused of High Treason and high crimes and misdemeanours, all of which carried a possible death penalty. However, the first Jacobite Uprising took place in 1715, and the government was too busy for the next couple of years executing people and trying to get them to incriminate Harley to bother much with him directly. All attempts failed and no link could be found to connect him with the uprising. He was finally formally acquitted and released in 1717. George I made it plain he was not welcome at court, but he joined the Tory lords to defeat the Peerage Bill aimed at reducing the number of lords in parliament.

Robert Harley died, with no fanfare, at his house in Albemarle Street, Westminster, in 1724. He is buried at St Barnabus, Brampton Bryan, Herefordshire.[504]

Although most historians claim Robert Walpole to be the first prime minister, Harley also has a claim to that distinction. Except that in eighteenth-century Britain, it was a term of insult, thrown at Harley and Walpole by their political opponents. He was seriously disliked in his day. Lord Macauley called him 'a base and hardy hypocrite'. Sarah Churchill, not to be outdone, said he had 'a wonderful talent for confounding the common sense of mankind'.[505]

There is no argument that he was a patron of the arts. He built an unparalleled library preserving Renaissance, Anglo-Saxon and Middle English literature. Now called the Harley Collection, it was sold to the British Museum in 1753. He also promoted the careers of Jonathan Swift, Alexander Pope and John Gay and wrote his own, mostly unsigned, poetry.[506]

Alexander Pope wrote of him as Maecenas, now synonymous with the phrase *patron of the arts*. The original Maecenas was a Roman friend of the Emperor Octavius. The Harley Collection is now housed at the British Library and a portrait of Harley hangs at the entrance to the Manuscript Room.

Brought up as a Presbyterian, he was seen as a political defector from the Whigs, who wanted only Protestant monarchs, whereas the Tories wanted a hereditary line for the monarchy. His nickname was 'Robin the Trickster'. A Country Whig from a family of dissenters he might have been, but by 1710, he was the only man who commanded the confidence of High Church Tories.[507]

Elizabeth Percy, Duchess of Somerset

Styled Lady Elizabeth Percy, the future Duchess of Somerset was born in 1667, the only surviving child and sole heir of Jocelyn Percy, 11th Earl of Northumberland. In 1679, at the age of 12, she was married to Henry Cavendish, Earl of Ogle and son of the Duke of Newcastle. As part of the marriage settlement, he adopted the surname Percy, but died a year later and was buried at the Percy family home, Petworth. It is considered unlikely the marriage was consummated due to her age.[508]

Her next foray into marriage was twelve months after her first husband died. Thomas Thynne was in his mid-thirties. Elizabeth was 14. She immediately went to The Hague for a year to stay with Lady Temple and the marriage was not consummated. However, Thynne claimed his wife's property, which finally ended in a decision for Thynne with an order that his wife should come and live with him. She was 15 by this time and had certainly not been asked her opinion or consulted in the matter.

Karl Johann von Konigsmark was very taken with her – unsuccessfully – and sent Thynne two challenges. Thynne then sent six men to France to murder Konigsmark. On 12 February 1682, Thynne, riding in his coach down Pall Mall, was shot and died next day. The three murderers were hanged the following month, but Konigsmark was acquitted of being an accessory. Although there was very strong circumstantial evidence against him, the court was known to favour him. But the verdict was very unpopular. And it came back to bite Elizabeth years later when Swift accused her of murdering Thynne.[509] Rumours also abounded that Thynne had seduced a lady his friend Monmouth was interested in, leading to a popular ballad going the rounds:

> Here lies Tom Thynne of Longleat Hall
> Who ne'er would have miscarried;
> Had he married the woman he slept withal
> Or slept with the woman he married.'[510]

Only five months after Thynne's death, Elizabeth, still a virgin, embarked on her third marriage, this time to Charles Seymour, Duke of Somerset. He used her immense wealth to rebuild Petworth House, but it was not a happy union. He showed her no affection or gratitude. That said, they had seven children. Two died in infancy and two more died unmarried.

Elizabeth was among Anne's oldest friends. While a princess, Anne had gone to live with the Somersets at Syon House after a heated argument with

William and Mary. Elizabeth represented Anne at Queen Mary's funeral, since Anne was, sadly, suffering a miscarriage. There is no doubt that Somerset used his wife's position with Anne to further his own career, in just the same way Marlborough did using Sarah's influence with the queen.[511]

After Sarah was dismissed in 1711, Elizabeth was made groom of the stole and first lady of the bedchamber. Peace in Europe and the succession dominated the final years of Anne's reign. She found emotional repose very difficult since she always put duty first, but this was exacerbated by her instinctive shyness and physical decline. At this time, Elizabeth was her most important personal attendant. Lord Dartmouth said she was 'the best bred as well as the best born lady in England, and by much the greatest favourite when the Queen died'.

Anne's doctor, Sir David Hamilton, said that, in contrast to Sarah and Abigail, Elizabeth 'never press'd the Queen hard, nothing makes the Queen more Uneasie than that'. The new ministers tried to stop her appointment as groom of the stole. Swift wrote of Anne's response to that, 'The Queen said if … she could not have what servants she liked, she did not find how her Condition was mended'.

Elizabeth's influence grew despite the fact that Somerset was the first to leave Harley's sinking political ship. The duke had been hoping to succeed Godolphin, and when he failed, he took his bat and ball home to Petworth determined 'to keep out as many Tories and Jacobites in this new Parliament as I can'. Both the Whigs and Tories saw the Somersets as troublemakers, but the duke's influence with Anne was solely through his wife. Swift wrote of her that she 'quickly won so far upon the affections of Her Majesty, that she had more Personall Credit than all the Queen's servants put together'. This, if nothing else from a contemporary political pundit, scuppers the view that Abigail Masham held more sway than anyone after Sarah Churchill left the queen's service.

Somerset lost no time in using his wife's influence. Both were of the Whig persuasion whereas Abigail was a Tory. Sir David Hamilton said to the queen, 'I took notice of my Lady Massams Passion, as unsuitable to the Queen's Temper, and of the Duchess of Somerset's more Suitable', to which the Queen replied, 'Yes, by farr'.[512]

When Swift attacked the Somersets, he explicitly accused Elizabeth – calling her by the nickname 'Carrots' due to her red hair – of murdering her second husband, in *The Windsor Prophecy*. He went on to suggest she might poison the queen: 'I have been told they assassin when young and poison when old'. Anne was outraged and refused to consider him for a bishopric, but she had no power of veto over his appointment as Dean of St Patrick's Cathedral in Dublin.[513]

Finally, Anne grew tired of the Duke of Somerset's arrogance in opposing the peace in Europe, and tried to dismiss him. He responded by saying that if he went, Elizabeth would go, too. That, Anne could not countenance. But in a personal interview, in January 1712, he agreed to go and that Elizabeth could stay.[514] Dr David Hamilton advised Anne to keep Elizabeth 'for her own quiet', and the Duchess stayed with the queen until the latter's death.[515]

After Anne's death, one of her unsigned wills stated that Elizabeth should have half her jewels 'as the fittest person to wear them after her'. Elizabeth was the Chief Mourner at the queen's private funeral.[516]

Elizabeth was seen as proud but very skilled in dealing with Anne. She was a shrewd observer and a notorious gossip. When the friendship between Anne and Sarah was in serious decline, Anne wanted the fact that they seldom saw each other to be kept quiet. She wrote of Lady Fitzharding and the Duchess of Somerset as 'two of the most observeing, pryeing ladys in England'.[517]

Anne died in 1722 of breast cancer. She was 55.[518]

Much is made of Queen Anne's favourites; much of it inaccurate. Bucholz argues that the influence of the favourites was 'vastly overrated' by contemporaries.[519] However, DeRitter Jones, argues that it was this very misperception of the influence the favourites wielded that helped make them prominent in the political world of Anne's reign. Simply because they were perceived as being so important, made them political targets for satire and criticism, especially in the case of Sarah Churchill, and then again when Swift accused Elizabeth of Somerset of murdering her second husband.[520] And wouldn't the reign of Queen Anne be so much less lively had that not been the case?

If this section on the life and reign of Queen Anne has interested the reader, I can heartily recommend Edward Gregg's biography of her, which goes much deeper into the political see-saw of her reign than was appropriate in this book. Details are in the Select Bibliography.

Notes

1. Gunn, S. J., 'The Courtiers of Henry VII', *The English Historical Review* 108, no. 426 (1993), pp. 23–49. http://www.jstor.org/stable/573548.
2. Penn, Thomas (2011). *Winter King*. Penguin, p. 7.
3. Gunn S. J., 'The Courtiers of Henry VII', *The English Historical Review* 108, no. 426 (1993), pp. 23–49. http://www.jstor.org/stable/573548.
4. Borman, Tracy (2016). *The Private Lives of the Tudors*. Hodder & Stoughton, pp. 7–8.
5. Penn, *Winter King*, p. 2.
6. https://en.wikipedia.org/wiki/Edward_of_Westminster,_Prince_of_Wales.
7. Lockyer and Thrush (1997). *Henry VII* (3 edition). Routledge, Ch. 4.
8. Ibid.
9. Penn, *Winter King*, p. 20.
10. https://en.wikipedia.org/wiki/Titulus_Regius.
11. https://en.wikipedia.org/wiki/Battle_of_Stoke_Field.
12. https://en.wikipedia.org/wiki/Perkin_Warbeck.
13. Penn, *Winter King*, p. 39.
14. http://conorbyrnex.blogspot.com/2014/11/28-november-1499-execution-of-edward.html.
15. Penn, *Winter King*, p. 275.
16. https://thehistoryofengland.co.uk/resource/the-indispensable-john-morton/.
17. https://thewarsoftheroses.co.uk/dr-john-morton-cardinal-and-archbishop-of-canterbury/.
18. Penn, *Winter King*, p. 49.
19. https://en.wikipedia.org/wiki/John_Morton_(cardinal).
20. https://thehistoryofengland.co.uk/resource/the-indispensable-john-morton/.
21. https://thehistoryjar.com/2016/03/12/sir-reginald-bray-tudor-advisor-architect-and-spymaster/.
22. Penn, *Winter King*, pp. 35–6.
23. https://thehistoryjar.com/2016/03/12/sir-reginald-bray-tudor-advisor-architect-and-spymaster/.
24. https://en.wikipedia.org/wiki/Reginald_Bray
25. Penn, *Winter King*, pp. 148–151.
26. https://en.wikipedia.org/wiki/Giles_Daubeney,_1st_Baron_Daubeney.
27. https://en.wikisource.org/wiki/Dictionary_of_National_Biography,_1885-1900/Daubeney,_Giles.
28. https://thehistoryofengland.co.uk/resource/henry-vii-and-his-loyal-councillors/.
29. https://en.wikipedia.org/wiki/Giles_Daubeney,_1st_Baron_Daubeney.
30. https://en.wikipedia.org/wiki/Richard_Foxe.
31. https://www.britannica.com/biography/Richard-Foxe.
32. https://www.medieval.eu/young-henry-viii/.

33. Weir, A. (2008). *Henry VIII: King and Court*. Vintage, p. 2.
34. https://throughtheeyesofanneboleyn.wordpress.com/2016/07/26/prince-arthur-the-tudor-king-who-never-was-guest-post-by-sean-cunningham/.
35. Ibid.
36. Starkey, D (2002). *The Reign of Henry VIII: Personalities and Politics*. Vintage, p. 121.
37. Borman, Tracy (2016). *The Private Lives of the Tudors*. Hodder & Stoughton, pp. 218–9.
38. Harris, Sir Nicholas (2024). *The Privy Purse Expenses of King Henry VIII from November 1529 to December 1532*. Hardpress.
39. https://www.hrp.org.uk/blog/henry-viii-medicines/#gs.cfhndm.
40. https://tudortreasures.net/dr-henry-viii-and-his-medicines/.
41. Letters and Papers, Foreign and Domestic, Henry VIII, Vol 14, Part 2, 153; O'Caellaigh. Seamus (2017). *Pustules, Pestilence and Pain: Tudor Treatments and Ailment of Henry VIII*. MadeGlobalPublishing. ISBN 978-8494729843.
42. https://www.ncbi.nlm.nih.gov/pmc/articles/PMC2789029/.
43. Richardson, Glenn (2020). *The Field of Cloth of Gold*. Yale University Press, Introduction.
44. *History Magazine*, July 2020, pp. 20–28.
45. https://leeds-castle.com/news/did-henry-viii-stay-at-leeds-castle-en-route-to-the-most-spectacular-event-of-the-century-in-1520/.
46. https://blogs.bl.uk/digitisedmanuscripts/2021/05/index.html.
47. Weir, *Henry VIII: King and Court*, p. 395.
48. Bush, Michael, 'Tax Reform and Rebellion in Early Tudor England', *History* 76, no. 248 (1991),pp. 379–400. http://www.jstor.org/stable/24421380.
49. Weir, *Henry VIII: King and Court*, p. 398.
50. Ward, Anne (1996). *The Lincolnshire Uprising 1536*. Louth Naturalists' Antiquarian and Literary Society, p. 6.
51. Ibid., p. 11.
52. https://www.henryviiithereign.co.uk/pilgrimage-of-grace-timeline.html.
53. Ward, *The Lincolnshire Uprising 1536*, p. 18.
54. https://www.henryviiithereign.co.uk/pilgrimage-of-grace-timeline.html.
55. Ward, *The Lincolnshire Uprising 1536*, pp. 37–8.
56. Stride, P., Lopes Floro, K (2013), 'Henry VIII, McLeod Syndrome and Jacquetta's Curse', *Journal of the Royal College of Physicians of Edinburgh*, 43, pp. 353–60. http://dx.doi.org/10.4997/JRCPE.2013.417. © 2013 Royal College of Physicians of Edinburgh.
57. Ibid.
58. Hutchinson, Robert (2019). *Henry VIII: The Decline and Fall of à Tyrant* (Kindle edition). Weidenfeld & Nicholson, Ch. 1.
59. Ibid., Ch. 1.
60. Ibid., Ch. 12.
61. https://www.parliament.uk/about/living-heritage/evolutionofparliament/originsofparliament/birthofparliament/overview/reformation.
62. Davies, C. S. L., 'A New Life Of Henry VIII', *History* 54, no. 180 (1969): pp. 31–48. http://www.jstor.org/stable/24406509.
63. Ibid.
64. Ives, E. W (1979). *Faction in Tudor England*. The Historical Association, London, p. 2.
65. Ibid., p. 5.
66. Ibid., p. 11.
67. Ibid., p. 16.

68. https://www.thinkswap.com/uk/a-levels-edexcel/history/a-level/how-significant-were-factions-court-king-henry-viii-years-1509-1547.
69. Ives, *Faction in Tudor* England, p. 18.
70. https://www.historic-uk.com/HistoryUK/HistoryofEngland/Queen-Mary-I/.
71. Shephard, Robert. 'Court Factions in Early Modern England', *The Journal of Modern History* 64, no. 4 (1992), pp. 721–45. http://www.jstor.org/stable/2124905.
72. https://www.poetryfoundation.org/poets/thomas-wyatt.
73. https://www.luminarium.org/renlit/wyattbio.htm.
74. Brigden, Susan. '"The Shadow That You Know": Sir Thomas Wyatt and Sir Francis Bryan at Court and in Embassy', *The Historical Journal* 39, no. 1 (1996), pp.1–31. http://www.jstor.org/stable/2639938.
75. Ibid.
76. http://www.tudorplace.com.ar/Bios/WilliamButts.htm.
77. Weir, *Henry VIII: King and Court*, pp. 285–6.
78. Ibid., p. 336
79. https://en.wikipedia.org/wiki/Prebendaries%27_Plot.
80. Ibid.
81. Borman, *Private Lives of the Tudors*, p. 171.
82. https://obgyn.onlinelibrary.wiley.com/doi/abs/10.1111/j.1471-0528.1985.tb01350.x.
83. http://www.tudorplace.com.ar/Bios/WilliamButts.htm.
84. https://thefreelancehistorywriter.com/2018/03/16/dr-william-butts-royal-physician/.
85. Ibid.
86. https://en.wikisource.org/wiki/Dictionary_of_National_Biography,_1885-1900/Butts,_William.
87. Furdell, Elizabeth Lane (2001). *Royal Doctors 1485–1714*. University of Rochester Press, pp. 26–7.
88. https://en.wikipedia.org/wiki/Nicholas_Carew_(courtier) .
89. Starkey, *Reign of Henry VIII*, p. 51.
90. Noble, Graham, 'Sir Nicholas Carew: Tudor Conspirator?', *History Review*, Issue 54, March 2006. https://www.historytoday.com/archive/sir-nicholas-carew-tudor-conspirator.
91. https://en.wikipedia.org/wiki/Nicholas_Carew_(courtier).
92. Starkey, *Reign of Henry VIII*, p. 77.
93. https://www.theanneboleynfiles.com/rivalry-charles-brandon-anne-boleyn-sarah-bryson/?utm_content=cmp-true.
94. Starkey, *Reign of Henry VIII*, p. 89.
95. Ives, Eric (2004). *The Life and Death of Anne Boleyn*. Blackwell, p. 327.
96. Starkey, *Reign of Henry VIII*, p. 94.
97. Weir, *Henry VIII: King and Court*, pp. 416–7.
98. https://www.luminarium.org/encyclopedia/carew.htm.
99. Weir, *Henry VIII: King and Court*, p. 446.
100. https://en.wikipedia.org/wiki/Nicholas_Carew_(courtier).
101. Lee, Stephen (2006). The Mid Tudors: Edward VI and Mary: 1547–1558. Routledge.
102. 'Classic Stories: The Story of the Tudors', *BBC History Magazine*, p. 57.
103. Ibid.
104. Borman, *Private Lives of the Tudors*, p. 174.
105. Hourly History (2019). *King Edward VI: A Life from Beginning to End*. Ch. 1.
106. Ibid., Ch. 3

107. Ibid.
108. The Story of the Tudors, p. 60.
109. Ibid., p. 61.
110. Hourly History, *King Edward VI*, Ch. 5.
111. The Story of the Tudors, p. 63.
112. Hourly History, *King Edward VI*, Ch. 8.
113. Borman, *Private Lives of the Tudors*, p. 239.
114. Markham, Sir Clements (1907). *King Edward VI: An Appreciation*. Smith, Elder & Co, p. 8, p. 168 onwards.
115. Ibid.
116. Markham, *King Edward VI*, p. 58.
117. Ibid., pp. 178–9.
118. Ibid., p. 197.
119. https://en.wikipedia.org/wiki/Barnaby_Fitzpatrick.
120. https://www.tudorsociety.com/11-september-barnaby-fitzpatrick-friend-of-edward-vi/?utm_content=cmp-true.
121. https://biography.wales/article/s-SIDN-HEN-1529.
122. https://en.wikipedia.org/wiki/Henry_Sidney.
123. https://biography.wales/article/s-SIDN-HEN-1529.
124. Foster, Roy (Professor) (1990). *Modern Ireland: 1600–1972*. Penguin.
125. https://biography.wales/article/s-SIDN-HEN-1529.
126. https://en.wikipedia.org/wiki/John_Gates_(courtier).
127. https://thefreelancehistorywriter.com/2020/08/21/sir-john-gates-tudor-courtier/.
128. https://en.wikipedia.org/wiki/Henry_Brandon,_2nd_Duke_of_Suffolk.
129. https://onthetudortrail.com/Blog/2018/05/10/the-sons-of-charles-brandon.
130. 'Lady Jane Grey's Last Hours', *Advocate of Peace (1847-1884)* 10, no. 2 (1879): pp.16. http://www.jstor.org/stable/27906035.
131. https://en.wikipedia.org/wiki/Lady_Jane_Grey.
132. *History Magazine*, November 2016, pp. 50-55.
133. The Story of the Tudors, pp. 66–67.
134. Borman, *Private Lives of the Tudors*, p. 245.
135. https://en.wikipedia.org/wiki/Mary_I_of_England.
136. Borman, *Private Lives of the Tudors*, p. 93.
137. https://en.wikipedia.org/wiki/Mary_I_of_England.
138. Anna Whitelock, and Diarmaid MacCulloch, 'Princess Mary's Household and the Succession Crisis, July 1553', *The Historical Journal* 50, no. 2 (2007): pp. 265–87. http://www.jstor.org/stable/4140130.
139. Vroom, Emma. *The Marian Court in Context*. http://earlham.edu/wp-content/uploads/2021/03/the-marian-court-emma-vroom-fall-2015.pdf.
140. https://www.tudorsociety.com/edward-courtenay-1st-earl-of-devon-1526-1556/.
141. https://en.wikipedia.org/wiki/Mary_I_of_England.
142. Spielmann, Richard M., 'The Beginning of Clerical Marriage In the English Reformation: The Reigns of Edward and Mary', *Anglican and Episcopal History* 56, no. 3 (1987), pp. 251–63. http://www.jstor.org/stable/42610201.
143. Ibid.
144. Ridley, Jasper (1987). *Elizabeth I*. Constable, p. 67.
145. Cavill, P. R., 'Heresy And Forfeiture In Marian England', *The Historical Journal* 56, no. 4 (2013), pp. 879–907. http://www.jstor.org/stable/24528854.

146. Vroom, *The Marian Court in Context*.
147. Clifford, Henry (1887). *The Life of Lady Jane Dormer; Duchess of Feria*.
148. https://en.wikipedia.org/wiki/Mary_I_of_England.
149. Courtauld, Simon (2021). *Lady of Spain: A life of Jane Dormer, Duchess of Feria*. Mount Orleans Press.
150. https://en.wikipedia.org/wiki/Jane_Dormer.
151. https://en.wikisource.org/wiki/Dictionary_of_National_Biography,_1885-1900/Dormer,_Jane.
152. https://en.wikipedia.org/wiki/Jane_Dormer.
153. https://en.wikisource.org/wiki/Dictionary_of_National_Biography,_1885-1900/Dormer,_Jane.
154. Courtauld, *Lady of Spain*.
155. https://en.wikipedia.org/wiki/Jane_Dormer.
156. https://en.wikisource.org/wiki/Dictionary_of_National_Biography,_1885-1900/Dormer,_Jane.
157. https://en.wikipedia.org/wiki/Susan_Clarencieux.
158. https://thefreelancehistorywriter.com/tag/susan-clarencius/.
159. Grey, Jane, and S. J. Gunn, 'A Letter of Jane, Duchess of Northumberland, in 1553', *The English Historical Review* 114, no. 459 (1999), pp. 1267–71. http://www.jstor.org/stable/580249.
160. https://thefreelancehistorywriter.com/tag/susan-clarencius/.
161. Ibid.
162. https://en.wikipedia.org/wiki/Stephen_Gardiner.
163. https://www.britannica.com/biography/Stephen-Gardiner.
164. https://www.catholic.com/encyclopedia/stephen-gardiner.
165. https://www.britannica.com/biography/Stephen-Gardiner.
166. https://en.wikipedia.org/wiki/Stephen_Gardiner.
167. https://spartacus-educational.com/Robert_Barnes.htm.
168. Bates, J. Barrington, 'Stephen Gardiner's Explication and the Identity of the Church', *Anglican and Episcopal History* 72, no. 1 (2003), pp. 22–54. http://www.jstor.org/stable/42612300.
169. https://www.britannica.com/biography/Stephen-Gardiner.
170. https://www.prisonersofeternity.com/blog/marian-burnings/.
171. Bates, 'Stephen Gardiner's Explication and the Identity of the Church'.
172. Edwards, John (2016). *Archbishop Pole*. Routledge.
173. https://en.wikipedia.org/wiki/Reginald_Pole.
174. https://www.luminarium.org/encyclopedia/cardinalpole.htm.
175. https://www.luminarium.org/renlit/cranmerwiltshire.htm.
176. https://www.luminarium.org/encyclopedia/cardinalpole.htm.
177. https://en.wikipedia.org/wiki/Reginald_Pole.
178. Ibid.
179. https://en.wikipedia.org/wiki/Reginald_Pole.
180. Edwards, *Archbishop Pole*.
181. https://en.wikipedia.org/wiki/Reginald_Pole.
182. Pogson, Rex H., 'Reginald Pole and the Priorities of Government in Mary Tudor's Church', *The Historical Journal* 18, no. 1 (1975), pp. 3–20. http://www.jstor.org/stable/2638465.
183. Ibid.

184. Edwards, *Archbishop Pole*.

185. Farr, Edward (1845). *Select Poetry*. The Parker Society, Cambridge University Press, p. 173.

186. http://news.bbc.co.uk/1/hi/magazine/6936537.stm.

187. Taylor-Smither, Larissa J., 'Elizabeth I: A Psychological Profile', *The Sixteenth Century Journal* 15, no. 1 (1984), pp. 47–72. https://doi.org/10.2307/2540839.

188. https://en.wikipedia.org/wiki/Elizabeth_I.

189. https://en.wikipedia.org/wiki/Queene%27s_Day

190. https://www.bbc.co.uk/history/british/tudors/elizabeth_i_01.shtml.

191. https://archives.nd.edu/episodes/visitors/rhb/essays03.htm.

192. Ridley, *Elizabeth I*, p. 82.

193. Starkey, D (2001). *Elizabeth*. Vintage, p. 237.

194. Neale, J. E., 'Parliament and the Succession Question in 1562/3 and 1566', *The English Historical Review*, October, 1921, Vol. 36, No. 144, pp. 497–520. https://www.jstor.org/stable/552580.

195. Ibid.

196. Ibid.

197. Ridley, *Elizabeth I*, p. 107.

198. Starkey, *Elizabeth*, pp. 277–79.

199. Hurst, John F., 'The Elizabethan Settlement of the Church of England', *The American Journal of Theology* 3, no. 4 (1899), pp. 679–94. http://www.jstor.org/stable/3153025.

200. Ibid.

201. Ridley, *Elizabeth I*, pp. 86–88.

202. Campbell, Heidi Olson, '"Of Blessed Memory": The Recasting of Elizabeth I as England's Protestant Patron Saint, 1603–1645', *Anglican and Episcopal History* 91, no. 4 (2022), pp. 429–54. https://www.jstor.org/stable/27176133.

203. Ridley, *Elizabeth I*, pp. 98–107.

204. Borman, *Private Lives of the Tudors*, p. 254.

205. Borman, Tracy (2023). *Anne Boleyn and Elizabeth I*. Hodder & Stoughton, p. 128.

206. https://thehistoricalnovel.com/2018/04/10/quotes-in-context-elizabeth-i/.

207. Peterson, Kaara L., 'Elizabeth I's Virginity and the Body of Evidence: Jonson's Notorious Crux', *Renaissance Quarterly* 68, no. 3 (2015), pp. 840–71. https://doi.org/10.1086/683853.

208. Borman, *Private Lives of the Tudors*, p. 340.

209. Peterson, 'Elizabeth I's Virginity and the Body of Evidence'.

210. https://spartacus-educational.com/TUDstubbsJ.htm.

211. McGovern, Jonathan, 'Allegory as Counsel: "The Garden Plot" and the Anjou Marriage Negotiations of Queen Elizabeth I', *Studies in Philology* 117, no. 4 (2020), pp. 743–68. https://www.jstor.org/stable/26973841.

212. McLaren, Anne, 'The Quest for a King: Gender, Marriage, and Succession in Elizabethan England', *Journal of British Studies* 41, no. 3 (2002), pp. 259–90. https://doi.org/10.1086/341150.

213. https://warfarehistorynetwork.com/article/sir-francis-walsingham.

214. Alford. Stephen (2013). *The Watchers: A Secret History of the Reign of Elizabeth I*. Penguin Books, p. 11.

215. Ibid.., p. 47.

216. https://thehistoryjar.com/2023/04/28/the-throckmorton-plot/.

217. Ibid.

218. Alford, *The Watchers*, pp.160–176.
219. Tiernan, R. Kent, 'Walsingham's Entrapment of Mary Stuart: The Modern Perspective of a Deception Analyst/Planner', *American Intelligence Journal* 34, no. 1 (2017), pp. 146–56. https://www.jstor.org/stable/26497131.
220. https://www.nationalarchives.gov.uk/education/resources/elizabeth-monarchy/the-tide-letter/.
221. https://www.history.com/news/queen-elizabeth-spy-network-england.
222. Tiernan, 'Walsingham's Entrapment of Mary Stuart'.
223. https://blogs.bl.uk/digitisedmanuscripts/2022/02/the-gallows-letter.html.
224. Borman, *Private Lives of the Tudors*, p. 344.
225. Alford, *The Watchers*, pp. 239–40.
226. https://en.wikipedia.org/wiki/Blanche_Parry.
227. https://www.bbc.co.uk/news/uk-wales-42805908.
228. Borman, Tracy, *The Private Life of the Tudors* p. 109.
229. https://en.wikipedia.org/wiki/Elizabeth_I.
230. Ballard, George (1752). *Memoirs of Several Ladies of Great Britain*, pp. 177–79.
231. https://htt. .gov.uk/1111.aspx.
232. Borman, *Anne Boleyn and Elizabeth I*, p. 109.
233. Norton, Elizabeth (2017). *The Lives of Tudor Women*. Head of Zeus, p. 174.
234. Borman, *Anne Boleyn and Elizabeth I*, pp. 223–4.
235. Ballard, *Memoirs of Several Ladies of Great Britain*.
236. https://htt. .gov.uk/1111.aspx.
237. https://en.wikipedia.org/wiki/Helena_Snakenborg .
238. https://historyofparliament.com/2024/03/14/elizabeth-i-helena-ulfsdotter-marchioness-of-northampton/.
239. https://en.wikipedia.org/wiki/Helena_Snakenborg.
240. https://historyofparliament.com/2024/03/14/elizabeth-i-helena-ulfsdotter-marchioness-of-northampton/.
241. https://en.wikipedia.org/wiki/Helena_Snakenborg.
242. https://historyofparliament.com/2024/03/14/elizabeth-i-helena-ulfsdotter-marchioness-of-northampton/.
243. Ibid.
244. https://en.wikipedia.org/wiki/Helena_Snakenborg.
245. Younger, Neil (2022). *Religion and Politics in Elizabethan England: The Life of Sir Christopher Hatton*. Manchester University Press, Introduction.
246. Guy, John (2016). *Elizabeth: The Forgotten Years*. Penguin, Chapters 3 and 4.
247. https://spartacus-educational.com/TUDhatton.htm.
248. https://en.wikipedia.org/wiki/Christopher_Hatton.
249. https://spartacus-educational.com/TUDhatton.htm.
250. https://www.britannica.com/biography/Christopher-Hatton.
251. https://en.wikipedia.org/wiki/Christopher_Hatton.
252. McCaffrey: Christopher Hatton: Oxf DNB 2004-14.
253. https://spartacus-educational.com/TUDhatton.htm.
254. https://www.britannica.com/biography/Christopher-Hatton.
255. https://en.wikipedia.org/wiki/Christopher_Hatton.
256. Sellar and Yeatman (1998). 1066 and All That: A Memorable History of England. Methuen; ISBN 978-0413772701.
257. Keates, Jonathan (2015). William III and Mary II: Partners in Revolution. Penguin.

258. https://londonist.com/london/history/king-james-submarine-thames.
259. Schwarz, Marc L., 'James I and the Historians: Toward a Reconsideration', *Journal of British Studies* 13, no. 2 (1974), pp. 114–34. http://www.jstor.org/stable/175090
260. Lee, Maurice, 'James I and the Historians: Not a Bad King after All?', *Albion: A Quarterly Journal Concerned with British Studies* 16, no. 2 (1984), pp. 151–63. https://doi.org/10.2307/4049286.
261. https://en.wikipedia.org/wiki/Henry_Stuart,_Lord_Darnley.
262. Wilson, D H (1963). *King James VI & I*. Jonathan Cape.
263. https://en.wikipedia.org/wiki/James_VI_and_I.
264. Matusiak, John (2015). *James I: Scotland's King of England*. The History Press.
265. https://www.rct.uk/collection/people/anne-of-denmark-queen-of-great-britain-1574-1619.
266. https://en.wikipedia.org/wiki/James_VI_and_I.
267. Fincham, Kenneth and Peter Lake, 'The Ecclesiastical Policy of King James I', *Journal of British Studies* 24, no. 2 (1985), pp. 169–207. http://www.jstor.org/stable/175702.
268. Burgess, Glen, 'Divine Right of Kings reconsidered', *English Historical Review*, 1992, Vol 107, No 425, pp. 837–861.
269. http://www.historyisnowmagazine.com/blog/2021/3/14/james-vijames-is-love-life-the-british-king-whose-lovers-were-men.
270. https://en.wikipedia.org/wiki/Esmé_Stewart,_1st_Duke_of_Lennox.
271. Matusiak, *James I*, Ch. 2.
272. https://en.wikipedia.org/wiki/Esmé_Stewart,_1st_Duke_of_Lennox.
273. Matusiak, *James I*, Ch. 2.
274. https://en.wikipedia.org/wiki/Esmé_Stewart,_1st_Duke_of_Lennox.
275. http://www.historyisnowmagazine.com/blog/2021/3/14/james-vijames-is-love-life-the-british-king-whose-lovers-were-men.
276. Matusiak, *James I*, Ch. 2.
277. http://www.historyisnowmagazine.com/blog/2021/3/14/james-vijames-is-love-life-the-british-king-whose-lovers-were-men.
278. https://en.wikipedia.org/wiki/Esmé_Stewart,_1st_Duke_of_Lennox.
279. https://www.historylearningsite.co.uk/stuart-england/robert-carr-earl-of-somerset/?utm_content=cmp-true.
280. https://en.wikipedia.org/wiki/Robert_Carr,_1st_Earl_of_Somerset.
281. Matusiak, *James I*, Ch. 4.
282. https://www.historylearningsite.co.uk/stuart-england/robert-carr-earl-of-somerset/?utm_content=cmp-true.
283. Matusiak, *James I*, Ch. 4.
284. https://en.wikipedia.org/wiki/Robert_Carr,_1st_Earl_of_Somerset.
285. Matusiak, *James I*, Ch. 4.
286. https://en.wikisource.org/wiki/1911_Encyclopædia_Britannica/Somerset_Robert_Carr,_Earl_of.
287. MacIntyre, Jean, 'Renaissance and Reformation / Renaissance et Réforme', *New Series / Nouvelle Série*, Vol. 22, No. 3 (summer / été 1998), pp. 59–81.
288. https://www.hrp.org.uk/blog/george-villiers-first-duke-of-buckingham/#gs.gei79i.
289. Ibid.
290. https://www.historic-uk.com/HistoryUKHistoryofEngland/George-Villiers-Duke-Of-Buckingham/.
291. https://issuu.com/oksassociation/docs/retrospect_winter_2022-23/s/17791758.

292. https://www.westminster-abbey.org/abbey-commemorations/commemorations/villiers-family/.

293. https://www.historic-uk.com/HistoryUKHistoryofEngland/George-Villiers-Duke-Of-Buckingham/.

294. https://en.wikipedia.org/wiki/Charles_I_of_England.

295. Hourly History. *Charles I: A life from Beginning to End*. Biographies of British Royalty. ASIN: B07GPT2ZZ3.

296. Young, Michael B., 'Charles I and the Erosion of Trust, 1625–1628', *Albion: A Quarterly Journal Concerned with British Studies* 22, no. 2 (1990), pp. 217–35. https://doi.org/10.2307/4049598.

297. Hourly History: Charles I: A life from beginning to end: ASIN B07GPT2ZZ3

298. Smith, David L., 'The Fourth Earl of Dorset and the Personal Rule of Charles I', *Journal of British Studies* 30, no. 3 (1991), pp. 257–87. http://www.jstor.org/stable/176042.

299. Hourly History, *Charles I*.

300. Holmes, Clive, 'The Trial And Execution Of Charles I', *The Historical Journal* 53, no. 2 (2010), pp. 289–316. http://www.jstor.org/stable/40865689.

301. Wedgwood, C. V., 'European Reaction to the Death of Charles I', *The American Scholar* 34, no. 3 (1965), pp. 431–46. http://www.jstor.org/stable/41209297.

302. Matusiak, *James I*, Introduction.

303. https://en.wikipedia.org/wiki/Jane_Whorwood.

304. https://www.english-heritage.org.uk/visit/places/carisbrooke-castle/history/jane-whorwood/.

305. https://www.historytoday.com/archive/jane-whorwood-king's-smuggler.

306. https://en.wikipedia.org/wiki/Jane_Whorwood.

307. Fox, John (2022). *The King's Smuggler: Jane Whorwood, Secret Agent to Charles I*. The History Press, 2nd edition, Ch. 1.

308. https://www.english-heritage.org.uk/visit/places/carisbrooke-castle/history/jane-whorwood/.

309. Fox, *The King's Smuggler*.

310. https://www.english-heritage.org.uk/visit/places/carisbrooke-castle/history/jane-whorwood/.

311. https://en.wikipedia.org/wiki/James_Stanley,_7th_Earl_of_Derby.

312. http://www.historyofparliamentonline.org/volume/1604-1629/member/stanley-james-1607-1651.

313. https://en.wikipedia.org/wiki/James_Stanley,_7th_Earl_of_Derby.

314. http://www.historyofparliamentonline.org/volume/1604-1629/member/stanley-james-1607-1651.

315. https://en.wikipedia.org/wiki/James_Stanley,_7th_Earl_of_Derby.

316. https://earlofmanchesters.co.uk/the-earl-the-massacre-of-bolton-and-the-price-that-was-paid-in-blood .

317. https://www.theboltonnews.co.uk/news/5923957.war-crime-led-to-earl-of-derbys-execution/.

318. http://www.historyofparliamentonline.org/volume/1604-1629/member/stanley-james-1607-1651.

319. https://en.wikipedia.org/wiki/Henry_Jermyn,_1st_Earl_of_St_Albans.

320. http://www.historyofparliamentonline.org/volume/1604-1629/member/jermyn-henry-1605-1684.

321. https://en.wikipedia.org/wiki/Henry_Jermyn,_1st_Earl_of_St_Albans.

322. Matusiak, John (2017). *The Prisoner King: Charles I in Captivity*. The History Press.
323. https://en.wikipedia.org/wiki/Henry_Jermyn,_1st_Earl_of_St_Albans.
324. http://www.historyofparliamentonline.org/volume/1604-1629/member/jermyn-henry-1605-1684.
325. Matusiak, *The Prisoner King*.
326. https://en.wikipedia.org/wiki/Henry_Jermyn,_1st_Earl_of_St_Albans.
327. Ibid.
328. https://en.wikipedia.org/wiki/Henry_Jermyn,_1st_Earl_of_St_Albans.
329. https://www.britannica.com/biography/Henry-Jermyn-Earl-of-Saint-Albans.
330. Matusiak, *The Prisoner King*.
331. https://en.wikipedia.org/wiki/Henry_Jermyn,_1st_Earl_of_St_Albans.
332. https://www.britannica.com/biography/Henry-Jermyn-Earl-of-Saint-Albans.
333. https://en.wikipedia.org/wiki/Henry_Jermyn,_1st_Earl_of_St_Albans.
334. https://www.britannica.com/biography/Henry-Jermyn-Earl-of-Saint-Albans.
335. https://en.wikipedia.org/wiki/Henry_Jermyn,_1st_Earl_of_St_Albans.
336. Matusiak, *The Prisoner King*.
337. https://en.wikipedia.org/wiki/Commonwealth_of_England.
338. https://en.wikipedia.org/wiki/Oliver_Cromwell.
339. https://www.bbc.co.uk/history/british/civil_war_revolution/cromwell_01.shtml.
340. https://www.britannica.com/place/United-Kingdom/Commonwealth-and-Protectorate.
341. https://en.wikipedia.org/wiki/Commonwealth_of_England.
342. Worden, Blair, 'Oliver Cromwell and the Protectorate', *Transactions of the Royal Historical Society*, 20 (2010), pp. 57–8.3 © Royal Historical Society 2010, doi: 10. 1017/S00804401 10000058.
343. https://en.wikipedia.org/wiki/Commonwealth_of_England.
344. https://www.britannica.com/place/United-Kingdom/Commonwealth-and-Protectorate.
345. https://en.wikipedia.org/wiki/Commonwealth_of_England.
346. http://www.olivercromwell.org/wordpress/articles/oliver-cromwell-kingship-and-the-humble-petition-and-advice/.
347. https://en.wikipedia.org/wiki/Oliver_Cromwell .
348. Worden, 'Oliver Cromwell and the Protectorate'.
349. https://en.wikipedia.org/wiki/Commonwealth_of_England.
350. https://en.wikipedia.org/wiki/Oliver_Cromwell.
351. Hourly History, *Charles I*.
352. https://blogs.bl.uk/digitisedmanuscripts/2019/10/drawing-a-blank.html.
353. Greenspan, Nicole, 'Charles II, exile and the problem of allegiance', *The Historical Journal*, March 2011, pp. 73–103: https://www.jstor.org.stable/23017283.
354. Hourly History, *Charles I*.
355. https://www.rmg.co.uk/stories/topics/king-charles-ii-public-personal-life-british-monarch.
356. Hourly History, *Charles I*.
357. https://www.rmg.co.uk/stories/topics/king-charles-ii-public-personal-life-british-monarch.
358. Hourly History, *Charles I*.
359. https://www.rmg.co.uk/stories/topics/king-charles-ii-public-personal-life-british-monarch.
360. https://en.wikipedia.org/wiki/John_Wilmot,_2nd_Earl_of_Rochester.

361. Larman, Alexander (2015). *Blazing Star: The Life and Times of John Wilmot, Earl of Rochester*. Head of Zeus.
362. https://en.wikipedia.org/wiki/John_Wilmot,_2nd_Earl_of_Rochester.
363. Larman, *Blazing Star*.
364. https://en.wikipedia.org/wiki/John_Wilmot,_2nd_Earl_of_Rochester.
365. Murray G. H. Pittock, 'John Wilmot and Mr. Rochester', *Nineteenth-Century Literature* 41, no. 4 (1987), pp. 462–69. https://doi.org/10.2307/3045228.
366. https://en.wikipedia.org/wiki/Louise_de_Kérouaille,_Duchess_of_Portsmouth.
367. https://www.wrongsideoftheblanket.com/louise-de-kerouaille.
368. https://en.wikipedia.org/wiki/Louise_de_Kérouaille,_Duchess_of_Portsmouth.
369. Ibid.
370. https://en.wikipedia.org/wiki/Thomas_Osborne,_1st_Duke_of_Leeds.
371. Clark, G. N., *The English Historical Review* 60, no. 238 (1945): pp.408–10. http://www.jstor.org/stable/556604.
372. https://www.historyofparliamentonline.org/volume/1660-1690/member/osborne-sir-thomas-1632-1712.
373. https://www.pepysdiary.com/encyclopedia/12994/.
374. https://en.wikipedia.org/wiki/Thomas_Osborne,_1st_Duke_of_Leeds.
375. https://en.wikipedia.org/wiki/James_II_of_England.
376. Ibid.
377. https://www.britannica.com/biography/James-II-king-of-England-Scotland-and-Ireland.
378. https://en.wikipedia.org/wiki/Bloody_Assizes.
379. https://en.wikipedia.org/wiki/James_II_of_England.
380. Speck, W. A., 'The Orangist Conspiracy against James II', *The Historical Journal* 30, no. 2 (1987), pp. 453–62. http://www.jstor.org/stable/2639203.
381. Ibid.
382. https://en.wikipedia.org/wiki/James_II_of_England.
383. https://en.wikipedia.org/wiki/Katherine_Sedley,_Countess_of_Dorchester.
384. https://www.theklean.com/red/seductress/Katherine-sedley.
385. Van der Kiste, John (2021). *James II and the First Modern Revolution: The End of Absolute Monarchy*. Pen and Sword History.
386. https://en.wikipedia.org/wiki/Katherine_Sedley,_Countess_of_Dorchester.
387. Van der Kiste, *James II and the First Modern Revolution*.
388. https://en.wikipedia.org/wiki/Katherine_Sedley,_Countess_of_Dorchester.
389. https://www.theklean.com/red/seductress/Katherine-sedley.
390. *The Dublin Literary Gazette*, no. 17 (1830): 262–64. http://www.jstor.org/stable/30064465.
391. https://people.elmbridgehundred.org.uk/biographies/catharine-sedley/.
392. https://en.wikipedia.org/wiki/John_Drummond,_1st_Earl_of_Melfort.
393. Ibid.
394. https://en.wikipedia.org/wiki/Earl_of_Melfort.
395. https://en.wikipedia.org/wiki/John_Drummond,_1st_Earl_of_Melfort.
396. Van der Kiste, *James II and the First Modern Revolution*, Ch. 8.
397. Ibid., Ch. 9.
398. https://www.dib.ie/biography/drummond-john-a2780.
399. Ibid.
400. https://www.dib.ie/biography/drummond-john-a2780.
401. https://en.wikipedia.org/wiki/John_Drummond,_1st_Earl_of_Melfort.

402. Miller, John (1989). *James II: A Study in Kingship*. *Methuen* Publishing Ltd, New edition, p. 225.
403. https://en.wikipedia.org/wiki/Earl_of_Melfort.
404. https://en.wikipedia.org/wiki/Richard_Talbot,_1st_Earl_of_Tyrconnell.
405. https://www.irishtimes.com/culture/books/in-defence-of-fighting-lying-mad-richard-talbot-the-last-cavalier-jacobite-rake-and-scourge-of-cromwell-1.2018673.
406. https://en.wikipedia.org/wiki/Richard_Talbot,_1st_Earl_of_Tyrconnell.
407. Ibid.
408. Ibid.
409. Ibid.
410. Lenihan, Padraig (2014). *The Last Cavalier: Richard Talbot 1631–91*. University of Dublin College Press.
411. Keates, Jonathan (2015). *William III and Mary II: Partners in Revolution*. Penguin reprint, ASIN B00O4MHBEI.
412. Ibid.
413. https://en.wikipedia.org/wiki/William_III_of_England.
414. https://alpennia.com/blog/why-cant-manbe-more-woman-17th-c-friendship-ideals.
415. https://en.wikipedia.org/wiki/Mary_II.
416. Keates, *William III and Mary II*.
417. https://en.wikipedia.org/wiki/Mary_II.
418. https://en.wikipedia.org/wiki/William_III_of_England.
419. https://en.wikipedia.org/wiki/Mary_II.
420. https://en.wikipedia.org/wiki/William_III_of_England.
421. Richard Price, 'An Incomparable Lady: Queen Mary II's Share in the Government of England, 1689–94', *Huntington Library Quarterly* 75, no. 3 (2012), pp. 307–26. https://doi.org/10.1525/hlq.2012.75.3.307.
422. https://en.wikipedia.org/wiki/Mary_II.
423. Keates, *William III and Mary II*, Ch. 3
424. Keates: Ch. 4
425. Ibid.
426. https://en.wikipedia.org/wiki/William_III_of_England.
427. Keates, *William III and Mary II*.
428. https://en.wikipedia.org/wiki/William_Bentinck,_1st_Earl_of_Portland
429. Carlton, Charles (2023). *Royal Mistresses*. Routledge, Ch. VI.
430. https://www.nottingham.ac.uk/manuscriptsandspecialcollections/collectionsindepth/family/portland/biographies/biographyofhanswilliambentinck,1stearlofportland(1649-1709).aspx.
431. https://en.wikipedia.org/wiki/1696_Jacobite_assassination_plot.
432. Gregg, Edward (2001). *Queen Anne*. Yale Monarchs Series, Yale University Press, pp. 21–2.
433. https://www.nottingham.ac.uk/manuscriptsandspecialcollections/collectionsindepth/family/portland/biographies/biographyofhanswilliambentinck,1stearlofportland(1649-1709).aspx.
434. https://research.rkd.nl/ [search Willem Bentinck].
435. Rosenheim, J. M. (2009). [Review of The Anglo-Dutch Favourite: The Career of Hans Willem Bentinck, 1st Earl of Portland (1649-1709); Redefining William III: The Impact of the King-Stadholder in International Context, by D. Onnekink & E.

Mijers]. Restoration: Studies in English Literary Culture, 1660-1700, 33(1), 43–46. http://www.jstor.org/stable/43293979

436. https://en.wikipedia.org/wiki/Arnold_van_Keppel,_1st_Earl_of_Albemarle.

437. Gregg, *Queen Anne*, p. 115.

438. https://en.wikipedia.org/wiki/Arnold_van_Keppel,_1st_Earl_of_Albemarle..

439. https://www.unofficialroyalty.com/arnold-van-keppel-1st-earl-of-albemarle-favorite-of-king-.

440. https://en.wikipedia.org/wiki/Arnold_van_Keppel,_1st_Earl_of_Albemarle.

441. https://www.unofficialroyalty.com/arnold-van-keppel-1st-earl-of-albemarle-favorite-of-king-.

442. https://en.wikipedia.org/wiki/Arnold_van_Keppel,_1st_Earl_of_Albemarle.

443. https://www.unofficialroyalty.com/arnold-van-keppel-1st-earl-of-albemarle-favorite-of-king-.

444. https://www.friendsoflydiardpark.org.uk/news/blog-post/elizabeth-villiers-another-royal-mistress/.

445. Carlton, *Royal Mistresses*.

446. Ibid.

447. Ibid.

448. https://www.unofficialroyalty.com/elizabeth-hamilton-countess-of-orkney-mistress-of-king-william-iii-of-england/.

449. https://en.wikipedia.org/wiki/Elizabeth_Hamilton,_Countess_of_Orkney.

450. https://www.friendsoflydiardpark.org.uk/news/blog-post/elizabeth-villiers-another-royal-mistress/.

451. https://en.wikipedia.org/wiki/Elizabeth_Hamilton,_Countess_of_Orkney.

452. https://www.friendsoflydiardpark.org.uk/news/blog-post/elizabeth-villiers-another-royal-mistress/.

453. McClain, Molly, 'Love, Friendship, and Power: Queen Mary II's Letters to Frances Apsley', *Journal of British Studies* 47, no. 3 (2008), pp. 505–27. http://www.jstor.org/stable/25482827.

454. Bucholz, R. O., '"Nothing but Ceremony": Queen Anne and the Limitations of Royal Ritual', *Journal of British Studies* 30, no. 3 (1991), pp.288–323. http://www.jstor.org/stable/176043.

455. Gregg, *Queen Anne*, p. 1.

456. Ibid., p. 2.

457. Ibid., p. 7.

458. Ibid., p. 13.

459. https://en.wikipedia.org/wiki/Anne,_Queen_of_Great_Britain.

460. Gregg, *Queen Anne*, p. 27.

461. Ibid., p. 33.

462. https://en.wikipedia.org/wiki/Anne,_Queen_of_Great_Britain.

463. Gregg, *Queen Anne*, p. 79.

464. https://en.wikipedia.org/wiki/Anne,_Queen_of_Great_Britain.

465. Gregg, *Queen Anne*, p. 111.

466. Ibid., p. 343.

467. https://en.wikipedia.org/wiki/Anne,_Queen_of_Great_Britain.

468. Gregg, *Queen Anne*, p. 171.

469. Ibid., p. 174.

470. https://en.wikipedia.org/wiki/Anne,_Queen_of_Great_Britain.

471. Gregg, *Queen Anne*, p. 134.
472. https://en.wikipedia.org/wiki/Anne,_Queen_of_Great_Britain.
473. https://en.wikipedia.org/wiki/Blenheim_Palace.
474. Gregg, *Queen Anne*, p. 276.
475. Ibid., p. 283.
476. Ibid., p. 287.
477. Ibid., p. 307..
478. Ibid., p. 299
479. https://en.wikipedia.org/wiki/Anne,_Queen_of_Great_Britain.
480. Gregg, *Queen Anne*, pp. 375–77.
481. Ibid., p. 394.
482. Ibid., p. 401–03.
483. Radice, F. R., 'The reign of Queen Anne', *History* 20, no. 77 (1935), pp. 29–39. http://www.jstor.org/stable/24401391.
484. https://en.wikipedia.org/wiki/Abigail_Masham,_Baroness_Masham.
485. Gregg, *Queen Anne*, pp.110–13.
486. https://www.friendsoflydiardpark.org.uk/news/blog-post/abigail-masham/.
487. Gregg, *Queen Anne*, pp. 246–53.
488. Ibid.
489. Gregg, *Queen Anne*, pp. 273–76.
490. https://en.wikipedia.org/wiki/Abigail_Masham,_Baroness_Masham.
491. Ibid., pp. 301–04..
492. Ibid., p. 332
493. Gregg, *Queen Anne*, pp. 398–99.
494. https://en.wikipedia.org/wiki/Abigail_Masham,_Baroness_Masham.
495. https://en.wikipedia.org/wiki/Robert_Harley,_1st_Earl_of_Oxford_and_Earl_Mortimer.
496. https://engelsbergideas.com/notebook/the-first-prime-minister/.
497. https://en.wikipedia.org/wiki/Robert_Harley,_1st_Earl_of_Oxford_and_Earl_Mortimer.
498. https://engelsbergideas.com/notebook/the-first-prime-minister/.
499. https://en.wikipedia.org/wiki/Robert_Harley,_1st_Earl_of_Oxford_and_Earl_Mortimer.
500. Gregg, *Queen Anne*, pp. 226–7.
501. Ibid., p. 237.
502. https://en.wikipedia.org/wiki/Robert_Harley,_1st_Earl_of_Oxford_and_Earl_Mortimer.
503. McInnes, Angus. 'The Political ideas of Robert Harley', *History* 50, no. 170 (1965), pp. 309–22. http://www.jstor.org/stable/24405239.
504. https://en.wikipedia.org/wiki/Robert_Harley,_1st_Earl_of_Oxford_and_Earl_Mortimer.
505. https://engelsbergideas.com/notebook/the-first-prime-minister/.
506. https://en.wikipedia.org/wiki/Robert_Harley,_1st_Earl_of_Oxford_and_Earl_Mortimer.
507. https://engelsbergideas.com/notebook/the-first-prime-minister/.
508. https://en.wikipedia.org/wiki/Elizabeth_Seymour,_Duchess_of_Somerset.
509. https://en.wikisource.org/wiki/Dictionary_of_National_Biography,_1885-1900/Thynne,_Thomas_(1648-1682).

510. https://en.wikipedia.org/wiki/Thomas_Thynne_(died_1682).
511. https://en.wikipedia.org/wiki/Elizabeth_Seymour,_Duchess_of_Somerset.
512. Gregg, *Queen Anne*, pp. 330–32.
513. https://en.wikipedia.org/wiki/Elizabeth_Seymour,_Duchess_of_Somerset..
514. Gregg, *Queen Anne*, pp. 351–52.
515. https://en.wikipedia.org/wiki/Elizabeth_Seymour,_Duchess_of_Somerset.
516. Gregg, *Queen Anne*, pp. 397–98.
517. Ibid., p. 274.
518. https://en.wikipedia.org/wiki/Elizabeth_Seymour,_Duchess_of_Somerset.
519. Bucholz, '"Nothing but Ceremony": Queen Anne and the Limitations of Royal Ritual'.
520. DeRitter, Jones, '"Wonder Not, Princely Gloster, at the Notice This Paper Brings You": Women, Writing, and Politics in Rowe's "Jane Shore"', *Comparative Drama* 31, no. 1 (1997), pp. 86–104. http://www.jstor.org/stable/41153847.

Select Bibliography

Alford. Stephen (2013). *The Watchers: A Secret History of the Reign of Elizabeth I*. Penguin Books, ISBN 9780141043654.

Ballard, George (1752). *Memoirs of Several Ladies of Great Britain*.

Borman, Tracy (2023). *Anne Boleyn and Elizabeth I: The Mother and Daughter Who Changed History*. Hodder & Stoughton, ISBN 9781399705080.

Borman, Tracy (2016). *The Private Lives of the Tudors*. Hodder & Stoughton, ISBN 9781444782899.

Brennan, Laura (2023). *James II and VII: Britain's Last Catholic King*. Pen and Sword History, ASIN B0C95BHHYG.

Carlton, Charles (2023). *Royal Mistresses*. Routledge, ISBN 978-1032464275.

Clifford, Henry (1887). *The Life of Lady Jane Dormer: Duchess of Feria*.

Courtauld, Simon (2021). *Lady of Spain: A Life of Jane Dormer, Duchess of Feria*. Mount Orleans Press, ISBN 9781912945320.

Edwards, John (2016). *Archbishop Pole*. Routledge, ISBN 1409420574.

Foster, Roy (Professor) (1990). *Modern Ireland: 1600–1972*. Penguin, ISBN 9780140132502.

Fox, John (2022). *The King's Smuggler: Jane Whorwood, Secret Agent to Charles I*. The History Press, 2nd edition, ISBN 9780750999403.

Furdell, Elizabeth Lane (2001). *Royal Doctors 1485–1714*. University of Rochester Press, ISBN 9781580460514.

Gregg, Edward (2001). *Queen Anne*. Yale Monarchs Series, Yale University Press, ISBN 0300090242.

Harris, Sir Nicholas (2014). *The Privy Purse Expenses of King Henry VIII from November 1529 to December 1532*. Perlego, ISBN 9700000046009.

Hourly History. *King Charles I: A life from Beginning to End* (Biographies of British Royalty). ASIN B07GPT2ZZ3.

Hourly History. *King Charles II: A Life from Beginning to End* (Biographies of British Royalty). ASIN B07FQMJRRS.

Hutchinson, Robert (2019). *Henry VIII: The Decline and Fall of a Tyrant* (Kindle edition). Weidenfeld & Nicholson, ASIN B07JL33BTM.

Ives, Eric (2004). *The Life and Death of Anne Boleyn*. Blackwell, ISBN 0631234799.

Jordan, D. and Walsh, M. (2013). *The King's Revenge: Charles II and the Greatest Manhunt in British History*. Abacus, ISBN 9780349123769.

Keates, Jonathan (2015). *William III and Mary II: Partners in Revolution*. Penguin reprint, ASIN B00O4MHBEI.

Larman, Alexander (2015). *Blazing Star: The Life and Times of John Wilmot, Earl of Rochester*. Head of Zeus, ISBN 9781781859247.

Lee, Stephen (2006). *The Mid Tudors: Edward VI and Mary, 1547–1558*. Routledge, ASIN B00NBN81MW.

Lenihan, Padraig (2014). *The Last Cavalier, Richard Talbot 1631–91*. University of Dublin College Press, ISBN 9781906359836.

Loades, David (2004). Intrigues and Treason: The Tudor Court. Longman, ISBN 9780582772267.

Lockyer & Thrush (1997). *Henry VII* (3rd edition). Routledge, ISBN 9780582209121.

Markham, Sir Clements (1907). *King Edward VI: An appreciation*. Smith, Elder & Co.

Matusiak, John (2015). *James I: Scotland's King of England*. The History Press, ASIN B01491XJEE.

Matusiak, John (2017). *The Prisoner King: Charles I in Captivity*. The History Press, ISBN 9780750967686

Miller, John (1989). *James II: A Study in Kingship*. Methuen Publishing Ltd, New edition, ISBN 9780413623409.

Norton, Elizabeth (2017). *The Lives of Tudor Women*. Head of Zeus, ISBN 9781784081768.

O'Caellaigh. Seamus (2017). *Pustules, Pestilence and Pain: Tudor Treatments and Ailment of Henry VIII*. MadeGlobalPublishing, ASIN B0788X3MQW.

Penn, Thomas (2011). *Winter King*. Penguin, ISBN 9780141040530.

Richardson, Glenn (2020). The Field of Cloth of Gold. Yale University Press, ISBN 9780300248029.

Ridley, J. (1987). *Elizabeth I*. Constable, ISBN 009466370X.

Sellar and Yeatman (1998). 1066 and All That: A Memorable History of England. Methuen, ISBN 9780413772701.

Spencer, Charles (2015). *Killers of the King: The Men Who Dared Execute Charles I*. Bloomsbury, ISBN 9781408851777.

Starkey, D (2002). The Reign of Henry VIII: Personalities and Politics. Vintage, ISBN 24681097531.

Starkey, D (2009). Henry: Virtuous Prince. Harper Perennial, ISBN 9780007247721.

Van der Kiste, John (2021). *James II and the First Modern Revolution: The End of Absolute Monarchy*. Pen and Sword History, ASIN B09GPCC8X8.

Ward, Anne (1996). *The Lincolnshire Uprising 1536*. Louth Naturalists' Antiquarian and Literary Society, ISBN 0952011743.

Weir, Alison (2008). *Henry VIII: King and Court*. Vintage, ISBN 9780099532422.

Younger, Neil (2022). *Religion and Politics in Elizabethan England: The Life of Sir Christopher Hatton*. Manchester University Press, ASIN BOBHJHQJMY.

Dear Reader,

We hope you have enjoyed this book, but why not share your views on social media? You can also follow our pages to see more about our other products: facebook.com/penandswordbooks or follow us on X @penswordbooks

You can also view our products at www.pen-and-sword.co.uk (UK and ROW) or www.penandswordbooks.com (North America).

To keep up to date with our latest releases and online catalogues, please sign up to our newsletter at: www.pen-and-sword.co.uk/newsletter

If you would like a printed catalogue with our latest books, then please email: enquiries@pen-and-sword.co.uk or telephone: 01226 734555 (UK and ROW) or email: uspen-and-sword@casematepublishers.com or telephone: (610) 853-9131 (North America).

We respect your privacy and we will only use personal information to send you information about our products.

Thank you!